Learning About Apples   April to August, 1984

Magazine Published in 1984 by:
Roger Wagner

Book Produced by:
Brian Wiser & Bill Martens

 Apple PugetSound Program Library Exchange

The Apple's Apprentice

ACKNOWLEDGEMENTS

The Apple's Apprentice magazine was originally published by Roger R. Wagner and Emerald City Publishing in 1984, and edited by A.P.P.L.E. founder Val J. Golding. All magazines inside this book are copyright © 1984, 2018 Roger R. Wagner, and licensed to the public with Attribution-NonCommercial 4.0 International (CC BY-NC 4.0).

Thanks to the Original Contributors: Linda Anderson, Jack Cassidy, Cheshire Catalyst, Robert Cavey, Mike Collins, Tim Graham, Val J. Golding, Joe Holt, Pete Katz, Pamela Lambert, Richard Owen Lynn, Mike Newton, Bill Sanders (aka "Uncle Bill"), Jeff Sandys, Donna Sexton, David Sparks, George Spelvin, Ralph H. Swerdlow MD., Margot and Al Tommervik, Mike Thyng, Roger Wagner, Sergio Waisman, Laurie Wofford, The Apprentice Wizard, and The Wizard of Fairhill Castle.

Thanks to Chris Torrence and Roger Wagner for loaning the original magazines.
Produced in coordination with Roger Wagner.

The modified art on the front cover was originally featured on *The Apple's Apprentice* premiere issue. The modified alien on the back cover from the third issue was originally created by Mike Wilcot and Doug Westercamp as a scene from the game *Bezare*, a trademark of Roger Wagner Publishing.

The cover and book was designed by Brian Wiser.

PRODUCTION

Brian Wiser → Design, Scanning, Magazine Restoration
Bill Martens → Production, Table of Contents

DISCLAIMER

About Roger Wagner

Roger Wagner is a programmer who has deep roots in the Apple II community, going all the way back to the beginnings of the platform. In 1978, he started his own software publishing company, Southwestern Data Systems (SDS), as a vehicle for the distribution and sales of some of his first software products for the Apple II. These products included his *Programmer's Utility Pack* and *Apple-Doc*, which were sold on cassette tape.

For those of us who grew up with the Apple II in the 1970s and 1980s, Roger's software was a mainstay – his hands were everywhere in the Apple world. He also wrote *The Correspondent* and *MouseWrite* word processors for the Apple II. SDS sold software written by other authors, including Glen Bredon's popular *Merlin* assembler, The Routine Machine Applesoft extensions by Peter Meyer, *ASCII Express* and *Z-Term* by Bill Blue, as well as games like *BEZARE* by John Beznard and *NORAD*.

During those early years, he also wrote articles for many major magazines of the day, including *Call-A.P.P.L.E.*, *Nibble*, *inCider*, *A+*, and *GS+*. Wagner is best remembered for his long-running "Assembly Lines" column in *Softalk*, which focused on teaching the first generation of Apple II users how to program in 6502 assembly language.

In 1984, Roger partnered with A.P.P.L.E. founder and *Call-A.P.P.L.E.* magazine editor, Val Golding, to create a magazine dedicated to teaching children of all ages about programming – *The Apple's Apprentice*. Roger was the publisher and Val was the editor. Articles were fun and informative with columns such as: Spells and Potions, The Sourceror's Apprentice, Ask the Wizard, and The Crystal Ball. The educational aspect and philosophy behind *The Apple's Apprentice* followed the same goal as Apple's with the Apple II computer – to educate and inspire. While the magazine only had three issues, the quality of the production, articles, and art stands out as a reminder of how good an educational magazine can be.

He later renamed his software company to Roger Wagner Publishing, and continued to provide quality software for both the 8-bit Apple II and the 16-bit Apple IIGS. His most famous contribution to the IIGS was the HyperCard-inspired program, *HyperStudio*, which linked pictures, audio media, and text with clickable links, a foretaste of the hyperlinked Web that was to arrive in the 1990s. Wagner later developed it for Windows and Mac, and promoted its use in schools – teaching students to create presentations and to learn about computers. He further developed *HyperDuino*, an Arduino-based hardware extension for the *HyperStudio* to let people control real-world devices with their projects. Roger continues to educate the younger generation, developing and teaching Arduino-type projects.

HyperStudio 5 for Mac continues to evolve from its Apple II roots. Roger released *HyperStudio AUTHOR* that allows for the creation of simple and beautiful interactive iPad books with HTML5-based media that can be merged into *Apple's iBooks Author*. For more information, visit: rogerwagner.com.

About the Producers

Brian Wiser

Brian Wiser is a long-time consultant, enthusiast and historian of Apple, the Apple II and Macintosh. Steve Wozniak and Steve Jobs, as well as *Creative Computing, Nibble, InCider,* and *A+* magazines were early influences.

Brian designed, edited, and co-produced many books including: *Call-A.P.P.L.E. Magazine: 1978 Compendium, What's Where in the Apple: Enhanced Edition, Nibble Viewpoints: Business Insights From The Computing Revolution, Cyber Jack: The Adventures of Robert Clardy and Synergistic Software, Synergistic Software: The Early Games, The Colossal Computer Cartoon Book: Enhanced Edition,* and *The WOZPAK: Special Edition* – an important Apple II historical book with Steve Wozniak's restored original, technical handwritten notes.

He passionately preserves and archives all facets of Apple's history, and noteworthy related companies such as Beagle Bros and Applied Engineering, featured on AppleArchives.com. His writing, interviews and books are featured on the technology news site CallApple.org and in *Call-A.P.P.L.E.* magazine that he co-produces. Brian also co-produced the retro iOS game *Structris*.

In 2005, Brian was cast as an extra in Joss Whedon's movie *Serenity*, leading him to being a producer and director for the documentary film *Done The Impossible: The Fans' Tale of Firefly & Serenity*. He brought some of the *Firefly* cast aboard his Browncoat Cruise and recruited several of the *Firefly* cast to appear in a film for charity. Brian speaks about his adventures to large audiences at conventions around the country.

Bill Martens

Bill Martens is a systems engineer specializing in office infrastructures and has been programming since 1976. The DEC PDP 11/40 with ASR-33 Teletypes and CRT's were his first computing platforms with his first forays in the Apple world coming with the Apple II computer.

Influences in Bill's computing life came from *Creative Computing* magazine, *Byte* magazine and *Call-A.P.P.L.E.* magazine as well as his mentors Samuel Perkins, Don Williams, Joff Morgan, and Mike Christensen.

Bill is a co-producer of many books including: *Call-A.P.P.L.E. Magazine: 1978 Compendium, The WOZPAK: Special Edition, Nibble Viewpoints: Business Insights From The Computing Revolution, What's Where in the Apple: Enhanced Edition,* and co-programmer for the iOS version of the retro game *Structris*. He has written many articles which have appeared in user group newsletters and magazines such as *Call-A.P.P.L.E.*.

Bill worked for Apple Pugetsound Program Library Exchange (A.P.P.L.E.) under Val Golding and Dick Hubert as a data manager and programmer in the 1980s, and is the current president of the A.P.P.L.E. user group. He reorganized A.P.P.L.E. and restarted *Call-A.P.P.L.E.* magazine in 2002. He is the production editor for the A.P.P.L.E. website CallApple.org, writes science fiction novels in his spare time, and is a retired semi-pro football player.

CONTENTS

June 1984 – Volume 1, No. 2

August 1984 – Volume 1, No. 3

The Apple's
Apprentice

FORWARD

by Roger Wagner

1984... Only six years after my first encounter with the Apple II, and here I was, making a go at a magazine that, at least in my mind at the time, would be for younger users of the Apple computer. We had a great team: Val Golding (former editor of *Call-A.P.P.L.E.*), the inspiration and encouragement of Al and Margot Tommervik (publishers of *Softalk* magazine), Joe Holt and Mike Newton (interns at the offices of Roger Wagner Publishing ("RWP") and forthwith talented programmers and writers), Robert Cavey (creative artist whose work appeared in a number of different RWP products), David Sparks (he wrote the first published review of *HyperStudio GS*), Bill Sanders (sharp-witted and prolific author of many books and columns), and many others, whom you will discover in the pages of this fascinating glimpse into a special corner of the Apple II world that existed in 1984.

At the time, I thought we were creating a magazine for kids, but looking at it now, it seems it was in fact a magazine for those with a youthful, playful, and adventurous mind.

The magazine existed for just a brief time. I had the "excellent" sense of timing to start an Apple II magazine at the same moment the Macintosh and the famous "1984" commercial had everyone's attention. As you'll see from the full-color pages throughout the magazine, I was also a bit overambitious in spending compared to revenue. Tom Weishaar, creator of *Open Apple*, and the founder of KansasFest, was much wiser in creating a black-and-white, lower-cost newsletter that far outlived *The Apple's Apprentice*.

Still, looking through these issues again after 30+ years brings back many memories, and I'm actually impressed by the quality and range of the articles and content that we produced. It's something of a time capsule from what is now a past century, that still brings me pleasure to revisit today in the year 2018.

I hope you will discover the same sense of delight and wonder in looking through the pages of this rare magazine in this even more rare compendium. There are many things and even a secret or two to be found again amidst the pages.

Those of us who lived through the time of the early days of the Apple II and personal computing each played a small part in what was to be the future of computing, and yet, none of us imagined just what would grow from those simple beginnings.

Many thanks to Brian Wiser, Bill Martens, Chris Torrence, and the others of the Apple II community that still thrives, for making this edition real.

As you read *The Apple's Apprentice*, imagine a time long ago when computers were new, full of mystery, magic, and the promise of adventure!

Roger Wagner
July 2018

Volume 1, No. 1

April 1984

the Apple's Apprentice

For Kids and Apples

$2.50

- Apogee and Apples, Oh Gee!
- MagiGraphics
- Bumbling Through BASIC

Premier Issue!

We Don't Strive for State-of-the-Art. . .
. . .We Define It.

The Complete Graphics System

This brand-new version of our non-programmers' graphics tools includes both best-selling and highly rated products: The Complete Graphics System II and Special Effects, combined into one easy-to-use package. All the command structures have been updated so that selections are made directly by pointing at choices from a graphics screen, or options are described on convenient help screens. This version is so advanced that users will hardly need a manual at all, yet they'll have the most diverse and powerful set of graphic capabilities readily at their fingertips. And we've combined all different versions into one single package that works with joysticks, paddles, trackball, the Apple Graphics Tablet, Apple Mouse, Houston Instruments' HiPad, and the Koala Pad. Priced at $79.95, it's sure to remain the most-used graphics development tool for the Apple.

The Graphics Magician

The new version of The Graphics Magician takes all the abilities of the original version, adds to them, and simplifies their use for even the least technically-oriented programmers. Animation and picture-drawing routines from this best-seller are being used in published products from over two dozen companies, including the likes of Sierra On-Line, Sir-Tech, Milton-Bradley, Mattel, Spinnaker, Adventure International, and many others. The big news is that versions are now being released for Macintosh, Atari, IBM, and Commodore personal computers, with graphics files transferable between computers. That means that a programmer's graphics work on one computer no longer needs to be redone on other computers . . . they can just be transferred with The Graphics Magician. Retail price is $59.95 for the Apple.

Paper Graphics

Paper Graphics is a brand-new graphics screen-to-printer printing utility. As you would expect from Penguin, it's the most advanced and easy-to-use of any such utility available today. An advance, incomplete version has already received an A+ rating from Peelings II, which called it "the most complete of the graphics-dump programs reviewed to date". Besides being compatible with virtually every interface card/black and white printer combination imaginable (we challenge you to find one that it won't work with), Paper Graphics includes magnification, cropping, screen editing, labeling, framing, combination dumps of both graphics screens, and the ability to pack and unpack pictures. At $49.95, you shouldn't settle for less.

Transitions

Transitions is the most advanced graphics presentation system yet on microcomputers. With it, you can easily create self-running or manually operated slide shows or presentations by combining up to eight picture disks (packed or unpacked) and 44 different transitions (screen wipes) between slides. Users can even see a graphic "catalog" of their picture disks, consisting of miniature versions of the pictures on each disk presented on the graphics screen. For a very professional-looking presentation, no other program will do. Transitions retails for $49.95, and together with The Complete Graphics System and Paper Graphics makes the most versatile set of graphics programs anyone could own for their Apple computer.

Additional Typesets and Map Pack

Two add-ons are available for The Complete Graphics System, at $19.95 each. Additional Type Sets contain over 50 extra typefaces that can be used with the text routines in CGS. Map Pack contains over 100 hi-res maps already on packed graphics screens.

penguin software ™
the graphics people

830 Fourth Avenue, P.O. Box 311, Geneva, IL 60134 (312) 232-1984

Call-A.P.P.L.E.

Official Publication Of

Apple PugetSound Program Library Exchange
Worlds Largest Apple User Group

A.P.P.L.E. PROVIDES THE *MOST COMPREHENSIVE* USER SUPPORT SERVICES

THE INTERNATIONAL MAGAZINE
- **CALL—A.P.P.L.E.**

TROUBLESHOOTING 10 HOURS-A-DAY 7 DAYS
- **HOTLINE**

MAJOR DISCOUNTS ON
- **HARDWARE & SOFTWARE**

DISCOUNT SUBSCRIPTIONS TO
- **SOURCE DATABASES**

- **24 HR. BULLETIN BOARD**

FOR THOSE IN PUGETSOUND COUNTRY
- ✓ CLASSES & SPECIAL INTEREST GROUPS
  ✓ MONTHLY MEETINGS
  ✓ THE APPLE GENERAL STORE

$25 PER YEAR + $26 FIRST YEAR DUES DELIVERS A FULL MEMBERSHIP WITH ALL PRIVILEGES. SUBSCRIPTION ONLY, $21

JOIN A.P.P.L.E. NOW & RECEIVE 10 FREE DISKS

YES I WANT TO JOIN. . . A.P.P.L.E.

☐ **MEMBERSHIP $51 FOR THE FIRST YEAR**
($25 One-Time Application Fee + $26 First Year Dues)

☐ **SUBSCRIPTION ONLY $21 PER YEAR**
Call Toll Free. . . . 1-800-426-3667

Tell operator you are joining through SOFTALK for you're FREE DISKS.

⎯ # _____

VISA # _____

NAME _____ PHONE _____

ADDRESS _____ Exp. Date _____

CITY_____ STATE_____ ZIP_____ Exp. Date _____

Mail This Coupon To: A.P.P.L.E. 21246 - 68th Ave. S.   KENT, WA 98032   Free Disk Special Expires 6/30/84

ADVERTISE TO OUR QUALIFIED BUYING MEMBERSHIP
John Elliott National Sales (206) 872-2245

Vol. I, No. 1   April 1984

PREMIER ISSUE!

The Apple's Apprentice is published monthly by:

Emerald City Publishing, Inc.
P.O. Box 582-AA, Santee, CA 92071,
(619) 562-7785.
Entire Contents copyright © 1984 by
Emerald City Publishing, Inc.

Roger Wagner, publisher
Val J. Golding, editor
Donna Sexton, Advertising Director
Pamela Lambert, Circulation Manager
Margot and Al Tommervik, godparents
(bless them!)

Subscriptions: $24/12 issues, $46/24 issues

From the Tower

the Apprentice Wizard

Making an Issue Of it

What an experience, putting together a new magazine the first time! You'll see it may take a while to get in the groove, get up to speed. That's why we're going to ask for your help. *The Apple's Apprentice* is going to be like nothing you've seen before, and that's because *you're* going to help create and guide your own magazine.

After you have a chance to read through this issue, write us a letter and let us know what you think. Did you like what you saw? What did you dislike? What can we add that would make it more interesting? What do you want to know about the Apple? What are your main interests... games, comic strips, graphics, programming, exploring inside? Along the same line, what do you use your Apple for? Is it your own machine, or your folks? (And speaking of your folks, we want to hear from them, too, but: *you've* gotta countersign their letter, just to let us know they're ok, ok?)

Let's see, what else? Oh, yes... (here comes another cry for help): you can be famous and see your name in print...we need some "Cheap Tricks" that will help your friends and schoolmates to learn to use the Apple better, or maybe a funny short program you have written. It doesn't even need to do anything much, as long as it does it differently (think about that for a minute), and we'll reward you for each item published with a six month extension to your subscription, or a new six month subscription for you or a friend.

Speaking of issues, this issue is dated April, 1984. For those of you who expected to see *The Apple's Apprentice* somewhat earlier, our apologies. It really does take some doing to get a new magazine to lift off. To those who expect to see a May issue, our apologies again. Our next issue will be dated June or July, and will be monthly thereafter.

Department Department

We've got a lot of neat ideas for your magazine, and you'll see many of them in this issue. Most of them will appear every month. Let's list a few:

- MICRO CHIPS
  Bob Cavey's amusing color comic about Apples
- BACK TALK
  your chance to sound off on any subject. If it's interesting, we'll print it. You'll also have a chance to reply to someone else's letter
- YE OLDE GAME SHOPPE
  news and reviews about games and gaming with an occasional contest thrown in for good measure
- SPELLS 'N' POTIONS
  open the huge oak door and find inside magical cures for ills such as how to prevent the screen from scrolling
- THE CRYSTAL BALL
  a glance through our crystal ball will pass on to you predictions of Apples in your future, games to come, the latest in peripherals, and products of interest to kids
- ASK THE WIZARD
  here's where we help *you*...If, for example, you can't figure out how to set up the ampersand (&) command?...ask the wizard

Now we come full circle: help! In this issue. be bring you as our "featured attraction," **Apogee? Yes, and Apples, Oh Gee!** Author *Mike Newton* has done a splendid job, telling you of the trauma and travail (use your dictionary) that went into the organization of a special effects production company and their later effort that resulted in pictures like *Star Wars, Battleship Galactica,* and *Star Trek.* Let us know if you like it. Or if you don't. Or if you'd like to hear about a 14–year old who sold an assembly language game commercially.

Deportment Department

The Apple's Apprentice is going to be a *different* magazine. Not only is it the first Apple magazine for kids, but it's the first magazine for kids where you can be the boss. Not only will we try to be responsive to your needs, we'll level with you on every word. Like the next — and very important — paragraph.

We need money. We're not a big company starting a new magazine that can afford to pour a few hundred thousand dollars into getting a project off the ground. To put out a quality magazine, for kids, and by kids, we have to sell subscriptions and advertising. We want you to look upon yourself as a co–owner. We want you to work with our staff and sell *The Apple's Apprentice*. The best salesmen in the world are those that believe in their product, and we have a product for you to shape and believe in. If you like what you see, ask your friends, your schoolmates, your teachers, to subscribe. If you really want to work at it, we'll give you a one month extension to your subscription for each new subscription you send us. Remember, for a limited time, a 12–issue introductory subscription is only $18, 25% off the regular rate.

We can predict now some changes in a typical conversation at a prom or dance such as : "Gee, Margie, how about a milkshake and Big Mac (excuse us, Merlin) after the dance?" to: "Gee, Margie, I really want to show you this new Apple magazine..." Anyway, you dig the scene...Anything you do for us will be returned to you in reading and computing delight.

So here we go...dig in and send us a report card...

Apogee? Yes, Apples, Oh Gee!

Mike Newton

How can one introduce the special effects studio that has produced some of the finest special effects shots ever seen on the wide screen? Perhaps with the same words one uses to describe their photography. Words like stunning, breathtaking, innovative and revolutionary. If these won't do, look around for one that conveys the ultimate impression: reality beyond belief.

What super-computers would it take to support this ensemble of celluloid sorcery? A *Cray One*? A *PDP-11*? Would you believe a 128-byte *Cosmac Elf*?

If you answered yes, you may be a just a little bit too gullible. You are correct, however, that a microcomputer is the workhorse — the "brains," so to speak — employed by this leading edge technological toyshop. A microcomputer called the Apple][.

You probably already know all about it, but back in 1978, few had. Along came bold Matt Beck, who proposed its use as a motion control device, a duty which, as it turned out, the Apple was well suited to. In those early days, not many people, perhaps excepting those who subscribed to *Byte* or *Kilobaud* paid much heed to micros, let alone considered a micro for the responsible task of controlling a motion picture camera.

The name of the company all of this has been leading up to, is *Apogee*. You may have also heard about Apogee before, and small wonder. In its short life span, it has produced special effects for such illustrious productions as *Star Wars*, *Battleship Galactica*, *Star Trek: the Motion Picture*, *Avalanche Express*, *Philip Marlow*, *Never Say Never Again*, and the unforgettable *Caddyshack*.

The work that is done by Apogee, and the history of how it all came about, is fascinating. To make it all simple and neatly categorized, we'll break our discussion into three parts: the history of Apogee, how the special effects systems work, and the tasks performed by the Apple itself.

A Star (Wars) is Born

In 1975, a talented young filmmaker envisioned an epic space adventure more ambitious than any science-fiction movie heretofore. This was none other than the now-revered George Lucas. He knew only he wanted to create the most realistic possible special effect for his movie, but knew of no facility capable of producing the quality desired. The solution, therefore, was to create his own.

Gary Kurtz, producer of Star Wars, happened to know of John Dykstra, a gifted cinematographer

> ### ...the history of how it all came about is fascinating.

who had worked on the legendary *2001: A Space Odyssey*. The highly recommended Dykstra was hired, and *Industrial Light and Magic* was formed around him in July, 1975. John had the responsibility for assembling a group of the most talented and respected professionals in the special effects field, who would ultimately produce some of the greatest special effects ever

done. Clearly, for the next couple of years, his work was cut out for him.

By the time Dykstra organized his team, they numbered close to one hundred, with an average age of just 27. The production crew had no time clock and no dress code. They were held together by their loyalty to Dykstra and their motivation to produce flawless special effects. (Funny,

> ### Lucas knew only he wanted to create the most realistic possible special effects.

I've seen the same characteristics in programmers!)

In order to achieve the effects Lucas desired, it was necessary to construct a device famous now as the *Dykstraflex*. It was an innovation in motion picture cameras, in that instead of requiring models to be moved past the camera, the camera itself moved in all directions, panned and tilted past the now stationary models. To incorporate the mechanical precision and memory needed by the camera brought out the genius of Al Miller, who electronically mated an elaborate system of digital clocks and multi-track recorders.

More than a year into the production, Lucas found that ILM had spent over half of their two million dollar budget, yet produced only three so-so special effects shots. After finding the facility so informal, unorganized, and unpoliced, Lucas decided to take over and personally oversee and manage the operation himself, which resulted in greatly increased tension between Dykstra and Lucas.

In the end, ILM took 22 months, including the six months needed to develop the necessary equipment, to finally finish the total of 365 special effects. When Star Wars was done, Dykstra and many of the crew left ILM to form their own independent organization, *Apogee*.

Battlestar Galactica, thus far the

. . .it was necessary to construct a device famous now as the Dykstraflex.

most expensive production ever made for television, was done at Apogee, using the same equipment that had proved so effective with Star Wars. After Galactica came Star Trek: the Motion Picture, at which point Matt Beck joined the Apogee crew. Having worked previously with microcomputer hardware, Beck encouraged Apogee to utilize this technology in their motion control system.

After having examined the state of microcomputers at that time, and because of numerous difficulties using the single board *Demon* computer,

Academy Award winner John Dykstra has ventured far from his beginnings as an industrial designer to become one of the most sought-after special effects wizards in the world. Apart from his Oscar for Star Wars and Academy Award nomination for Star Trek, Dykstra has garnered innumerable certificates and science-fiction awards for his contributions to filmmaking. As the Emmy award winning effects designer and producer of Battlestar Galactica, which enjoyed distinction as the most expensive and technologically ambitious television series ever made, Dykstra pioneered new areas of motion control photography which culminated in the creation of a camera that bears his name. The Dykstraflex Camera has become a mainstay of special effects photography, and has permitted filmmakers to capture illusions never before possible.

As an undergraduate student, Dykstra studied architectural design while maintaining a strong interest in still photography. Shortly after college, he worked with the National Science Foundation in a psychological study of man's response to certain architectural forms, a study that sought

to discover by use of miniatures, desirable formats for urban architecture. After his involvement with the N.S.F. came a brief apprenticeship with Douglass Trumbull as an industrial designer on the film Silent Running. This film became a predecessor to the films that would dominate the

late seventies and usher in the eighties.

After completion of Silent Running, Dykstra worked for the Ruben H. Fleet Space Theatre in San Diego on a program entitled "Voyage to the Outer Planets." This experience provided him with a background in celestial photography that would later prove most valuable.

Following his work at the Space Theatre, Dykstra resumed his association with Douglas Trumbull and went on to produce amusement park rides, aircraft simulator films, and experimented extensively in three dimensional filmmaking.

It was at this time Dykstra became involved with George Lucas on Star Wars, and what followed exceeded their greatest expectations. Not only did they produce a film among the most prosperous of all time, but exceeded the limitations of current technology in the greatest special effects extravaganza ever staged.

Following his involvement with Lucas, came the 1978 formation of Apogee Incorporated, which brought nine of the world's top special effects experts under one roof. Today they operate from a 30,000 square foot production facility, capable of turning out complete motion pictures. As president of Apogee, Dykstra oversees all productions and is presently involved in a variety of film projects.

When not consumed with a hectic production schedule, he enjoys flying aircraft, racing cars and motorcycles, and playing music in his residential recording studio.

they decided to try their luck with an Apple][, which, as it turned out, was to be the key to their ultimate success. With its (then) high density disk drives and superior high resolution graphics, the Apple was soon put to use in the Star Trek scene where a light-energy beam wreaks havoc aboard the Enterprise.

The motion of the image distorter was controlled by an Apple...

The energy beam was actually a man holding a Xenon tube in front of himself. In order to disguise the tell-tale portions of the figure which appeared around the tube, they constructed an x-y-z rig that bent the picture around the light beam. The motion of the image distorter was controlled by an Apple using fast-running Integer Basic. Since none yet existed, Matt built a parallel interface for the Apple, and wrote a program to interpolate the positions of the beam for each frame of film.

Following completion of this job, the Apple proved itself as a valuable and reliable piece of equipment. Al Miller took Beck's rudimentary interface and expanded it into a full-blown system, and from that time on, it became an integral part of the motion control system.

With the vast experience gained

with Apple hardware and software, a subsidiary company, *Hollywood Hardware*, was formed. This new company has recently begun to market some of the hardware used so effectively in creating their motion picture and television special effects. Among these peripheral cards is a 16 channel A/D (analog to digital) converter with 12 bits of resolution, and a 48 line parallel interface (both of which are used in their motion control system), and the *Ultra-ROM Board*.

The latter item is of particular interest and extremely useful to Applesoft programmer types, since it includes on board *GPLE*, a BASIC edit utility which will make you wonder how you ever managed without it. (GPLE is also available on diskette from *Beagle Brothers*.) Included also on the Hollywood Hardware board are several useful ampersand routines such as a multiple byte memory search, print-using, and if/then/else, etc. All told, there is 32k of ROM space available, all transparent to the user.

Special Effects Techniques (...where do computers fit in?)

Most of the spectacular and dazzling special effects shots from Apogee were made possible by their computerized motion control system. Why a computer controlled camera? The answer to that lies deep in the heart of the very processes required to create special effects.

The illusion of motion with models is done with *relative* motion. In other words, instead of moving the models

The illusion of motion with models is done with relative motion.

themselves, which tend to be somewhat immobile and cumbersome, the camera itself moves. Apogee's highly flexible camera employs twelve independent axes of motion, and can be programmed to "make passes" at models with such utter precision that only a computer could handle it. The importance of this will be obvious later.

A typical space scene, with space ships, stars, asteroids, lasers, etc., actually consists of many, many elements of film combined photographically. There is usually one strip of film shot for each object that appears in the picture. Sometimes as many as 30 separate rolls must be combined in an optical printer to produce the final illusion of deep space (or for that matter, near Earth).

Exactly how are these individual elements combined? The process that film makers must go through is surprisingly close to the efforts of game program authors who achieve the high quality graphics and animation that you admire.

This process is usually called *blue-screening* in the film industry, while in computer graphics circles it is known as *and/or animation*. For those of you who can relate more easily to computer concepts, graphics parallels will be used for purposes of illustration.

For example, let's say we want a ship to start off in the distance in the bottom of the frame, then zoom by over our heads. To do this with our relative motion system, we would begin by backing the camera far in front of the model, so that it appears to be very far away. The camera would have to be aimed parallel to the ground, with the model at the bottom of the frame.

The camera would begin to move toward the model, decreasing shutter speed as it advances, which creates the illusion of increasing speed. As the camera moves forward, it also begins to lower at a faster rate, all the while

remaining parallel to the ground. This gives the impression that the model has suddenly gained tremendous speed and has accelerated vertically.

If we wanted to get fancy and cause the model to veer to the right, we would just slowly roll the camera to the left while the film was rolling. As you can see, these delicate camera movements are far too complex to be

...these delicate camera movements are far too complex to be controlled by anything other than a computer.

controlled by anything other than a computer. This illustrates the concept of relative motion with the system, but what of multiple elements? Here's where things get hairy.

Suppose that we want the ship to zoom by in front of us, while at the same time, passing a large, revolving asteroid (not forgetting the starlit background).

Let's see how this might be done by a computer graphics program. The

first image to be generated is the starfield, twinkling at random intervals. Next, an *and-mask*, the same size as the asteroid in the frame, would be anded to the screen to black out the area where the asteroid will appear, while leaving the remainder of the screen intact. The area where the asteroid is to be placed would be filled with zeroes, and the balance of the and-mask would contain ones. After the area occupied by the asteroid has been blanked out, we would use an *or-mask*, which would represent the asteroid in this particular frame of movement. This would be ored to the screen, resulting in the image of an asteroid in space.

The anding and oring is important...

The anding and oring is important because we don't want any stars to show through the asteroid, which would spoil the illusion of solidity and make the asteroid appear transparent.

Now to add to our speeding ship! Remember it is constantly moving away from us, moving diagonally upward from the lower left of the screen, and constantly growing smaller, thus each and every and-mask and or-mask will differ from frame to frame.

Now we "and" the and-mask to the screen to clear the area the space ship will occupy in a given frame. The and-mask must be used at this precise spot to be effective. Then we can "or" the image of the ship for this frame at the appropriate spot, just as we did for the asteroid. We don't want the asteroid to be seen through the ship,

...there are several ships on the screen at any given time.

should the ship happen to pass in front of it. Likewise, we don't want stars to twinkle through the ship.

Actually, this is far simpler than any scene Apogee might do. Usually, there are several ships on the screen at any given time, plus the complications of laser fire, vapor trails, space debris, explosions, and other unnatural space phenomena.

There are several important things to take note of. First, the elements are anded or ored sequentially from the furthest back to the closest in front. This brings to mind sprites, with their priority levels and multi-planed 2½ dimensional look.

Secondly, these objects must be placed in precisely the correct locations on the screen, and at the proper speed, so as to appear synchronized and harmonized with the rest of the shot. That's where the Dykstraflex proves itself.

Now that you understand how the scene can be created with computer graphics, let's see how the photographic process might be applied to the same set of circumstances.

The blue screening process is what makes it all possible. The blue screen is a backdrop which emits a pure light frequency. This special light wavelength leaves no image or color on the

...the photographic process can be applied to the same set of circumstances.

film itself. Instead, the camera has a special beam splitter in it whose purpose is to separate the images. One image is transfered to regular film, while the other develops on a black and white film that produces an inverse silhouette, called a *traveling matte*. This traveling matte is then used as the and-mask, while the regular color film becomes the or-mask.

These images are processed by the optical department, layer by layer. The device used to combine the frames of film is called an optical printer. The background is first anded with the matte of the object furthest from the camera, then its or-mask is photographically combined with the image. This process continues until all elements of the scene have been merged in, and the shot completed.

So far we have made little mention of the vital role played by the Apple][, and alas, that must wait for the next issue. (Like the daily comics, you don't get the whole story at once!) But keep tuned to the *Apple's Apprentice* frequency; you won't want to miss hearing about the part *your* computer plays.

Assembling Teens:
The Sourceror's Apprentice

Mike Newton

It was not too long ago, and not too far away, but the magic has been forever engraved in the Chronicles of Time. Woz was a very young wizard, but his youth did not keep him from creating magic so wonderful and so different that many of the older wizards were insanely jealous. Woz wasn't so selfish with his wizardry, though; he wanted to share it with the rest of the world. His Apple was given to many, so that they too might learn of its wonders and magic. Now it is time for you as well to learn of its magic, and become the Sourceror's Apprentice.

Any magician will tell you that the most important part of magic is learning the magic words and how to use them properly. As the Sourceror's Apprentice, you will learn how to speak to the circuits that are at the heart of the Apple][plus and Apple //e computers, and become a wizard yourself at programming in assembly language.

Programs are written with ...an editor/assembler.

"What is assembly language and why should I use it?" you've probably asked yourself many times. Maybe you already know there is a *microprocessor* within the computer, called the *6502*. Microprocessors are the real brains and "intelligence" of the computer, and are also called CPU's or MPU's. They "eat" electricity, "think" in binary and "talk" to other parts of the computer through wires and circuits, and *registers* or *memory cells*.

You've probably seen programs in BASIC before. It looks pretty simple. In fact, you may be tired of it already because it sometimes seems so slow.

At the same time, you probably wonder what assembly language *looks* like. Before we get into that subject, let's first talk about *machine language*. Machine language is the only thing that the CPU *really* understands. Machine language looks just like an endless stream of numbers, but to the CPU, the numbers contain information that tells it what it's supposed to do, and what numbers it is supposed to use to perform calculations. It's not easy to understand a program in its machine language form, not even for experienced wizards.

...there is a microprocessor within the computer...

So how do you program in machine language? You usually don't. The preferred (and simpler) language to program in is called assembly language. Programs are written with what is called an *editor/assembler*, using using ordinary words (something like BASIC), and the editor/assembler turns all those words and text into machine language numbers. *Merlin* is an example of a good editor/assembler. Using an editor/assembler, you will see how much easier it is to write in assembly language than straight machine language.

Why would you want to program in assembly language anyway? Well, since the CPU directly understands it, it is much, much faster than BASIC. most games with graphics, for example, wouldn't look good in BASIC, because they would be too slow. Besides just being super fast, assembly is often shorter and smaller than BASIC. Not only that, but in BASIC,

you are limited to using the existing "commands," whereas in assembly, you can do, the way *you* want to do it, anything the computer can do.

There are a few more reasons that make it fun to program in assembly language. For one, you are as "close" to the hardware as you can be in software. It often fills you with a feeling of awe to see your program playing directly with the innards of the computer at speeds so fast it makes you dizzy. Now that's magic for you!

What is inside the 6502? If you take the top off your Apple so that you can look in and see the *motherboard*, the biggest, black chip you will find (labeled "6502" in white writing) is the 6502 itself. Inside the 6502 are several important electronic control and memory devices, but rather than confuse you with difficult words and explanations about the 6502, I will compare it to the lower dungeons I run. There are so many similarities that you can learn about the 6502 through my dungeon comparison.

Down in the dungeon there are a bunch of strange beasts called *Hexels*. What's so strange about them? Well, instead of having ten fingers like we do, Hexels have 16 fingers, and that's just one of their strange features.

They're funny little creatures who never have much to do, so to keep them out of trouble, I try and find things to make them productive. What do they do down there? They run the Post Office department for the whole Castle.

The drawing I made for you,

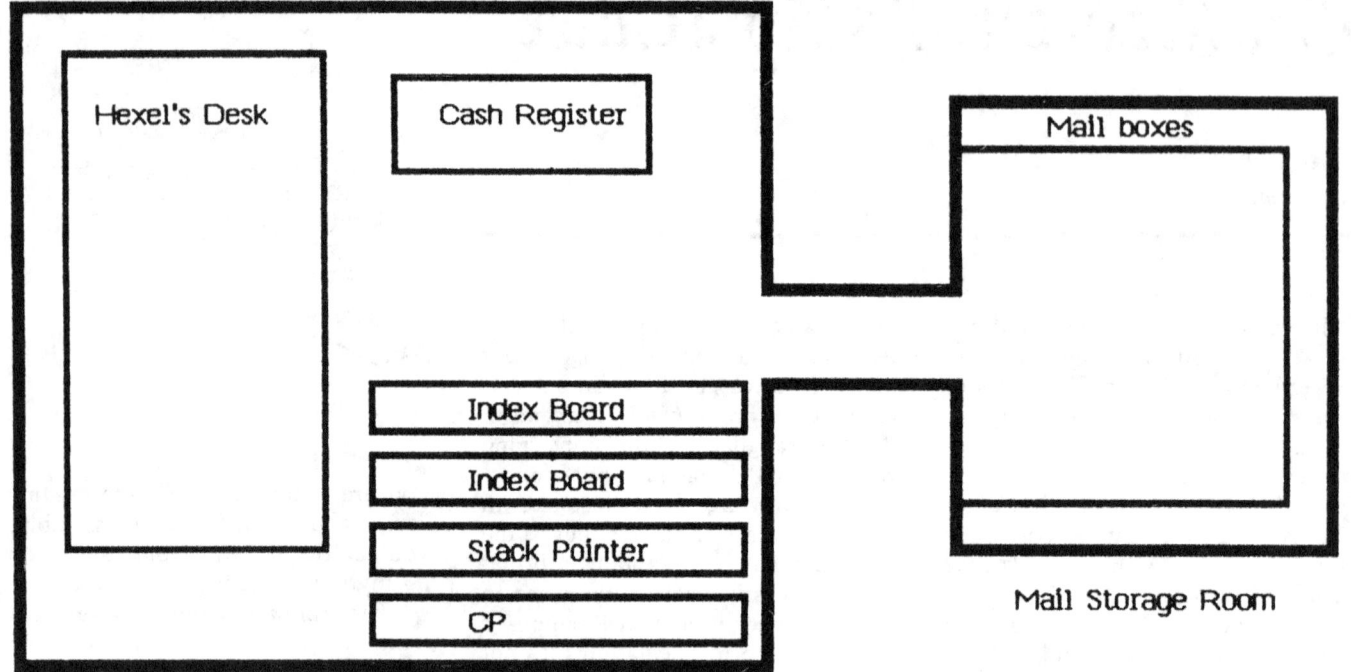

Mail Control Room

6502 Microprocessor

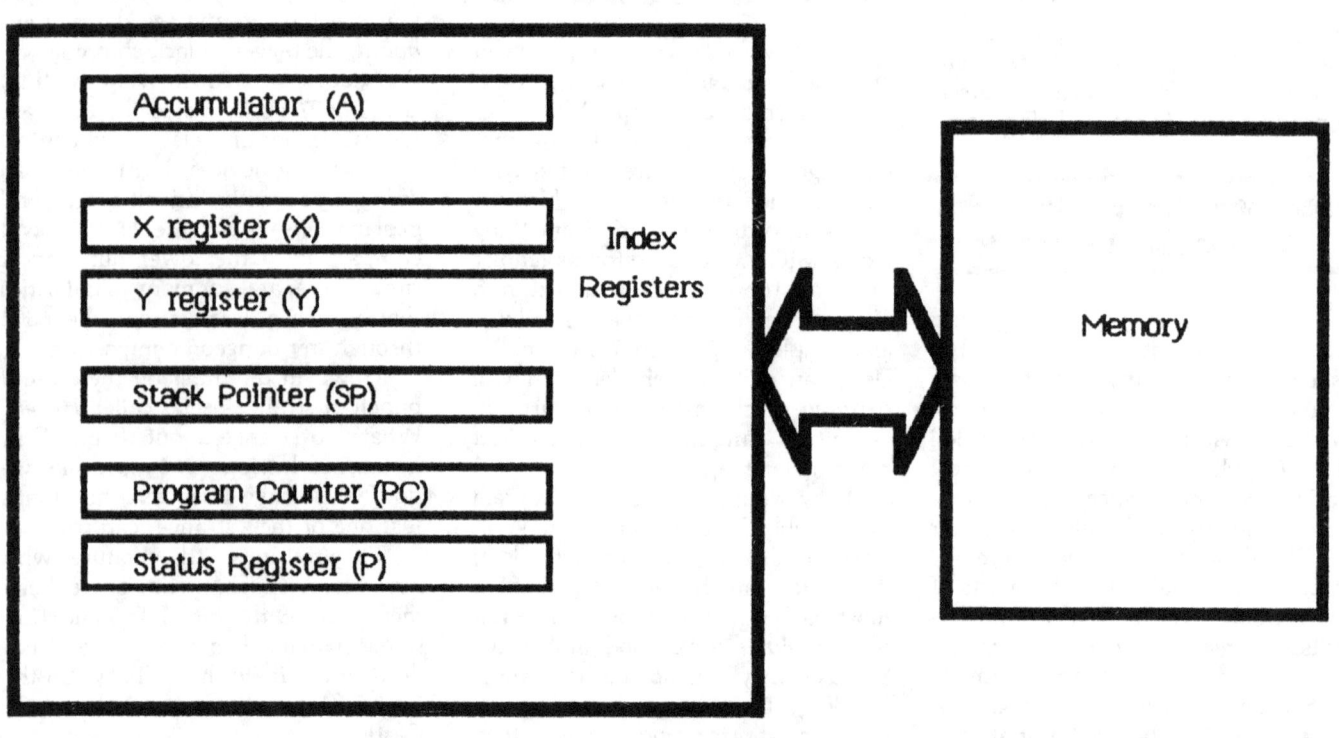

FIGURE 1

which I'll call *figure 1*, is an illustration of the mail control room and of the 6502. If you ask me, they look very similar. We'll talk first about the mail control rooms. You can see that there is one main control room, and that there is another room adjoining. This room is where all the mail is actually stored, in little mail boxes on the walls. We'll call this the storage room.

There is always a Hexel in the control room doing the mail. What does he do? It seems that since we do live in a royal castle, he often needs to read the mail through to make sure that no important information leaks out. For the same reason, he sometimes needs to change what is written in the letters.

Since Hexels are not very smart, they always need to be told what to do. When this Hexel comes in every morning, I leave a piece of paper telling him which mail box to get his instructions from. He goes to that mail box, and instead of taking out a letter, he finds my instructions. So you see, the same storage boxes often contain both letters and instructions.

Sometimes Hexels need to calculate things like postage cost. They aren't smart enough to do it in their heads, so they use the Cash Register in the mail room. There's only one, so when they use it, they have to be very careful not to lose any important information that might be in it.

There are two small blackboards in the control room, called the Index Boards. Because they are very small, only one number at a time can be written on them. They are used to help the Hexels remember where some of the mail slots are.

There is a special blackboard called the Stack Pointer which is sometimes used to process special mail, like the things the King sends. These special kinds of letters are always kept in mail boxes that are very close to the mail room. Since these letters are very important, this board helps the Hexel remember which letter was last put on the stack of letters. The most recent letter put on the stack is always the first one to be pulled off and mailed.

A Hexel's memory is often not very good, so there is another blackboard they write on to show which mailbox they are currently working on. This holds only one number at a time, and is called the CP (for Current Postbox).

Later on, we'll examine in detail what some of their jobs are, but in the meantime you've already gotten a pretty good idea of what they do in that dark and damp area.

The 6502 has things called registers. . .

Now let's talk about the 6502, and you'll see at once what a remarkable coincidence it is that the Hexel's job and that of the 6502 are so similar. Instead of having mailboxes for storage, it has electronic memory. Not only is memory used to store numbers and data, but like the mailboxes, it also holds the instructions or *program*.

The 6502 has things called registers that are just like the chalk boards and cash register in the mail room. Registers hold numbers, one at a time. The one that is used for all math and arithmetic calculations is called the *Accumulator*.

Just as the mail room had two blackboards called indexes, the 6502 has two *Index Registers*. They are called the "X-Register" and the "Y-Register." They are used to hold data or numbers or to "point" at places in memory. They are most often used for things called *Table Look-up*. You'll hear more about that later.

The 6502 even has a *Stack Pointer* that works just like the one in the mail room. It is used to point at very special data in a special place in memory. The pointer always points at the piece of data most recently pushed on the stack and which will be pulled off first. This is called a *LIFO* structure, which stands for "last in, first out."

In the mail room, we had a "CP" to tell the Hexels which current postbox they were working on. If you reverse the initials you will get *PC*. Now the 6502 calls this the *Program Counter*, and it tells the 6502 where in memory the current program instruction is that it is executing. In other words, if there was a program that was running, and the program was in memory at location 300, the PC would contain the number 300.

There is still another special register in the 6502 called the *Processor Status Register*. It is often called just the *Status Register* or for short,

the *P-Register*. This register knows almost everything that is going on in the 6502, which register is processing what kinds of numbers, and it gives this information out by hoisting *flags*. The P-Register has seven flags that are numbered from 0 to 7. For example, by checking to see if the "Z" flag is raised, you can find out that the last number processed was equal to zero. If the number is negative, then the "N" flag will equal one. This is also called being set or turned on. These are ideas we will talk about later, so don't worry about them for now.

That's pretty much what's inside the 6502. How everything works together will be easy to understand, once I tell you more about how the mail room works. You might be confused at first, and you might have to read some things several times to really understand, but who ever said being a wizard was easy? I've been at it for over two centuries now, and I still get stuck.

You must remember that being a wizard requires a lot of time and patience. You must never give up. The road may be long and hard, but the knowledge that you gain will be well worth the time and effort involved. Knowledge is power, my master always used to tell me.

If you are really serious about learning assembly language, you need an editor/assembler, so that you can type in the example programs I will be showing you. I would recommend that you get *Merlin* from Roger Wagner Publishing. It was named after a very dear friend of mine, and he'd be quite flattered if you got it. He always was a bit of a show-off.

The Hexels are getting hungry again, so I'll having to be leaving soon. This time of night they seem to get very restless, and it's best not to leave them alone. Last time I left them by themselves, a whole colony of leprechauns disappeared, and I have a feeling I know what happened to them.

Prepare yourself for more soon, my young apprentice. Oops, I can hear those Hexels now, banging on my walls for food. They certainly do press their luck at times. Perhaps I'll have to turn one of them into a frog, just to remind them who their master is!

Anyway, before those rascals damage my dungeons, I must bid you farewell until next time. . .

Is the Hex Clock Hexed

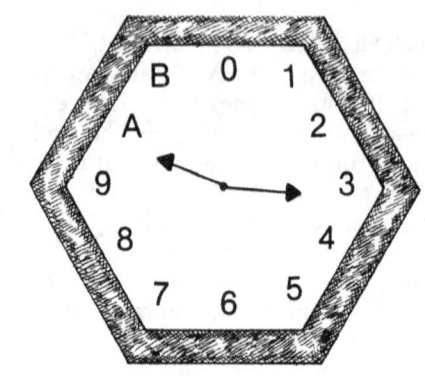

Whoopee! Another contest! Prizes? You bet! For the first three earliest postmarked, correct solutions, you'll win 12-, 6- or 3-month subscriptions (or extensions) to *The Apple's Apprentice*. All entries must be postmarked no later than June 1st, 1984, and mailed to:

Hex Contest
The Apple's Apprentice
P.O. Box 582–AA
Santee, CA 92071

Now that you know where to send it, here's what to do: Type in Paul Raymer's Hex Clock program on this page, and RUN it. Does it run ok? Does it keep fairly good time? Good enough. Now you tell us:

- what's wrong with the program?
- what do we do to fix it?
- did it help you learn about hex numbers?

Well, gosh, that's simple . . . you better get with it!

```
]LIST

100  REM

HEX CLOCK BY PAUL RAYMER

200  TEXT : HOME : CLEAR
210  A$ = "0001020304050607080900A0
     B0C0D0E0F101112131415161718 1
     91A1B1C1D1E1F202122232425262
     728292A2B2C2D2E2F30313233343
     5363738393A3B3C"
220  M = 1:H = 1:E$ = CHR$ (32)
230  B$ = "         ": REM 7 SPACES
     !
240  INVERSE
250  REM

==========
BACKGROUND
==========

260  FOR X = 1 TO 15
270  FOR Y = 1 TO 40
280  VTAB X: HTAB Y: PRINT E$
290  NEXT Y: NEXT X
300  NORMAL
310  REM

======
INSETS
======

320  FOR X = 4 TO 12
330  VTAB X: HTAB 3: PRINT B$;: HTAB
     12: PRINT B$;: HTAB 23: PRINT
     B$;: HTAB 32: PRINT B$
340  NEXT X
350  REM
```

```
==========
START CLOCK
==========

360  VTAB 20: HTAB 1: INPUT "STAR
     TING HOUR (1-12) ";SH:H = 2 *
     SH + 1
370  VTAB 20: HTAB 1: INPUT "STAR
     TING MINUTE (0-59) ";SM:M =
     2 * SM - 1
380  VTAB 20: HTAB 1: INPUT "DISP
     LAY DECIMAL TIME? (Y/N) ";DE
     $: IF DE$ = "Y" THEN DE = 1
390  VTAB 20: HTAB 1: CALL  - 868

400  M = M + 2: IF M > 120 THEN H =
     H + 2:M = 1
410  IF H > 26 THEN H = 2
420  VTAB 8: HTAB 6: PRINT  MID$
     (A$,H,1);
430  VTAB 8: HTAB 15: PRINT  MID$
     (A$,H + 1,1);
440  VTAB 8: HTAB 26: PRINT  MID$
     (A$,M,1);
450  VTAB 8: HTAB 35: PRINT  MID$
     (A$,M + 1,1);
455  IF  INT (M / 2) < 10 THEN  VTAB
     23: HTAB 1: CALL  - 868: IF
     DE = 1 THEN  PRINT  INT (H /
     2);" 0"; INT (M / 2): GOTO
     470
460  VTAB 23: HTAB 1: CALL  - 868
     : IF DE = 1 THEN  PRINT  INT
     (H / 2);" "; INT (M / 2)
470  REM

=====
TIMER
=====

480  IF FL = 0 THEN  NORMAL
490  IF FL = 1 THEN  INVERSE
500  VTAB 17: HTAB 5
510  FOR D = 1 TO 31 STEP 2
520  PRINT  MID$ (A$,D,2);"   ";
530  FOR Z = 1 TO 2489: NEXT Z: REM
     (= ADJUST HERE IF NEEDED
540  IF D = 15 THEN  VTAB 18: HTAB
     5
550  NEXT D
560  NORMAL
570  FL = FL + 1: IF FL = 2 THEN F
     L = 0
580  ST =  PEEK ( - 16384): IF ST >
     127 THEN DE = DE + 1: POKE  -
     16368,0: IF DE > 1 THEN DE =
     0
590  GOTO 400
600  VTAB 23: HTAB 1: END
```

The Duncan Letters

Joe Holt

Duncan my friend!

It is always so good to hear from you. How is the young squire?

I take it from your last letter that you've begun your apprenticeship. Wonderful! May I wish you all the best of luck with your new studies? Good Luck! Keep me posted on your progress, will you?

I remember my apprenticeship... There weren't many teachers back then — what I learned, I learned on my own. You are very fortunate indeed to live in this day and time, where a bright young mind such as yours can learn and grow... I know I've told you this too many times already, but remember: Without your mind, you're nothing. Use it!

Laurelin is fine, as are the rest of the people here at the castle — little Valarel seems to have a knack for keeping our spirits high. Everyone is preparing for the coming winter and the snows she'll bring with her. I do hope it won't be as bad as the one three seasons ago.

Ah, the fire in the hearth feels so good to these cold bones of mine! Let me tell you, there is nothing quite like sitting lazily in front of a fireplace, pen in hand, while the cold winds that come off the mountains blow against the outer walls.

Oh, let me tell you about something that has caused quite a stir around here:

Yesterday, just as the sun was setting behind the distant slopes of the Far Mountains, a young man appeared outside the castle gate. His clothes gave him away immediately as being a traveling minstrel, no doubt seeking shelter within our walls

from the cold. His hair was fair, and his countenance happy, despite the weather.

A minstrel he was, but the stories he told were not of dragons and hidden treasures and valiant heroes!

He spoke of a far-off land beyond the Northern Edge where, he claimed, the streets are paved with something he called "silicon" (your knowledge is more recent than mine, do you know what it is?) and the workers there have eight fingers on each hand (I'll have to ask the Sorceror if any of his Hexels have escaped). He said the people of this land often talk to fruit, or at least that's what I think he said. He did say they often carry on conversations with their apples! Can you imagine that? What's more, he said these apples talk back! Sometimes I wonder if the guards shouldn't let so many "strangers" through our gates.

He told us that these are not ordinary apples, but were specially designed to help people do all sorts of things, and that they are the creation of a young wizard named Woz. This fellow Woz, I think he ought to see the court apothecary! Really, the stories the minstrels are telling these days are getting harder and harder to believe. One should never take tales told by a man in leotards too seriously.

Whoever he was, he just left this afternoon. He said he misses his own lands, and wishes to return there as soon as he is able to get passage with a farmer or merchant going his way.

Whether these stories are true or not, they've apparently had some effect on the people here.

Everyone is anxious to see one of these "magic apples" the minstrel promised he'd bring back with him the next time he passes through the "silicon valley". That's what the Sorceror calls the place, and it seems to fit.

I can't deny that I am also a bit excited to see one of them. Being an artist, the minstrel's stories of the colorful artwork these apples can conjure up has left me curious. The minstrel has guaranteed me that anything I can put on paper, an apple can do also, only quicker and without the mess of mixing paints!

Oh, and something else I remember him saying: the pictures on these apples move! I didn't believe him either, but he promised me that what he was telling me was the absolute truth, and that he saw it happen himself. This is just too much for one as unacquainted with magic as I am to imagine.

Anyway, I'm hoping that I'll be able to use one of the apples which he brings back. I know that there are plenty of people in the Castle who hope the same, so I suppose I'll just have to wait my turn. Next time you visit me, I hope to have some beautiful artwork to show you which a "magic apple" helped me create!

I can't say I'm sorry to see him leave, however. What with all the excitement, things were beginning to get left undone. My own quarters are a mess! Now that he's gone, I hope things will return to normal, although I think that it will be a lot worse when he returns. The stories of these apples are just too good to be true! I suppose we'll all just have to wait and see.

Please write me as soon as possible — it is always so nice when the page stops by with a letter from my favorite cousin!

You are young — don't let life get old too soon! Study hard, and learn as much as you can. With knowledge, you can do anything!

your friend and cousin,

Joseph

P.S. Do your parents a favor and listen to them once in a while, all right?

Spells and Potions

George Spelvin

A word of introduction for this little column. What I intend to do here is to pass on little "tricks of the trade," such things as the simple and well known POKE 33,33, which narrows the text window and keeps you from getting big ugly gaps in your PRINT statements when you trace your cursor over the program line you have just LISTed.

Did you know you could POKE characters directly to the screen? Yes, indeed. Take a look at your (or your folks) Apple][Reference Manual, page 15. There is a chart there that I constantly refer to. It shows the ASCII values of Apple characters as they are displayed on the screen, inverse, flashing and normal. Note the are not the same values that Applesoft uses.

Next, turn the page and look at the chart on page 16. This is called a *memory map*, and it shows you in decimal and hex, the memory locations used for screen display. If you select location 1024 (from page 16), and POKE it with 220, guess what is displayed? Right on... the backslash (\). I'll leave the rest of the experimentation and the ideas to you. Let me know how you make out.

Just time for one more, this issue.

Next time, I'll have more room. So many people have asked me how you can keep a program from being LISTed, so I'll tell you one way. Maybe at some other time I can give you more ideas.

Applesoft has what is called a *protection flag*. It is located at at 214 decimal ($D6). If your program POKEs 216 with 255 (actually any value greater than 127), any command issued from the keyboard (direct mode), such as LIST, SAVE, CALL, etc., will RUN the program. This will not work under ProDOS, and I don't know why. But look out! Make sure you have SAVEd the program before you test it, because once that "flag" is set, you can't do anything except reset or turn the power off.

Next time, I'll have a few more neat tricks to show you. I hope you'll tune in.

Ask the Wizard

Dear Wizard:

When I do a PEEK of 37 and do a VTAB later, it never seems to come out right, it's like I'm always a line off. Can you tell me why?

Sure can. It's because BASIC and the monitor count differently. Usually BASIC counts starting with one, while the monitor (because it uses hexadecimal numbers) starts with zero. Here's what really happens: On the text screen, the *cursor vertical* (decimal location 37) is a register or storage location in the monitor that keeps track of where the current screen line is. The range is from 0 (top line) to 23 (bottom line). VTAB is a BASIC command, and BASIC thinks the screen begins with line 1 and ends with line 24, so there is a conflict.

If you want to identify a screen line and VTAB to it later, do it like this: Set a variable to the screen line (X = PEEK (37), then when you want to go back to that line, VTAB X + 1. That's all there is to it!

Send your questions to "Ask the wizard," P.O. Box 582–AA, Santee, CA 92071.

An Intro to Low-Res Graphics:
MagiGraphics
Roger Wagner

Welcome to *MagiGraphics!* This column will appear each month in *The Apple's Apprentice* with the idea of teaching you a little about how graphics are done on an Apple computer.

You see graphics everywhere these days, whether it's in a super new Hi-Res arcade game, intriguing educational software, or even the software used by businesses.

By reading *MagiGraphics* each month, you'll not only have a better understanding of how graphics are created in these programs, but learn how to create entertaining graphics effects in your own programs!

In talking about the various subjects in this column, we'll assume that you know a little about how to write a program in Applesoft Basic, and that you know how to turn on the computer and type a program in, run it, and save it for future use.

You might be wondering about the name "MagiGraphics" for this column. It's a blending of the words "magic" and "graphics," but it's also interesting to note that the beginning of the final name then becomes *magi.* Although the word "magi" is usually associated with the three wise men in the bible story, magi actually comes from the Middle English and Latin words for sorceror! Magic is still an appropriate term though. In fact, one of the definitions for "magic" in the dictionary is "Any mysterious and overpowering quality that lends singular distinction and enchantment."

We at *Apple's Apprentice* think that the Apple computer is definitely something that has a singular distinction and enchantment to it. The computer is truly one of the most powerful things for improving your own personal creativity and productivity to come along, and the ability to use of graphics is certainly one of the more inspiring parts of that magic!

The Principles Behind Graphics

The essence of graphics is the principle of communicating information or ideas by using visual *patterns* instead of text. When you look at text, your mind uses the *words* on the page or screen to represent the things being talked about. With graphics, we use the visual image itself of an object or symbol to communicate the idea.

From the phrase "a picture is worth a thousand words," you get the impression that people have found pictures to be effective ways of communicating. One of the best recent examples of this is the success of the Macintosh and Lisa computers from Apple, and their extensive use of graphics symbols, called *icons,* to convey the ideas and instructions that ordinarily would have been done with text screen menus and volumes of instruction manuals.

Graphics images can be representations of objects we are familiar with, like houses or airplanes, or they can help us to visualize objects that have yet to be created, like the computer design systems that automobile manufacturers use to design the cars of the future. They can even be abstract patterns that have no exact meaning, they're just interesting to look at.

Graphics can include stationary images like a pie chart, or the objects can move on the screen, thus creating the effect of *animation.*

Finding the Right Spot

To create a pattern, you must have some control over where lines and shapes are drawn on the screen. To get this control, we use what is sometimes called a *coordinate system.* A coordinate system is just a big word for describing the slicing up of the screen on which we would like to draw something into a big grid, where every available spot for drawing a dot is numbered.

Usually, the screen is numbered to reflect the smallest area that can be colored in at once. This smallest area is sometimes called a *pixel.* The more pixels present in a picture, the clearer the image. The number of pixels per square inch is also referred to as the *resolution* of the picture.

Lo-Res graphics on the Apple is a short-hand term for "Low Resolution Graphics." It's called Lo-Res because the screen is only divided up into a grid that is 40 units (or pixels) wide by 40 units high. It's hard to draw anything very detailed in Lo-Res.

Hi-Res graphics is short for "High Resolution Graphics" because the screen is divided up into much smaller pixels. In Hi-Res, the screen is 280 pixels wide by 162 pixels high.

The advantages of Lo-Res are that there are more colors available, and the range of colors to deal with is smaller (40 x 40) for Lo-Res, as opposed to 280 by 162 for Hi-Res). In Hi-Res though, you can create much more detailed pictures. A pie chart or good arcade game is, for all practical purposes, impossible in Lo-Res graphics.

In both systems, each screen pixel is identified by its own pair of numbers, called a *screen coordinate.* This screen coordinate tells the computer (and you) exactly where to find or draw a given dot on the screen. The first number in the pair tells you how far over the dot is. The second number tells how far down on the screen the dot it. Drawing a dot (or pixel) on the screen is usually called *plotting* a point.

For example, in Lo-Res graphics, a dot with the screen coordinate (0,0) would be at the upper left corner of your screen. A dot with the screen coordinate (39,39) would be in the lower right corner. You'll also notice here that instead of counting from 1 to 40, the pixels are numbered from 0 to 39. There's no really great reason for this, other than it was easier for the people who designed and built the Apple computer in the first place.

Can you guess what the screen coordinates of the lower left corner and the upper right corner would be? There is a box with the answer on page 20, but think about it now for a moment to see if you've got the idea of how screen coordinates work.

Making the Computer Do Something!

To see a real example of how graphics work on your Apple, let's try doing a few experiments in Lo–Res graphics. You know, whenever you wonder whether something might work a certain way on your computer, one of the very best ways to find out is to just try it out! Experiments aren't just for scientists and science students. They're also good for helping *you* find out exactly what your computer will and won't do!

To start, type in and run this simple Applesoft program:

```
10  GR
20  FOR I = 0 TO 15
30  COLOR = I
40  PLOT I,20
50  NEXT I
```

What this program does is to plot 16 boxes on the screen. The FOR–NEXT loop creates all the number values we need to get the 16 colors available in Lo–Res graphics. Line 30 sets COLOR equal to each successive value, and line 40 PLOTs the point. Notice how the screen coordinate is used in the PLOT command. Although in Lo–Res, the PLOT command actually draws a small box (because the pixel is so large), we'll generally refer to each plotted point as a 'dot'.

When I = 0, the program will plot a dot at (0,20). This would correspond to a dot at the far left part of the

screen, half way down. If you count the number of dots drawn on your screen by this program, you'll probably only see 15. That's because the first color plotted is *black*. Since the screen also has a black background, you don't see any change when the black dot is plotted!

Making Things Move

Now a row of dots on the screen certainly isn't all that exciting. That's why adding motion to any graphics screen makes things look so much better. The question is, how do you make the dots move?

The answer is you don't. What's that you say? You think we're playing with your mind? Well, we might be, but it's still true. You know your television or video monitor doesn't move around. And take our word for it, the letters and graphics figures you see on the screen don't *physically move* from one place to another.

What actually happens is that they're in fact erased from one position, and then *re-drawn* at a new location. If the new location is close enough to the first location (like right next to it for instance), then you're eye tells you that the letter or object has moved. Very tricky these computers! Don't feel bad though, movies work practically the same way!

To see what we mean, try this program:

```
10  GR
15  FOR J = 15 TO 25
20  FOR I = 0 TO 15
30  COLOR = I
40  PLOT I,J
45  COLOR = 0
47  PLOT I,J
50  NEXT I
55  NEXT J
```

Now it should look like things are moving. You should be able to tell by looking at the program though that no command like "MOVE" has been used. Instead, we've added a few lines that when combined with the original program, erase each line immediately after its drawn.

In this case, instead of drawing each row of dots at the middle of the screen, we use the counter in the FOR–NEXT loop that has 'J' as its counter to move the row down one line each time the J loop goes through one loop.

This brings us to a very important point: [If the X or Y value for a screen coordinate is changed by '1' each time the dot is plotted in a repeating loop, the dot will appear to move.]

continued on page 22

```
LIST

5    REM
RACER 1 GAME BY ROGER WAGNER

10   TEXT : HOME : GR : COLOR= 3
15   VTAB 21: HTAB 20: PRINT "HIGH
         SCORE: ";HS
20   X1 = 0:Y1 = 0:S1 = 0
30   K$ = "":D1$ = "R": REM


100  REM
MAIN SCAN LOOP


105 KEY =  PEEK ( - 16384): IF KE
      Y > 127 THEN  POKE  - 16368,
      0:K$ =  CHR$ (KEY - 128)
110  IF K$ =  CHR$ (27) THEN  RUN

115  IF K$ = "I" THEN D1$ = "U"
120  IF K$ = "M" THEN D1$ = "D"
125  IF K$ = "J" THEN D1$ = "L"
130  IF K$ = "K" THEN D1$ = "R"
135  IF D1$ = "U" THEN Y1 = Y1 -
      1: IF Y1 < 0 THEN Y1 = 0
140  IF D1$ = "D" THEN Y1 = Y1 +
      1: IF Y1 > 39 THEN Y1 = 39

145  IF D1$ = "L" THEN X1 = X1 -
      1: IF X1 < 0 THEN X1 = 0
150  IF D1$ = "R" THEN X1 = X1 +
      1: IF X1 > 39 THEN X1 = 39: REM


300  REM
DRAW PLAYER #1

305  IF  SCRN( X1,Y1) < > 0 THEN
       COLOR= 15: PLOT X1,Y1: VTAB
      22: PRINT  CHR$ (7);"CRASH!"
      : GOTO 600
310  PLOT X1,Y1
315  S1 = S1 + 1: VTAB 21: PRINT "
      SCORE:";S1
500  GOTO 100: REM

600  REM
ANOTHER GAME?

605  IF S1 > HS THEN HS = S1
610  PRINT "ANOTHER GAME? (Y/N)";

615  HTAB 20: GET A$
620  IF A$ = "Y" THEN 10
630  IF A$ = "N" THEN  END
640  GOTO 615
```

Logical Variables the Illogical Way:

Bumbling Through Basic

Val J. Golding

Perhaps as you read our title, you thought "What is a bumbler? A bumbler is a no–where man..." Well, you're right and wrong, at the same time. Consider this: your first day in a new school, you find unfamiliar hallways, maybe you've just moved from another city. You've checked in with the registrar, been assigned a home room. Next task: Find the home room and go through the first–day motions of traveling from class to class.

So you go through a doorway and see somewhat forbidding doors lining each side of a hall. You're looking for 117, and on each side of the hall, you note doors labeled 101 and 162. Neither of these are close to 117, so you wander down the hall, grasping your registration form, until you reach the end. Corridors extend both left and right from the hallway, so you turn left and walk a few feet and find opposite one another, rooms 145 and 162. Wow! You're still no closer. Or are you? You've pretty much eliminated two possibilities, right? Right. So you walk back a few steps and peek into the other corridor, and the first thing that greets your eye is room 123. "Aha, I'm pretty close," you may think. And you're right. As you walk a little further, you see 121, 119 and (oh yeah!), 117! You've been bumbling, friend!

So what is bumbling, and what does it have to do with programming or the Apple? You've just done it! You've been looking for a classrooom, you checked out three hallways, and on the third try, you struck it rich; you found what you were looking for. And so it is with the BASIC programming language. To program well, you

have to follow certain established ideas. But when it comes down to the nitty–gritty, you have to explore on your own. You have to often determine by trial and error whether or not something will work.

You have to determine by trial and error whether or not something will work.

There are times when you will find it expedient to ignore the rules entirely and follow your mind. Usually you will find what you are looking for. And in the meantime, you will have absorbed certain concepts: *this does this* and *this doesn't do this*. Your program may not be the best solution to a problem, but as long as it runs and does its job, that is the important thing. Later, you can (and should) go back over it and reduce things to the least common denominator, add REM lines so six months from now, you can figure out what's going on, renumber it, modularize it, in fact, rewrite it from scratch, *as long as you have a program that fits your needs* and runs correctly.

You always read about the *right* way to do things. Baloney! There are as many ways to program, and be creative in the process, as there are to drive a car. You can start easily from a

...there are different avenues to explore...

stop sign, accelerate to 25 miles per hour, brake gently for the next stop, and so on, until you arrive at your destination. Or you can peel it until you hit 25 and tromp on the brakes for the next light, or you can peel off and hit your top speed, stopping for nothing until you reach your destination. All three methods usually get you

where you're going (unless you run afoul of the law), but the arrival times will vary and the degree of safety will differ. The point is, there are different avenues to explore, and, at least in terms of programming, we urge you to do that. We want to give you a few examples to help you get the drift. Let's talk a bit about variables, and next time we chat, we'll drop a few hints, in our bumbling way, that will help you debug a program.

Variables are your friends. With descriptive names, they can jog your memory months later or help someone else working with your program. A variable may have a name up to 238 characters long, but Applesoft looks at only the first two characters of a variable name. Applesoft would think **RETRIEVE** and **RECOVER** were the same variable. In writing big programs, a utility like Roger Wagner's *Apple Doc* can be a big help to index and cross–reference your variables. Note that if you get into the habit of using long (and meaningful) variable names, you gotta watch out for that old bugaboo, the *reserved word*, otherwise known as an Applesoft command. If perchance one slips into your variable name, watch out! Try this one and see what happens:

```
920  PATTERN = 45
```

There are two classes of variables (simple and subscripted) in Applesoft, and four types: real, integer (designated by %), string (designated by $), and FN. *Different classes and different types of variables may have the same name.* For instance, Applesoft would individually recognize variables named A, A%, A$, FN(A), A(0), A%(0), and A$(0). There are times where we will purposely use a real variable and an integer variable with the same name, because they relate closely to one another.

As we said a few lines back, descriptive names are good memory jog-

Answer to question on page 19

Lower left corner: (0,39)
Upper right corner: (39,0)

gers. Typically in a FOR/NEXT loop, we will write something like

```
320  FOR I = 1 TO 45 : INPUT A(I)
     : NEXT
```

but why not write it like this:

```
320  FOR ITEM = 1 TO 45 :
     INPUT AUTHCODE(ITEM) :
     NEXT
```

Doesn't that really make a lot more sense and make the program easier to understand? Another little trick you

---

...substitute an integer variable to conserve memory.

---

can use — and the larger the program, the more important this becomes — is to substitute an integer variable to conserve memory. An integer (%) array will use three less bytes of memory for each element (numeric subscript) of the array. If you use integer variables, program execution speed will be slowed a trifle, but you'll probably never notice. Incidentally, the terms

array variable and *subscripted variable* mean almost the same thing and we use them interchangeably here. An *element* is a single subscript in an array, e.g., A$(21), 21 being the element or subscript.

Let's find our way back to bumbling, step by step. Did you know you can use your Apple as a lie detector? True. (ha-ha.) Of course, you may have to clue your Apple in beforehand, but if you want to check something out, Applesoft (and Integer Basic) will set a *truth flag*. To give you an idea of what we mean, type in from the keyboard:

```
A$ = "MARY"
PRINT A$ = "MARY"
```

What do you think the computer will print back? Remember, we're talking about a "truth test." If you think it will say "YES", you're wrong, but it will print "1". A truth variable can print (or return, as we like to say) only two things: the numbers "0" and "1." If the statement is true, a one will be printed, and if the statement is false, a zero will be returned. Try this:

```
PRINT A$ = "JOHN"
```

What do you think you'll see this time? 0? That's right, you're getting the idea.

Quite possibly, you're going to ask how you can use that idea in a program. Ok. Let's suppose you have an interactive (means the computer talks or responds to the user) program, and depending on whether Mary or John is using the program, different computer responses will be required. Let's look at two ways (there is always more than one way) in which we could perform a test in the program. The first, and most common method is with an IF/THEN statement like:

```
270  INPUT A$
280  IF A$ = "MARY" THEN
     TFLAG = 1
```

or you can write:

```
280  TFLAG = (A$ = "MARY")
```

This has the advantage of being just a little bit faster, and because no IF is involved, may be combined with other lines of code.

Here is where things get a little more hairy, 'cause we're going to talk

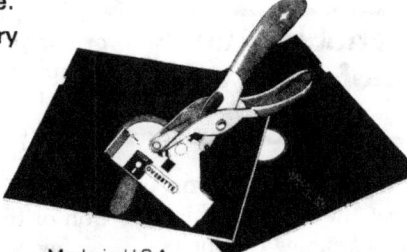

a little bit about *logical* variables. But before we get into that, we need to go off on a tangent, a side path, for a few minutes. Logical variables are simply extensions of truth variables, or truth variables with conditions attached.

...understanding logical variables was one of the toughest concepts we faced.

Logical variables are modified by statements like IF, AND, OR, and NOT. When we were learning to program, understanding logical variables was one of the toughest concepts we faced. In fact we still do have to stop and think about them. Often in writing a program where logic clearly dictates the use of AND, we find that OR would be the proper form to accomplish our programming goal. But here is how we bumble our way through. If AND does not produce the expected result, then try OR. If this works, then stop and *analyze why* it works, and find the flaw in your thinking. Remember the computer is (almost) always right!

First let's dispose of IF (in its logical sense) and NOT, because not only are they the simplest of the logical variables, they are also the most mysterious. Consider two BASIC statements:

```
760   IF A = 1 THEN GOTO 1000
770   IF B = 0 THEN GOTO 1200
```

Both of the two above statements can be expressed more simply as logical variables in the form:

```
760   IF A THEN GOTO 1000
770   IF NOT B THEN GOTO 1000
```

What these two statements convey literally is *if A has a value, then...* and *if B has no value, then...*

NOT has a second function as a *toggle*. A toggle is a switch that has only two possible states, on and off. Let's say in a program you want the user to be able to change a condition at will. Using a logical variable, *the program does not need to know the current state to be able to change it.* The

program statement which will do this for you is:

X = NOT X

If X = 0 then when this statement is encountered, it will be set to equal 1 or, if it now equals 1, it will be set to equal 0.

If your program needs to check whether more than one condition has been met, the IF statement can be modified, using the AND/OR combination. Generally, AND will test for and branch only when *both* conditions are true, while OR will branch to the indicated action on *either* condition being true.

```
620   IF (A AND B) THEN 1000
621   FLAG = (A AND B) :
      IF FLAG THEN 1000
630   IF (A OR B) THEN 1100
631   FLAG = (A OR B) :
      IF FLAG THEN 1100
640   IF (A OR (NOT B)) THEN 1200
651   FLAG = (A AND (NOT B) :
      IF FLAG THEN 1300
```

Now type in lines 1000, 1100, 1200 and 1300, all as STOP. When you reach one of these lines, Applesoft will print BREAK IN 1000, etc., so you'll know where your IF statement took you. Last, don't forget an INPUT or

Watch out for those parentheses.

otherwise establish the values for A and B. This is bumbling at its best (or worst). Watch out for those parentheses, they'll kill 'ya every time. Strictly confidential: We almost always end up with extra sets in the programs we write!

Here's a little quiz you can give yourself. Play it straight...write down each of the following questions and answer them, *then* RUN the above

...logical variables can help you out of many a tight spot.

program, and find out how well you did. If you can get the hang of this, you'll find logical variables can help you out of many a tight spot. You can

carry things a great deal further than we did here, and form some truly complex beasties, filled with ANDs, ORs and NOTs

A equals 1 and B equals zero.
Which line or lines will be executed.
A equals –5 and B equals zero.
Which line or lines will be executed.
A equals 0 and B equals zero.
Which lines or lines will execute.
A equals 0 and B equals 256.
Which line or lines will be executed.

So AND your hearts out; we're going to knock off for a while. We'll be back to bumble some more in a future issue, and next time around, we'll talk specifically about bug extermination.

MagiGraphics
from page 19

from page 19

If the dot is erased each time before it is re-drawn, the dot will look like a small object that moves. If you do not erase the old dot, then the "moving" dot will leave a trail.

You can use this "trail" to create a fun game. We call our version *RACER 1*. We have included a listing you can type in.

When the program is RUN, you'll see a line start out in the upper left corner, and head off towards the right hand part of the screen. The game is played by using the 'I,J,K and L' keys to steer the racer. If you let it run into a wall, *or even its own trail*, it will crash. You get more and more points depending on how long you can drive the racer without running into something.

The high score is printed at the bottom of the screen, so you can take turns with a friend, and see who can drive the longest without crashing.

There is a logical way to make sure you get as many points as possible with the least chance of crashing. Can you figure it out?

Next time, we'll explain how this program works, and also show you a two player version that lets two people each drive their own racers at the same time on the screen. This game is very much like the "light cycles" in the movie *TRON*, and the light cycle portion of the arcade game of *TRON* .

See you next time for another session of *MagiGraphics!*

Blast From the Past:
Phreaking Out

Cheshire Catalyst

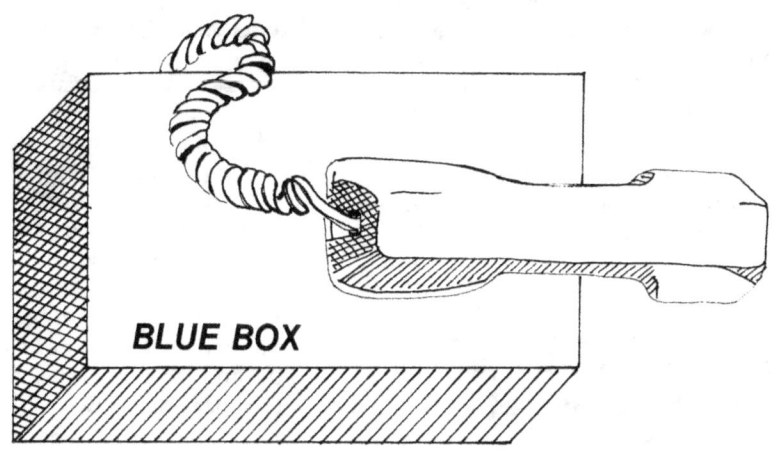

BLUE BOX

The international telephone network has been referred to as the world's largest computer. The Phone Phreaks, then, are the logical ancestors of today's modern computer hackers, since indeed, they were hacking the only available computer for anyone to hack on: The Telephone Network! If the public were made aware of how they "access" this "switching matrix," and otherwise shown the computer jargon that would pass for the simple human terms for "dialing," and "busy signal," they may possibly be made to understand that the jargon hype is a silly reason to be scared away from learning more about computers. The public "accesses" the most complex computer system on this planet every day, and

. . . phreaking is accessing the network in ways which were not intended . . .

almost without thinking. Certainly not thinking about it in computer-jargon, at any rate.

Phone phreaking is accessing the phone network in ways which were not intended by designers of the telephone network. In the late 50's, Bell Labs designed the Multi-Frequency (MF) Signaling System. These MF tones were designed to directly control the Long Lines switching network. The Touch Tone® telephone dial would put out a set of tones which were completely different from the MF signalling tones. So, while you would send TT signals to your local switching office, it would then send MF tones on up the line to instruct the network as

to what telephone number you wanted to be connected to.

The phone phreaks discovered the MF frequencies in the Bell System Technical Journal, a scholarly journal published by Bell Labs for network engineers so they will know what is going on with the network. When the MF signalling system was devised, it cost a lot of money to build the tone generators and decoders, even in the industrial quantities that Western Electric, supplier to the Bell System, was turning out. Not even Bell had forseen that solid state devices would drop in price so drastically that electronic hobbyists would be able to pick up the parts at Radio Shack and just throw together something that would sound to the receiving equipment like the Bell System's own equipment.

The Bell System Technical Journal, published with a blue cover, is called The Blue Book in the industry. It was no wonder, then, that the phreaks called their electronic wonder toy The *Blue Box*. It is interesting to note that the great wizard Woz was among those to develop, along with Cap'n Crunch, the first primitive blue boxes. But that is another story itself, and we'll leave that for the Woz himself to tell. To show how one of the original blue boxes worked, let's discuss how the network worked in general.

When you place a long distance call from your home, the number is captured by an "incoming register."

From the first few digits, it determines that you want to place a long distance call. It then MF's the digits up the wire, and the Long Lines equipment handles it from there. When the party at the other end picks up the phone, a "supervision" signal is sent back to your central office which means "They answered, so start billing."

Just silence on the line wouldn't do . . .

When you hang up the phone, your central office stops the billing machine, and signals are sent to "dissolve" the connection.

When you've hung up, the long lines machine now has to tell the machine at the other end that the call is finished. Just silence on the line wouldn't do, because there might be a couple of teen-agers who are just on the line breathing at each other, and the Bell System wouldn't want to disconnect the call and lose the revenue. What they do do is send a tone of 2,600 Hertz (cycles per second) down the line as an indication that the line is free.

What a phone phreak did, was dial a long distance call, usually to an 800 "Toll Free" number (hotel reservations number, or an airline). The 800 numbers start billing at the other end of the call, that is, when the receiving party picks up the call, billing computers at the calling party's end are instructed to disregard 800 calls on billing tapes. Getting back to our example, however, our phone phreak will call an 800 number. While it is ringing, and before anyone can pick up the phone at the other end, the phreak will transmit a tone of 2600 Hz into the phone line. The "blue box" usually contains a speaker which is held over the mouthpiece of the telephone. The machine at the other end of the circuit "hears" its signal that the calling party has hung up, and disconnects its end of the call.

. . . the phreak will transmit a tone of 2600 Hz . . .

When the phreak stops sending the tone, the machine figures, "Oh, this trunk circuit has now been siezed by the other end, so I will now set up to receive signals (MF tones) telling me where to route the next call." The phreak then enters the sequence of tones that will route his call anywhere in the world, and the telephone company computer system snaps to an electronic "Yes Sir!," and connects the call. Now the called party picks up the phone, and the "supervision" signal is returned to the originating central office, but since that billing machine only knows that an 800 call was placed, it discards the billing information. It is (or was) as simple (?) as that. Let's face it, the phone phreak had to know as much about the network as any telephone traffic engineer. Many of the phreaks, in fact, got caught when they reported network problems they discovered.

Ah, those were the good old days. Days when phone phreaks were real phone phreaks, and not just someone trying to rip off The Phone Company (or TPC, after the 1966 movie "The President's Analyst" in which The Phone Company was foiled in its attempt to rule the world). The phreaks were genuinely interested in how the network operated. However, all good things must come to an end, and the evolving digital telephone network did away with the transmission of "analog"

(sound) signals for the switching of telephone calls.

The phreaks were genuinely interested in how the network operated.

The new Common Channel Interoffice Signaling system (CCIS) is a new computerized method for The Phone Company to switch phone calls. For example, where there is a 500 pair cable between New York and Chicago, then pair number 1 would be connected to the computers at either end, and the computers would tell each other how to switch the other 499 pairs in the circuit. Besides being a faster method of communicating between the switching machines, computerized switching also did away with the "blue boxing" antics of the phone phreaks.

. . . computerized switching did away with "blue boxing" antics . . .

By that time, computers had appeared on the scene. The type of intellectual challenge that the phone network represented, was to be found in the home computers that were becoming affordable, as the phone network became more and more unexplorable.

As a case in point, John Draper of California was one of the nations best known phone phreaks after being written up in *the* definitive article on the subject in a 1971 issue of Esquire magazine. He called himself Cap'n Crunch, because he had found that a Bos'n whistle, given away free in Cap'n Crunch breakfast cereal, produced a tone of exactly 2600 Hertz! He subsequently found most of the other information he needed from Bell System publications, and by making himself obnoxious at Bell System switching offices. I've watched his interviewing technique on unsuspecting, and helpful service people, and it certainly is a wonder that he can take a person's natural inclination to be helpful, and turn it against a person's inclination to protect the proprietary nature of the information in his/her care.

Bell eventually caught him doing his nasty electronic stuff, and had him thrown in the slammer. If John hadn't been made such a folk hero by the press, it may not have gone so bad for

John Draper wrote Easy Writer.

him. On one of his sojournes into jail, (after having been caught in Pennsylvania "breaking parole") he was back in a California pokey in a work program. He was allowed out to work a job during the day, but had to be back inside the walls at night. At the time, there were no good word processing programs for the Apple computer, so John set out to write one. It was while in the work program that John wrote Easy Writer, which was the first really good word processor for the Apple.

A couple of years later, IBM was looking around for software to bundle with its PC (Personal Computer) so that they would have software available when it "Hit the street." By that time, there were better packages than Easy Writer for the Apple, and other micros, but I personally think that someone at IBM had a sense of humor. Either that, or they wanted to send a shot across that someone's bow.

AT&T and IBM were taking their corners in the fight of the century.

In the late 70's, it looked as if the 80's would be the "Battle of 56th St." On the North side of Madison Avenue and 56th St in New York City, there is the world headquarters building of IBM, and on the south side of 56th St, is the new AT&T Chippendale. With the FCC unable to draw the lines between Data and Voice Communications after two inquiries to try to do so, it looked as if AT&T and IBM were taking their corners in the fight of the century. The Justice Department breakup of AT&T disrupted this fight, and the whole arena changed shape.

Meanwhile, IBM decided John Draper, the infamous Cap'n Crunch, and his new software company "Cap'n Software" should design and program the word processing package for the new IBM PC. This could be taken as a slap in the face to AT&T, if anyone bothered to look at it, but no one I know in the industry has decided to look at it this way.

So we now have a digital telephone network, and former phone phreaks now involved with digital technology. One of the early dreams when CCIS was first announced, was for a phreak to take a Gunn Diode, and make a "Gunn," or a shoulder fired rifle type of transmitter with a microcomputer inside, and "fire" a signal at the local microwave tower, which would inject a digital message saying "When my friend in Los Angeles hangs up, ring me back." The computerized switching network is able to handle messages of that type, and other services which only recently have been offered to the public, mostly because Bell couldn't determine what to charge for them.

The reason this type of thing won't work is due to the national security aspect. It seems that the Russians have been listening in to our microwave transmissions over the years. All they had to do was tune in the channels, and let the computers take over. As the MF signals were sent, the Soviet gear would determine if the "target" phone number was of interest to them. this meant, if the number being called was a military installation, or government facility, a tape recorder could be started up on that circuit. Now the Bell System and national security boys are getting together, and all the data transmissions regarding how the calls will be switched will go via under ground circuits. This way, the data being sent underground will tell the circuit switchers at the microwave sites where the call will be routed next.

As the phone phreaks get deeper and deeper into the digital universe, they are being bought up (hired) by the complex world of data communications. They've learned more by themselves, than what was being taught in colleges just a few short years ago. They are infiltrating the "Real World," as well as the computer hackers of my aquaintance, who mostly are trying to put their old "hacking" days behind them in the closet, along with the rest of the skeletons, as they penetrate further into the corporate en-

vironment, where having been "one of those nasty hackers" may not be good for their corporate health. Fortunately, there is now a movement afoot to "clear" the good name of Hacking which has recently been tarnished by the media coverage of "hacking incidents."

The phone phreaks of yesteryear are the electronic crossword puzzle solvers of the pre-computer era. Now that computers are everywhere, that kind of intellectual challenge is provided by the most complex, and involving of all mind toys, The Computer.

Cheshire Catalyst is Richard Cheshire, a new York City based Telecomputer Consultant who publishes TAP, The Hobbyist Journal for the Communications Revolution (a technological revolution only, mind you). TAP has been published for informational purposes only since 1971, and is a source of information for phone phreaks, and computer hackers. Their address is:

TAP, Room 603, 147 West 42nd St, New York, NY 10036

This article is an exerpt from Digital Deli, a book edited by Steve Ditlea to be published by Workman Publishing.

Back Talk

Dear Val,

Being an average 16 year old with a somewhat limited computer background, I thought that I would sit down and drop you a line or two about what I would like to see in a computer magazine oriented toward the "younger generation." I think that the idea for such a magazine for the young (and the young at heart) is certainly worth whatever effort and expense there may be to bring it into fruition. Ideas concerning content, style, and frequency are probably coming to you by the dozen, however, please indulge me to give you another. Again, let me stress the point that I am not a computer expert, just one who has an interest in this new technology.

As a final thought, some of your readers may be considering careers in computers. I think that it would be nice if you, or a contributing author, would present some articles on the educational requirements necessary, and career opportunities that one could expect.

These are just a few of the thoughts that I have regarding your new magazine. I hope that they stimulate other possibilities for you. I also wish you the best of luck with the magazine, flourishing and eventful years, and a bright future.

Michelle Craft
Renton, WA

Dear Editor,

Thank you for the opportunity to tell you what I would like to see in a kids computer magazine. I would like to see things about other kids of all ages. I would like to see articles about programs written for learning, especially those that make learning fun. Of course, the latest on games and their reviews.

Thinking about games, I love puzzles, riddles, and crosswords. I would like to see articles that make you really think. I would like to see pictures and illustrations whenever possible, also something on BASIC troubleshooting we can do before calling our parents to the rescue.

Articles on many different [programming] languages and how we can use them. And last, but not least, I would mostly like to see a column on computer slang and its many uses and meanings.

Good luck to you and the *Apple's Apprentice*.

Marquisha Davis (age 9)
Van Nuys, CA

Strategy-arcade game for the whole family!

Fat City

Developed by Optimum Resource, Inc. Designed by Richard Hefter and Steve Worthington. For the Apple computer.

You run a crane for the Fat City Wrecking Co. Your job: knock down deserted buildings in 10 cities. But beware! The old buildings are occupied by a bunch of nasty rats. And they're going to bombard you with cans, tomatoes and rocks as you slam your wrecking ball into their crumbling homes.

Can you batter the buildings before running out of fuel? Can you rub out the rampaging rodents? Fat City is a game everyone in your family is going to love. Says Softalk: "A great deal of thought went into its development as its excellent playability attests. The game incorporates super graphics and strategy, fun and a new idea. The combination could well prove addicting."

Look for Fat City in finer computer stores everywhere. Or, order by calling toll-free 1-800-852-5000, Dept. AF-18. Only $39.95.

FatCity
WeeklyReader
Family Software

A division of Xerox Education Publications
Middletown, CT 06457

YE OLDE GAME SHOP

VAL J. GOLDING

Welcome, ye, to Ye Olde Game Shoppe. Swing wide the oaken door, my lovelies, taking care not to disturb the cobwebs, and feast thy eyes upon the goodies which lineth the walls. Wander to thy heart's content, lads and lasses, and when thou spoteth a program sufficient to curdle thy blood, feel free to place it in the magic apple and playeth away. Remember the wizard's words, my friends: "Thou breaketh, thou buyeth!" And now young ones, as the day wears on, let me direct thy attention to a special game, and to a contest thou shalt enjoy.

Fat City

Here is a game which should appeal to the destructive element in all of us. Imagine being let loose in a town doomed to be torn down and rebuilt, with a wrecking crane at your disposal (you know, the old-fashioned kind with a huge swinging ball), and no one around to stop you from climbing in the empty cab. What a ball! ('scuze the pun.) This is what *Fat City* is all about.

Visuals are great and the packaging is durable and attractive. Fat City comes with excellent documentation, decals, posters, and a warranty card for free replacement if your disk goes bad. It's $39.95 from *Weekly Reader Family Software*, 245 Long Hill Road, Middletown, CT 06457, or your dealer.

Play commences with a full fuel tank and the image of the city through the window of your cab. Keys or joystick control the motion of the crane up and down the street, and the height of the wrecking ball, which is swung with button zero. Points are scored for each portion of a building brought down, and the larger the piece the more points you get. But a word of caution: each swing of the ball uses fuel, and an attempt to bring down too large a piece will result in only a crack in the building.

One unexpected hazard is the rats. Yes, we said rats. You know rats are always the last to leave a sinking ship. Well it appears they are also the last to leave an abandoned building. In the meanwhile, they pass the time by throwing bricks and other debris at the crane. If you don't dodge, each hit costs you fuel. Ah, fuel. That's the other point we wanted to mention. There is always a fuel tank hidden behind one of the buildings, and you need to refill to be able to finish the job. Sneakily, the fuel tank is not in the same place each time you play.

When you manage to tear down an entire town, there is another waiting for your gentle touch, just ever-so-slightly tougher, up to a total of ten. The game is a joy to play, goat-getting and a whole bunch of fun. You need to spend a lot of time developing skills and technique before getting much beyond the first two or three cities.

Fat Chance!

A Contest! Here's one you can't pass up. We've spent many hours playing Fat City, but never made it passed round eight. Almost into nine, but not quite. (Those dawgone fuel tanks!) So here's a chance to win a free game or get a one year sub to *The Apple's Apprentice*. To the first reader who sends us a Fat City diskette with a score of 100,000 or more and shows round 10 completed, we'll award a free Weekly Reader Family Software game, and for the second diskette we receive, we'll give you a one year subscription or extension to *The Apple's Apprentice*. Each entry must contain the following:

• Your name, address and age

• A stamped, self-addressed envelope with sufficient postage to return your diskette, otherwise diskettes *can not* be returned
• Address your entry to:
  Fat Chance
  Emerald City Publishing, Inc.
  P.O. Box 582-AA
  Santee, CA 92071

Sounds almost too good to be true, doesn't it! But that's right, all you have to do is have fun and mail your disk to us. What more can you ask? (We'll probably hear about that!)

A Reading Adventure

For you adventure game players, we've found a new book to help you on your way through the caverns and rooms of games like *Time Zone* or *The Wizard and the Princess*. We couldn't believe it when we saw it — here are room maps and clues galore, advice and tips on playing each of the 14 popular games covered, all in large easy-to-read type, and many illustrations.

It's 167 pages, softbound, for $9.95, and published by *Datamost*, 20660 Nordhoff St., Chatsworth, CA 91311. The authors introduce the book with one very important note we'd like to pass on: "Try to solve each puzzle yourself, before looking up the answer." That's good advice, too, because you don't want to take the fun out of your game-playing, but "Shortcut" is good to have at the ready, if and when you need it. Betcha we put it to use soon!

And now the shadows grow long, a purple haze graces the Far Mountains, and our supper awaits us. We must shutter our windows, and be on our way.

An Introduction to Eamon Adventures

Michael Thyng

Probably the first modern computer game that "everyone" heard about was *Pong*. But *Pong* is a game of coordination and wrist exercise. Likewise, so are *Pac-Man*, *Invaders*, and *Defender*.

The first computer game was probably some main-frame version of *Star Trek*. I keep running into various versions on the different systems I work with. Even in 1977, when the Apple][was first introduced, sure enough, a cassette tape of *Apple][Trek* running in Integer Basic, was included.

No one locally seems to know where the various versions originated. They just arrived, courtesy of someone who knew someone who knew someone who had a copy from someplace. This simulation of travel around the universe, fighting for the Federation, was no doubt the first computer adventure game. An adventure game is a computer program that describes a place by displaying words on the screen and gives the adventurer — you — a limited vocabulary of directions. The computer describes what surrounds you at a given stopping point, and you decide which direction to go. The object of the game is usually to recover the greatest number of valuable items in a dangerous place and return to the starting point without being killed. There are variations on this theme, such as rescuing unjustly imprisoned hostages or some important official.

One of the popular adventure games is called EAMON. Like the typical adventure game, playing EAMON is a quest to amass the greatest amount of loot and return to the main hall alive. If you've never played an adventure game, EAMON is a good one to get your first experience on. It offers not only an easy first adventure, The Beginners Cave, but it also gives you the programs necessary to create your own EAMON adventure, with your own creatures, places, and valuable items to be found.

To begin the game you just type "RUN THE WONDERFUL WORLD OF EAMON." You immediately find yourself in the main hall. A sign says "register here." The computer tells you that you see people drinking beer, then it asks you if you want to join the people drinking or register? Now you have to make a decision. Depending on your response, you will either be guided into an adventure or else be killed by a stab in the back, and be forced to start over. When you figure out how to get past the first obstacle, you are told what the attributes are for your character. (An attribute is a *quality*, such as wisdom, that — as in the case of EAMON — can be given to a character.)

Each character will be assigned a number from 1 to 25 for each attribute. The EAMON attributes are Agility, Hardiness, and Charisma. Generally, the higher the number in each attribute, the better chance your character will have for survival when meeting other characters in the adventure. A female character with a lot of charisma may be able to soften the heart of the hairy gorilla and avoid being killed. Someone with low agility may not be able to move quickly enough to keep from being injured by a hostile character.

In the EAMON series adventures, you are given a list of directives or code words you use to play the game. The directives are such things as NORTH, SOUTH, GET, DROP, and the like. These tell the computer that you want to go north or south or pick something up or set something down. As the adventure progresses, you may find yourself in a long north/south tunnel with a passageway to the east and a door to the west; there is a can of brown liquid on the ground. Now you have to decide what to do. What's behind the door? To find out, just enter a "W." If you say "get can" you will pick up the can, which could hold a potion that might save your life at some future point in the game (like after the hairy gorilla beats you up) — or the brown liquid it contains may be a poison for which there is no antidote. Experience pays.

Unlike typical adventure games, EAMON does not stand alone. There are 40 or more unique adventures, on as many diskettes. You can travel from adventure to adventure just by successfully [remaining alive] returning from an adventure.

Each is available through Public Domain software. Public Domain means the programs belong to everybody, and the author asks no royalties (payment) for his work. Public Domain diskettes can be copied and given to your friends without violating any laws. EAMON diskettes are available from *Call -A.P.P.L.E.*, *The Apple Avocation Alliance*, and many Apple Computer user groups around the country.

The simple hints given here also, in general, apply to many of the other adventure games. If you haven't played adventure-type games before, here's your chance to get started at very little cost.

Better Begin With BASIC

Mike Collins

This column is about programming in the BASIC language on an Apple]l or Apple //e computer. Some of you may already be familiar with your Apple and may have already started to program on it, while others of you may have just gotten your computers recently, and haven't had a chance yet to play around on it. Or perhaps you have had an Apple at home or at school for a couple of years, but haven't wanted to do anything with it until now.

Everyone is different, but hopefully interested in learning to program in BASIC. That is why I decided to use this first column to try and teach you a little bit about the way we will be writing BASIC programs on our Apples.

First of all, it might help if we all know what a "program" really is. I looked program up in the dictionary, and got several answers, including *a brief outline of the order to be pursued or the subjects included,* and *coded instructions for a mechanism.* Both of these definitions are trying to say the same thing, but neither has made it very clear. As far as we are concerned, a program is *a sequence of instructions given to a computer to make it do something for us.*

For example, if you wanted to tell your Apple to type the word "HELLO" on the screen, we could write a program like this:

```
10   PRINT "HELLO"
20   END
```

That is a BASIC program that instructs or tells the computer to type the word "HELLO" on the screen where we can see it. As you can see it is pretty short, and very simple. When you have typed it in and then typed the *keyword* "RUN," it will *execute,* and you have written and run your first program!

So now your dad (or mom) has bought a computer, and told you when they were not using it, you could play with it. What are you going to do, play games? Sure, that's a good idea, 'cause a couple came with with the machine, and mom and dad don't really dig games that much.

But you know, after a few weeks, two or three games can get pretty dull. Then what? Well you Better Begin With BASIC. You already know all there is to know about DOS, or at least to put a disk in the drive and turn the power on, and then the same ol' silly game boots up.

Mebbe you better stop and think: is there anything more exciting you can do? The Apple computer really is a pretty high-falutin' piece of equipment. Do you really have any idea of what it can do, of what you can make it do?

Well, guys and gals, you Better Begin With BASIC. Applesoft Basic is a "programming language" that comes built into the Apple]l. Mostly it is made up of simple words or instructions like PRINT or TEXT or IF or THEN. You'll be amazed how little study is needed to write a simple program that will print your name on the screen. If you're really interested in seeing how much fun you can have learning to program your Apple, Mike Collins has agreed to take the time to show you.

The program is only two lines long, and each line has a number. It is standard practice for most programmers to number the lines in their programs in steps of ten, just in case they want to add something inbetween lines later on without having to retype the whole program.

For example, if I wanted to say hello to my friend Danny on the Apple, I could use the program we just wrote to do it. If I type RUN, then the word HELLO would appear on the screen, just as I explained a moment ago. What if I wanted to put Danny's name on the screen at the same time? If I could get the computer to type HELLO DANNY, then that would be a much nicer message than a plain, ordinary HELLO. That way, Danny would know I was saying "hello" to him, and not just anybody that happened to come along and type RUN on my Apple.

I could change the program to say HELLO DANNY in a couple of different ways. First, I could just rewrite line 10 to read:

```
10   PRINT "HELLO DANNY"
```

That would do the trick, and when I ran the program by typing RUN, I would see the message HELLO DANNY just as I had expected. Suppose I was lazy and didn't want to retype the line. I could do the same thing by adding another line between 10 and 20, which would tell the computer to type Danny's name after it had typed HELLO. The way to do this is to pick a number between 10 and 20, like 15, and type in:

```
15   PRINT "DANNY"
```

If I want to see the whole program together, I can type LIST, and the screen will show:

```
10   PRINT"HELLO"
15   PRINT"DANNY"
20   END
```

LIST is the instruction that tells the Apple to show me what my program looks like so far, and when I type RUN, I will see:

**HELLO
DANNY**

That's just what I wanted to see. By adding in a line number that was between the line that told the Apple to print HELLO, but before the one which told the machine the program was over (the END statement), I was able to tell the computer to say hello to Danny, rather than just hello.

The most important thing to learn from the program is the process we had to go through to make the computer do what we wanted. In order to make the machine say "hello," we had to tell it to PRINT "HELLO". Then, to have the Apple say hello to Danny, we had to find the part of the program after it said HELLO, but before it said END, and tell it to PRINT "DANNY." If we had tried to do the same thing just by typing PRINT "DANNY" at the beginning of the program, when we tried to RUN it, we would see:

**DANNY
HELLO**

which doesn't make very much sense. In other words, to make the Apple do what we wanted, we had to tell it each special step involved in doing the task, *in the order we wanted*. This looks pretty easy, and it is, but sometimes there are more than just these few steps involved in running a program.

For example, when we take out the garbage, all we usually think about is taking out the garbage. We don't go through the chore piece by piece, telling ourselves to:
1) get the garbage
2) carry the garbage outside
3) put the garbage in the can
4) go back inside

However, if we wanted to have the computer do the job for us, that is exactly what we would have to do. We would have to write a program to tell the computer each and every step it needs to do to make sure the garbage got emptied O.K. The program might look something like this:

```
10   GET GARBAGE
20   CARRY GARBAGE OUTSIDE
30   PUT GARBAGE IN CAN
40   GO BACK INSIDE
```

Even this is an over–simplification, because we forgot things like taking the top off of the garbage can and putting it back on, but you get the idea, and if our Apple were a robot which could pick things up and move them around, then the program might work. The important thing is to understand how to take a task, like taking out the garbage, and break it down into a series of little, tiny jobs. Once we have done all of that, then we can write the program that tells the computer what to do.

We can practice breaking things down into jobs by making up pretend programs to do things that we do without ever thinking about what we're doing. If you wanted to go to the kitchen to get a glass of milk, you could make up a program that would *simulate* your actions, like:

```
10    GO TO KITCHEN
20    OPEN REFRIGERATOR
30    GET MILK
40    CLOSE REFRIGERATOR
50    GET GLASS
60    TAKE TOP OFF BOTTLE
70    POUR MILK
80    PUT TOP ON BOTTLE
90    OPEN REFRIGERATOR
100   RETURN MILK
110   PICK UP MILK GLASS
120   DRINK MILK
130   GO TO SINK
140   TURN ON WATER
150   WASH GLASS
160   TURN OFF WATER
170   PUT GLASS IN CUPBOARD
180   LEAVE KITCHEN
```

When we write it out like that, we can see that there are a whole lot of different jobs involved in doing something simple like getting a glass of milk, so a computer must be told each and every step along the way. Even as detailed as we were, a real computer would have to be told even more than the instructions we put in out program. It would have to know where to get the milk glass, how to pour the milk, how to drink it, how to turn on the faucet to wash the glass, and a whole bunch of other things we never think about until we have to explain it to a computer.

Computer programmers have a saying: Garbage in, garbage out. This means that, because a computer can do only what you to it to do, if you tell it to do something that doesn't make any sense, then it will do something that doesn't make any sense. The key to programming your Apple is knowing exactly what you want your Apple to do for you, and working out exactly the way to tell it, so that it will understand what you mean.

In future columns I will help you to learn about what words or commands your Apple understands, so that you will know how to tell it what to do. Remember, the Apple is your servant; you can use it for many things.

In the meantime, have fun. That's what it's all about!

The Crystal Ball

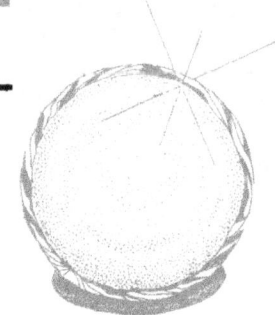

New Graphics System

Apollo Software Technology, a software research and develop company, recently published the Graph-Art System I, a graphic utility program for the Apple][Plus and //e. The program can help users create brilliant pictures for entertainment, business display, or computer art hobbyist.

It includes a 50+ coloring program, a fast eraser, an inverse picture producer, a tracing sheet, a slide show organizer, mix graphic/text, and much more. The program is on a disk, with a tutorial/instruction booklet, and demo pictures (both on disk and booklet). The suggested retail price for the system is $34.00. For further information, please write to Apollo Software Technology, P.O. Box 34057, Houston, Texas 77234.

Hallowe'en Year 'Round

The fun and magic of pumpkins, spiders, and skulls is now available the year "round with 'HALLOWE'EN" from MicroSPARC. This high-resolution arcade game is for a 64k Apple][, //e, or Franklin Ace.

The object of HALLOWE'EN is to lead a wizard through a 10-screen kingdom, snatching pumpkins and killing spiders and skulls along the way.

A novice wizard will fall prey to the pouncing spiders, bouncing skulls, and deadly choppers, unless he quickly becomes adept with his magic wand.

It can be played with one or two players, using joystick, paddles, or keyboard. Games can be redesigned extensively by varying options which include sound toggle, delay times for falling objects, choice of point values per object, and even the number of skulls, pumpkins, etc., on each of the 10 levels. The top five highest scores can be saved on disk.

HALLOWE'EN comes on a pumpkin-colored diskette and can be ordered for $29.95 from Micro-SPARC, Inc., 10 Lewis St., Lincoln, MA 01773, phone (617) 259-9710. Check, money-order, Visa and MasterCard accepted.

M.E.C.C. Catalog

The current MECC catalog contains 190 educational computing programs and training materials for the Apple][and other computers.

Request your free copy now by contacting Minnesota Educational Computing Consortium (MECC), 3490 Lexington Avenue North, St. Paul, MN 55112. (612) 481-3500.

AppleMouse][Announced

Apple Computer demonstrated a mouse and new software called MousePaint, which is now available for its Apple®][personal computers.

A mouse is a pointing device that can be used instead of a keyboard to select computer operations and modify information displayed on the screen. Apple's Lisa™ computer, introduced last year, ignited broad interest in the mouse among computer owners, software developers and other computer manufacturers. The Lisa is designed to be almost completely controlled by a mouse, one of the things that makes it much easier to use yet more powerful than conventional computers.

AppleMouse][will be packaged with MousePaint software that uses the mouse to design charts, diagrams, free-hand drawings and other visual aids for reports and presentations. Users can insert text in a drawing and can choose from a variety of character fonts and fill patterns. MousePaint simulates bit map graphics to support the Apple]['s high resolution capabilities.

Independent software developers are being encouraged to write applications that take advantage of the mouse. Most future Apple software programs for the Apple][family will offer the mouse as an option.

Apple also is developing a mouse to work with Apple /// personal computers.

Apple Color Plotter

Apple Computer has introduced a multi-color plotter for its Apple®][and Apple /// personal computers that produces presentation-quality graphs, charts, drawings and graphic designs on either paper or overhead transparencies.

The Apple Color Plotter, Model 410, is a versatile tool for anyone who gives presentations or needs to produce printed copies of multi-color graphics created with a personal computer.

The Apple Color Plotter is compatible with Apple Business Graphics, Apple Logo and many other software programs which utilize the high-resolution, multi-color graphics capabilities of the Apple][and Apple ///.

The plotter features four color pens that are interchanged automatically during operation. Commands given to the plotter by the graphics software determine pen selection, so a user does not need to stop the plotter's operation to change pens.

Designed for both plotting accuracy and speed, the plotter provides 0.004-inch resolution, 0.008-inch repeatability and 3.94 inches-per-second plotting speed. Its variable-width plotting bed and adjustable pinch roller mechanism permit a wide choice of media sizes up to 11" x 17".

The Apple Color Plotter uses a standard RS-232C serial interface and will connect to any personal computer that supports this interface. The plotter connects directly to the Apple ///'s built-in serial port. Apple's Super Serial Interface Card connects it to the Apple][Apple][+, or Apple //e.

The Apple Color Plotter is available now from U.S. authorized Apple dealers and through Apple's educational state buy programs. The U.S. suggested retail price for the plotter is $995. The plotter carries Apple's standard 90-day warranty, and Apple's extended service plan, AppleCare™, also is available.

New Educational Software

The Learning Company, producer of award-winning educational software packages, has introduced five new discovery learning programs... Reader Rabbit and The Fabulous Word Factory, Word Spinner, Number Stumper, Addition Magician and Colorasaurus.

With these new offerings, The Learning Company product line has two new reading programs, two new number programs and its first art program.

Reading Programs

Reader Rabbit and The Fabulous Word Factory is a completely new approach to teaching essential pre-reading and early reading skills to children aged 5 to 7. By helping Reader Rabbit match pictures and words, label boxes and load words into a word train, children learn to recognize and spell more than 200 three-letter words. The program sells for $39.95.

Word Spinner takes young readers, aged 6 to 10, on a whirl through the alphabet to learn the building blocks of reading. In building more than 500 three-letter words and 1,000 four-letter words, children learn to recognize word patterns and develop critical vocabulary and spelling skills. Emphasis is placed on proper positioning of vowels and consonants to enhance word pattern recognition. Priced at $34.95, the program runs on Apple II computers and is now available.

Number Programs

Number Stumper, the computer-age version of a classic 14th century game of chance, teaches basic addition and subtraction. Using animated dice, children aged 6 to 10 create and solve mathematical equations and develop abstract reasoning and strategic thinking skills. The program sells for $39.95.

Addition Magician is a fast-paced, race-against-the-clock number strategy game that teaches children the basic concepts of addition and flexible thinking about numbers. Children build magic walls around groups of numbers that add up to a target sum. The program, for children aged 6 to 10, is priced at $34.95.

With these additions, The Learning Company now offers 14 educational software packages. Its other programs are Juggles' Rainbow, Bumble Games, Bumble Plot, Gertrude's Puzzles, Gertrude's Secrets, Moptown Parade, Moptown Hotel, Magic Spells and the popular Rocky's Boots, called a "software classic" by The New York Times.

The Learning Company is headquartered at 545 Middlefield Road, Suite 170, Menlo Park, CA 94025. Telephone (415) 328-5410.

MICROCHIPS   by Robert Cavey

The Book
That's an Open Door to the Computer Future

KIDS & THE APPLE is its name, and its game is to prepare your child, or any child, to take his or her place as a member of the computer generation by teaching them the mysteries of the Apple* computer in ways they'll love and enjoy. Don't be surprised if you will also learn along with your child.

The kids of today are fascinated by computers to start with. And that's great, because it means **they're eager** to learn. But, until this book by Edward H. Carlson, learning about the Apple was a fumbling, bumbling effort for a child.

KIDS & THE APPLE was designed in every aspect to lead them gently, interestingly yet quickly into the computer world. First, it's a large 8½ by 11 book which can be opened flat for ease of use. Second, there are 35 chapters, each one building upon the knowledge of the prior chapter — and it's loaded with dozens and dozens of cartoons which make a point as they amuse.

At computer stores, or from:

The educational/book division of

DATAMOST INC.

9748 Cozycroft Ave.
Chatsworth, CA 91311   (213) 709-1202

Then, there are special sections for a parent or teacher to use so they can work along with the kids, if they wish, and help them over any rough spots.

Perhaps the major reasons the kids will love this book is that it is **truly** written so they can easily understand it (without a lot of confusing technical language) . . . and that they see on-screen-results almost immediately! Right away they realize they'll soon be programming their Apple, making their own games! . . . or creating other programs for school or work or to play.

The computer world is roaring toward us. To be successful at work, school or even play, a child will have to be knowledgeable about computers. Make sure your favorite child is prepared for the challenge. With KIDS & THE APPLE at his side, he'll enjoy learning and you'll know you've prepared him or her for a successful future.   Only $19.95.

*Apple is a trademark of Apple Computer, Inc.

The Macintosh has a new ring.

The ARTSCI **MAGICphone**™ creates an entirely new aspect to the APPLE Macintosh™, that provides a spectrum of voice/telephone communications.

Software is provided to manage and dial hundreds of phone numbers and will record and print the details (time, number, and charge) of each call. The phone log can be printed on a daily, weekly, or monthly basis. The mouse is used to select and dial any phone number, and **MAGICphone** uses TONE dialing to any of the lower-cost telephone carriers like SPRINT and MCI.

The **MAGICphone** also allows control of two separate phone lines. A "hold" feature for each line with lighted indicators is provided. You can then call someone to the phone or pick up an extension and continue the call. The **MAGICphone** can temporarily stop incoming calls, and the caller will hear a busy signal.

The **MAGICphone** can be used as a stand alone telephone without Macintosh control. Tone dialing and last number redial are standard features.

Installation is a snap. You simply plug the **MAGICphone** into your Macintosh speaker jack, and into your phone line.

Available now. $199.95.

ARTSCI, INC.
5547 Satsuma Avenue
North Hollywood, CA 91601
818/985-2922

MAGICphone was developed for ARTSCI by Digital Matrix Inc.
MAGICphone is a trademark of Artsci, Inc.
Macintosh is a trademark of APPLE Computer, Inc.

Volume I, No. 2

June, 1984

the APPLE'S APPRENTICE

Learning about Apples

$2.50 ($3.00 Canada)

Fantasy
learning
the Apple's Apprentice way!

Computer Camps
vacation learning fun

Apple's Newest!
the //c portable

- **GAMES**

- **CONTESTS**

- **PUZZLES**

- **COMICS**

- **PROGRAMS**

- **TRICKS**

The Apple magazine for kids 8 to 80

Penguin Scores Again!

	Releases	Hits	Errors
Fantasy	2	2	0
Arcade	1	1	0

Expedition Amazon—A fantasy role-playing game with a sense of humor. Guide your own expedition from Nihil, Texas to Pedro's Trading Post and through the jungles of Peru in search of priceless treasures and the fabled lost city of Ka!

Arcade Boot Camp—Tired of getting 30 seconds of arcade play for your quarter? Face forward, Civilian, and march over to your dealer for this one. Train in five areas vital to arcade skills: Driving, Chopper Flying, Shooting, Jumping & Ducking, and Obstacle Course.

Xyphus—Explore the Lost Continent of Arroya as you develop a band of warriors and spellcasters in preparation for the final confrontation with Xyphus, Lord of Demons! This fantasy role-playing game features four-player independent movement and six separate scenarios, each set in a different region with different types of creatures, weapons, and spells. A true breakthrough in its genre, **Xyphus** is destined to become a classic.

penguin software™
the graphics people

830 Fourth Ave.
P.O. Box 311
Geneva, IL 60134
(312) 232-1984

Expedition Amazon, Arcade Boot Camp, Xyphus, and Penguin Software are trademarks of Penguin Software, Inc.

Just when all computer games have started to seem the same, here's a thrilling new twist – software matched up with an exciting boardgame!

Every step on the big colorful gameboard, and the action-packed, on-screen adventures that result, depends on your skill and luck – and your opponents! Chivalry™ confronts you with challenges demanding the skills of a master gamesplayer as you battle thieves, witches, and trolls in 20 arcade-style games. 1 to 4 players.

Developed by Optimum Resource, Inc. Designed by Richard Hefter and Janie and Steve Worthington.

For the Apple® computer.

Look for Chivalry in finer computer stores everywhere. Or order by calling toll free 1-800-852-5000, Dept. AE-61. Only $49.95. Price includes disk, poster, gameboard, playing pieces, storage case and instructions.

Chivalry is a registered trademark of Optimum Resource, Inc. Apple is a registered trademark of Apple Computer, Inc.
A/M44AE61

WeeklyReader Family Software

A division of Xerox Education Publications
Middletown. CT 06457

Chivalry™ is alive!

ANNOUNCING

The Easiest Computer Language in the World.

Spellcaster is a new computer language that is easier to learn than LOGO or BASIC. With Spellcaster you can learn to program your own fast-action video games, intricate art designs, interactive courseware, and many other applications using graphics, color, movement or sound.

What makes Spellcaster so easy to learn?

- Spellcaster is the simplest language on the market. Young children use it to draw all over the screen. As they grow, the tutorial entices them into true programming.
- Everything a Spellcaster program does leaves marks on the screen. You watch all its inner workings in motion.
- Spellcaster's on-screen tutorial makes your computer teach you programming. It even teaches you how to program your own video games.
- Debugging a Spellcaster program is easy, because you can stop it, make it back up to the mistake (while you watch), change it, and let it run forward again.
- Spellcaster's manual, The Book of Spells, is light-spirited, color-coded and loaded with examples.

For $39.95 you get

The Book of Spells (Manual)

Copyable disk with:
  Spellcaster Language
  Tutorial program
  Video game subprogram library

One issue of The Spellswappers' Gazette *

1-800-635-0050

MC/VISA   (In VA call 1-703-433-8788)

At your dealer or direct from:
Shenandoah Software
1111a Mt. Clinton Pike
Harrisonburg, VA 22801

For Apple II, II+, IIe

The language: Spellcaster was designed from scratch to be easy to learn, yet formally complete. Its privitives are not numeric operations, but screen operations. Each change in state is visible to the programmer. Spellcaster is highly structured (nested conditions, loops with exit conditions, recursion) but the control structures are expressed with radical simplicity. "Teleporters" are unique language fea- tures that partially save and restore process state to permit real-time video game programming.

The environment: Imagine an editor and an interpreter so wed that every keystroke, as it is typed, is syntactically checked and executed, so you instantly see its effects. If you backspace, the pro- gram reconstructs its previous state — even in the middle of conditions and loops.

The tutorial: Keystrokes generated by the tutor- ial guide the user, stroke by stroke, through experi- ments in programming. The tutorial can generate macro's which execute on the spot. The pedagogical approach is to have beginners build their own video games.

---

* On the flip side of the Spellcaster disk is a free issue of The Spellswappers' Gazette, a diskette magazine of readers' games, comments and programming know-how.

Apple is a trademark of Apple Computer, Inc.

Volume I, No. 2   June, 1984

The Apple's Apprentice
is published monthly by:

Emerald City Publishing, Inc. P.O. Box 582-AA, Santee, CA 92071, (619) 562-7785. Entire Contents copyright © 1984 by Emerald City Publishing, Inc.

Roger Wagner, publisher
Val J. Golding, editor

Donna Sexton,
       Advertising Director
Pamela Lambert,
       Circulation Manager
Linda Anderson, Illustrator
Margot and Al Tommervik,
       godparents
            (bless them!)

Subscriptions: $24/12 issues, $46/24 issues

Cover art by:
William Giese

Scene from Transylvania™ A trademark of Penguin Software, Inc. Reproduced by their courtesy.

Table of Contents

From the Tower

Dawgone that sourceror! It seems his Dunglebaries have gotten loose again and raised all sorts of havoc. Our alarm clock is on the missing list, and we've overslept a full month! Never mind though, we've got some really neat stuff inside this issue that'll make you scream for more. We'll get back to that shortly.

The **Apple's Apprentice** made its debut at the ninth annual West Coast Computer Faire, held this last March in San Francisco, and was very well received. That tells us we're doing something right. But we want to do more than just "something" right. This is where you come in. We're going to repeat quite a bit of what we said last time, because it is important. To you, to us.

This is your magazine, where you can be the boss, where you can tell us what to do and where to go. And we will, just as much as we can, but we need to hear it from you. Fire off the brickbats and bouquets; let us have it. Tell us what's good and what's bad with the **Apple's Apprentice.**

If you read the premier issue, you'll notice we had a column **Back Talk,** which does not appear in this issue. Why? Simple. Nobody talked back to us. This is your forum where you can air your gripes or ask questions of other readers or share with them some of your own ideas and discoveries. We want your back talk. Talk back to Back Talk and we'll talk back to the back talkers and have a ball talking back!

The **Apple's Apprentice** is one place where you can learn about using your (or your parent's) Apple in a fun way. But summer is upon us, and with summer comes thoughts of summer camps, hiking, fishing, horseback riding, and computers. Computers? Yes, you heard us right, computers! One of the interesting developments of the computer age is the melding of traditional summer camps with computer instruction. What a gas, to have fun learning about computers in a camp environment!

Our own Donna Sexton (alias the Princess Donna) has taken the time to find out about this relatively new vacation concept, and tells you all about computer camps in her interview with Mark Zacovic, Executive Director of the Original Computer Camp, starting on the next page.

The mail that we've received so far tells us you like contests, so we've started a new column: **Daze of the Knights.** Each issue you will find at least one contest; we start with two in this issue. These are designed to really make you stop and think. Some may look like a "you can't get there from here" thing, others will . . . well, you'll just have to stick with us and see. But there will be prizes and points and all sorts of goodies to turn you on to enjoying programming and computers. And if you have an idea for a puzzle or contest, send it in. If we use your submission, you will be rewarded appropriately.

What's new in the Apple kingdom? Only a new Apple computer, that's all . . . In late April, Apple introduced the new Apple //c, a perfectly portable computer that weighs less than eight pounds and can run about 90% of all existing Apple software! If you want to see what it looks like, and learn more about it as well, GOTO page 9 and see what you find.

One new column that we have added is **Shortcut To Adventure,** excerpts from a new book which describes techniques for getting safely through the various rooms in popular adventure games such as Transylvania, featured this issue.

We want to alert you to a feature coming next month that you won't want to miss: **Uncle Bill's Column.** Uncle Bill is going to write about fun with Apples, making money, becoming famous, and seeing what you can get away with when you're parents aren't looking! Issues will include Piracy (a bio on Cap'n Hook), and burning down your school with a modem! Keep your eyes (and Apples) peeled for this 'un . . .

What you always wanted to know about Apples, but what the manual didn't tell you is the subject of **What To Do Till the Wizard Comes.** If you're just unpacking your brand-new Apple, stop right now and read this informative piece. And while you're at it, don't miss our regular features like **Ye Olde Game Shoppe,** Bob Cavey's color comic **Microchips,** or **Ask the Wizard.**

We're, as we told you last time, still the new kid on the block. Each of you have a vested interest in our success. The bigger we grow, the more we can offer you, so we again ask that you consider yourselves as our salespersons. If you enjoy the **Apple's Apprentice,** then tell your friends about it. Ask them to subscribe. We still offer, for a limited period, 12 issue subscriptions at $18, which save $6 from the regular rate, or $12 off the newstand price. If you send your chum's subscription to us and include your name and address, we'll extend your subscription by a month. Deal?

So tell us: what more can we do for you. We'll be around again soon to make good on your ideas.

Interview:
Journey to a Computer Camp

Donna Sexton

Once upon a time, the wizard of Fairhill Castle and the Princess Donna were in the wizard's tower, partaking of herb tea. Strolling over to the tall, arched window, the wizard opened wide the stained glass panes and stepped out on the balcony, gazed to the north, past the mist-shrouded Far Mountains, their peaks barely visible.

"Come hither, fair princess, enjoy with me the view," he bade. Wondering what indeed the wizard had spied, she slid gracefully from her chair to the balcony to join the wizard, standing there with his hand shading his eyes, staring into the distance.

"Look now to the north, far beyond the mountains," he spoke, "There lies a valley called Silicon, where, has been reported to me, there are these magical apples, which can do all sorts of wonderous things, and there, in this Silicon Valley, also I am told, the children are instructed in these apples and other magical devices.

"The young ones of the Silicon Valley are taught in places called 'Computer Camps,' words with which I am not familiar, and we must learn more about them, and about the apples.

"The minstrel Stephen has been moping about Fairhill castle these last days, yearning to return to his distant home, and grows impatient to journey on.

"It is my wish that you select one of good King Buckingham's knights to accompany the two of you, and journey to this land, so that you may bring me back first hand news of these strange camps."

So saying, the wizard dismissed the Princess with a wave of his gloved hand, and she moved away in silence to prepare for her adventure.

And so it came to be that the Princess Donna embarked upon her travels, and she indeed reached the land of apples and spoke with one known as Mark Zacovic, a person titled as "executive director", who rules bands of "instructors" at remote areas called "Original Computer Camps".

Seeking to please the wizard, the Princess Donna, upon her return, offered this report:

Apple's Apprentice: Let's start at the very beginning: I really know very little about you or the *Original Computer Camp*. I see that you're in your fifth year of operation. Considering that the home computer is a relative Johnny-come-lately, that speaks rather well for you. Perhaps I should begin with the five W's of journalism, who, what, why, where, and when. When and how did the camp get off the ground?

Zacovic: Well, it started in 1980, in Santa Barbara by Denison Bollay, who is a computer . . . shall we say computer whiz kid . . . and he just got the idea that camp and computers would be a good combination and started the camp and put it all together, and off he went, and we ran it in the Santa Ynez Valley area of Santa Barbara.

Apple's Apprentice: Do I understand you also have other camps in California, Colorado, Connecticut?

Zacovic: We have seven camps. We have one here in Santa Barbara, one in Sequoia (which is central California), one at Lake Tahoe, just on the Nevada

side of the border; we have one at Steamboat Springs, Colorado, one in New Milford, Connecticut, one in Greeley, Pennsylvania in the Poconos, and we have one on Lake Winnisquam, near Laconia in New Hampshire.

Apple's Apprentice: Well you're definitely broad-based; you seem to have the country well covered. Is it correct that you are not tied to any specific computer?

Zacovic: Yes, we are not a hardware-specific curriculum.

Apple's Apprentice: What kinds of computers are available for hands-on... as far as what kinds of computers you actually have...

Zacovic: We use Apple]I Plusses and we use Commodore 64's, basically.

Apple's Apprentice: Suppose I had an IBM PC and I wanted to sign up?

Zacovic: No problem, simply because we are *not* machine-specific. Our curriculum is really teaching a basic broad concept of the computer.

Apple's Apprentice: Tell me, are the classes held during the summer only, and how long do they last and when do they start?

Zacovic: The camp sessions are actually 12 days. The children are in on a Sunday and out on a Friday. They begin as early as June 17th and through about the middle of August. The curriculum is designed so they can take multiples of two weeks... They could take another two weeks right after the first two, and not be hindered or anything. In fact they could, if they wanted, go the

whole summer. We think that after six weeks there is apparently diminishing returns on the ones that are able to get to the computers.

Apple's Apprentice: Would you say there are beginning, intermediate and advanced levels?

Zacovic: Each child is interviewed upon arrival at camp by the assistant director in charge of computer instruction, for the child's individual interest and ability level with the computers. Then, for every two week session, we sort of make it a tailor-made curriculum or group of classes. He takes the results of his interviews, finds the general interest and is able to assign children into classes that they'll be in for the next two weeks. We may not have any intermediate Logos, for instance, so we wouldn't need to offer that module.

Apple's Apprentice: Do you find the 7-15 age group — the one listed in your brochure — easiest to teach? ...or what if a five-year-old or a 16-year-old wanted to go...

Zacovic: Again, those seem to be the best camp ages, but we have had younger children, and older children at camp. I really leave it to the parents to make that decision. If we had a five-year old, for example, I would alert the parents so they would be aware their child was the youngest in camp.

Apple's Apprentice: Can you give me an idea of what the 12 days consist of... what the daily schedule is like.

Zacovic: Well, the days are divided into

six 1½ hour activity periods. There are two required computer periods that they must attend, and two of them are mandatory recreation classes, and then the fifth period is an optional camper-choice activity where the child can choose more time on the computer, or more recreation — their choice — and the sixth period is really a camp-wide activity period, either a campfire, movies, or something like that.

Apple's Apprentice: And what about accomodations... are there dormitories or what?

Zacovic: It varies. We stay away from the college campuses; we really don't think that's camp, as camp should be. Four of our sites are traditional camps, designed and built as summer camps, you know, in mountain locations.

Apple's Apprentice: Let's take the one in California — where did you say that was?

Zacovic: Well, in California we have two — or three, counting the one just over the Nevada border. The one in Santa Barbara is at a private school, private preparatory academy, as is the one in Connecticut, and the one in Colorado, and those are dormitory settings, semi-private accomodations, bath down the hall, counselor in close proximity to the rooms; the children are still cabined according to their age, so that eight children of similar age would be a cabin group, although they would sleep in four different rooms. At the traditional camps, they do have cabins, and the counselor-camper ratio is about one to eight, and they are again cabined according to age.

Apple's Apprentice: I see. Not only are they learning computers, but they are in an actual camp setting.

Zacovic: Yes, and that is a big concern for the traditional camp people who have said: "Computer camp, that's not camp...," because we offer a full recreation program, and while they could — by choosing computer, every time they have an option — probably take up to six hours a day of computer instruction. But we balance it out; they must go to recreation activities; they must participate.

Apple's Apprentice: What do you find, what's the consensus of the average. Are they kids who are there because Mom and Dad want them there, or...

Zacovic: I think it's really 50-50. I think about half of them are there because the parents realize it's a real good idea, and

I think the other half are there because the campers themselves really appear very interested—they've initiated the whole idea of computer camps for their family.

Apple's Apprentice: My son is 15 now, and we've had an Apple for about two years, but I'm concerned because he's great with games — loves the games — but little else...

Zacovic: We don't allow game-playing at camp as a rule, although there are some free periods from time to time where they may play games, but what's more interesting for our campers is that we have an arcade game writing course; they actually write the programs and design their own games.

Apple's Apprentice: What do you find is the average age?

Zacovic: I'll give you a range... around 11 to 14, right in there.

Apple's Apprentice: Let's talk for a minute about price. I know many of our readers will be interested, and that is something that seldom appears in the ads. For a 12-day session, what does it usually run?

Zacovic: It ranges from 795 dollars to 1100 dollars. This depends on the campsite and which session. Now we have one session at the Sequoia camp which begins in early June, right after California schools are out, requiring a quick turnaround, so we discount that session to 795; the rest are 895.

Apple's Apprentice: And what does that include?

Zacovic: That's all-inclusive, room and board, computer time, computer instruction, recreation programs... there is a 50 dollar canteen fee which covers a nutritional item every day, supplementary course material, sundry items, their text books, note books, pens, paper, things like that.

Apple's Apprentice: I see. Now if I took the same course in say, New Hampshire, would the price differ?

Zacovic: It depends. All three of the camps back east happen to be 895 dollars, which is our average price. The camp in Colorado is 945 dollars; the camp in Tahoe is 845 dollars, and then the camp in Santa Barbara is 1100 dollars.

Apple's Apprentice: Tell me about the difference in sexes. I'll bet you any amount of money it's more boys than girls...

Zacovic: You win. It's mainly societal. Society tells girls that they're not sup-

posed to be good in math, and they're not supposed to be good with electronics and computers, but I think that's what happens. Also the tradition of summer camping itself is male oriented.

Apple's Apprentice: Are you saying you don't usually have any girls at all?

Zacovic: Oh no, no. We usually have about one to four, or a 25 percent ratio. It's interesting, I've never had any problems with the girls at camp, thinking they were different, or that there weren't enough other girls or whatever. They have their own cabin groups and women counselors; they're part of the program.

Apple's Apprentice: Is it co-ed... are the girls in the same computer classes with boys?

Zacovic: Absolutely. And also in the recreation classes with boys, as well.

Apple's Apprentice: But you're finding that the parents push more for the boys more than for the girls?

Zacovic: For some reason, yes, which I think is really awful.

Apple's Apprentice: Anything else... can you think of anything else you want to add?

Zacovic: Well, we have robots in camp, which is something you read about every day, but we have 12 robots — similar to R2D2 — like the ones you may have seen at the trade shows, and they are a lot of fun, as well as a learning experience. They are programmed with an Apple computer, they have three sensing devices... they have a sonar sensing device (like on a polaroid

camera), that they can "see" with, they have bumpers around their outsides where if they physically touch a wall or an object they will react; they also have an infra-red sensing device that looks at the floor, so that they can read markings off of the floor. Initially when we got them, robotics seemed like an advanced concept, but some of our people got together and were able to write the programs, so that even beginning campers at our camps were able to work with the robots, so as part of our introduction to microcomputing course, which is the basic course for all of the beginning kids that come in, they get several days work with the robots.

Apple's Apprentice: How exciting...

Zacovic: We have a standardized maze that we have at every camp, and then the children who are interested can enter a contest and write programs for the robot to run the maze in the shortest time, and we had about 20 or 25 semifinalists who submitted programs. We ran the heats back here in Santa Barbara and had three finalists that were so close in time that we sent each of them a robot and computer to practice with and re-write their programs and shave any time off of them. April first was the due date, so we're just getting those programs back. We're going to re-run the contest, and the writer of the program with the fastest time wins the robot!

Apple's Apprentice: What about handicapped children?

Zacovic: I had a young man who had lost a leg to cancer, and he was com-

pletely mainstreamed into the program, in fact there were several boys in camp that didn't even realize he had an artificial leg, but in general, we don't have the facilities to handle the more severely handicapped. Again, this is a decision we leave to the parents.

Apple's Apprentice: I tend to look at camp — any camp — as a chance for a child to go away and learn something educational, and have fun while they're doing it. To me, that's very important.

Zacovic: I think you're a wise parent, and I talk to many wise parents who are realizing they'd like to provide this summer camp opportunity for their child, and to be able to have the extra added bonus of computer education, and it's not an overboard thing; it's a healthy combination, well balanced. They get real excited about it because it's more value for the buck.

Apple's Apprentice: That's true. It's one thing to put out 800 dollars to go and have a good time, and it's another thing to know you're going to get some return — something out of it, too.

Zacovic: Right. And we really emphasize... that the children should be walking away with skills and knowledge that they're going to be able to take into adulthood... and this includes recreational as well as computer skills.

Apple's Apprentice: Well I think it sounds great, and I wish you all the luck in the world, although I don't think you're going to need it...

Zacovic: One last thing that I might as well mention is our ACA accreditation — the American Camping Association, the only national standards regulatory agency for camps in this country. They have about 250 different standards that you need to comply with to become accredited — they're all basic concerns any parent would have — you know, personnel, hygiene and safety, food preparation, and facilities management, all those types of things, and by having that accreditation symbol — sort of like the Good Housekeeping seal of Approval — from the American Camping Association...

Apple's Apprentice: Let's go a step further. What kind of credits do these people have that are teaching the actual computer classes?

Zacovic: In our particular situation, we have certain personnel standards that we have designed and developed that are in conjunction with the American Camping Association standards... our counselors and instructors must be over 19 years of age, because we really want adults at camp; the role models should not be children — and there are some camps that have younger people in counseling positions, which is something I think you need to be careful of... I interview everybody for camp positions for their compatibility with an outdoor setting, with an educational setting, how the personality is going to jibe, then, in addition, for the computer instructors, we have our curriculum writers here who interview them for their very specific skills.

Apple's Apprentice: Well, everything I've heard sounds well thought out and planned, and first cabin. From what you've said, I don't think I would have any apprehensions about entrusting mine to your care...

Zacovic: Well thank you. *Original Computer Camp* is like any personal belief, you work to make it good, to make it conform to your personal standards.

Those readers wishing further information, may call toll-free (800) 235-6965 {in California, (800) 824-3349}.

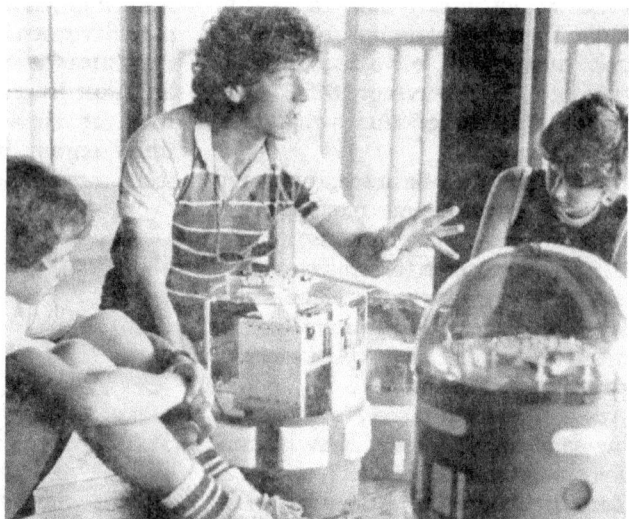

Robert Reali, Director of Curriculum Development at the Original Computer Camp, uses robots to demonstrate concepts of Artificial Intelligence to campers.

The children program the robots to "think" their way through an obstacle course as part of the training the youngsters receive in Artificial Intelligence.

Apple's Newest: the //c
What's To See?

Plenty is the answer to our rhetorical pun. Apple Computer's new *Apple //c* is the most revolutionary, evolutionary descendant of the Apple][line, first sold in 1977, an eight-year old design, so advanced for its time — antique by current technology standards — that today's versions, the Apple //e and //c, remain front-runners in an ever-more competitive market.

The Apple //c is the newest progeny of that illustrious line. Presumably, the "c" stands for "compact," although we've seen nothing from Apple to confirm that. However, compact it is, weighing in at a mere 7½ pounds. With its optional carrying case, 9- to 20-volt DC power pack interface, and a flat-panel display, to be available much later this year, the //c becomes a true portable with all the power and more of its big brother //e.

It differs from the //e in the following respects:

(1) The microprocessor is a 65C02 operating at 1.02 MHz. The 65C02 is an advanced model of the 6502, upward compatible, with new addressing modes and dozens of new opcodes, such as BRA (Branch Relative Always).

(2) It comes with 128k of RAM memory and 16k ROM.

(3) Also built-in is 80-column video display, switchable to 40-column mode.

(4) A 5¼" floppy disk drive is enclosed in the right side of the //c case, and a second drive may be plugged into the rear apron plug.

(5) The interior is not user-accessible without voiding the warranty, and there are no expansion slots. All available interfaces appear on the rear apron.

(6) Printers and modems may be connected to two serial interfaces, and two video ports provide for RGB or standard monitors, or an LCD flat panel display. An RF modulator is built-in. There is a mouse/paddle/joystick port as well.

(7) Two of the most innovative features are external switches which allow pre-selection of 40-80 column display mode, and standard or Dvorak keyboard.

The Apple //c is supplied with two operating systems: the familiar DOS 3.3 we all know, and ProDOS, Apple's recently released system which makes use of a hierarchical directory structure and other I/O speed-up features, plus file compatibility with the Apple ///.

For those interested, a complete list of 65C02 *opcodes* appeared in the May issue of *Call -A.P.P.L.E.* At least two assemblers for the 65C02 have made their appearance: *Big Mac* from A.P.P.L.E. and *Merlin* from Roger Wagner Publishing. If not here now, then expect one as well from S-C Software, who seem to always keep on top of things.

Additional information on the Apple //c may be found in the *Crystal Ball* column near the back of this issue, and we wish to thank Apple Computer, Inc., for the photographs that appear here, as well as the following historical and background material. From all appearances, the //c is a superior product and will remain highly competitive to both the IBM PC and the PCjr.

Introduction

In 1977, Apple Computer, Inc., introduced the Apple][computer — the first fully assembled personal computer. The Apple][took the power of computing out of the exclusive domain of highly trained experts and put it into the hands of people in all walks of life. As the number of computer users increased, Apple grew rapidly from its modest garage beginnings to become the youngest company to enter the ranks of the Fortune 500.

Increasing use placed increasing demands upon personal computers — to perform more tasks, to become easier to operate, to fit more conveniently into limited spaces and to meet all these demands quickly and inexpensively. The personal computer industry responded by introducing more diverse computer systems to satisfy the burgeoning needs.

Apple followed its Apple][with the][plus. This computer featured Applesoft as Apple's primary BASIC programming language, as well as automatic system start-up instructions in the new "autostart" monitor ROM.

Apple ///, a member of the][family, was introduced in 1981 as the first personal computer designed specifically for businesses. It appealed to business professionals who wanted the freedom and control of their own computer. Today's version, known as the Apple /// plus, contains several major improvements over the original.

In 1983, Apple brought out the Apple //e, so named to denote "enhanced." The //e added more memory, 80-column text capability and an expanded keyboard to the Apple][plus, all at a lower cost.

Now Apple introduces the //c. The company views this newest member in the Apple II family as the first serious computer for the home. It is a compact, transportable computer that goes beyond playing games and storing recipes to perform the same tasks executed by bigger personal computers: personal productivity, such as finances and word processing, plus home education. A leading European design company collaborated with Apple to create a special look for the //c computer and its matching accessories. This new look, called "snow white," will be the standard design of all of Apple's future products.

The transportable //c, smallest yet in this line, comes with 128k of memory and a built-in disk drive. From the beginning, Apple intended this newest member of the II family to complement the popular //e as well as fulfill new personal computing needs of an expanding market.

Concurrent with the introduction of the Apple //c hardware, Apple will feature 21 software products designed specifically for the //c. Described in a //c *Software Sampler* brochure, these packages encompass personal productivity, home education and entertainment applications. They consist of 17 products by independent software suppliers, plus four from Apple. Moreover, the //c can run most of the thousands of programs available on the Apple //e.

The Apple //c builds on the personal computer heritage of the Apple] [family while adding enhanced features to keep pace with the continually changing needs of computer users.

Apple //c Market

People are buying home computers at an increasing rate, and forecasts indicate this trend will continue through the next decade and beyond.

The number of personal computers in U.S. households is projected to grow from its 1983 level of 8 million to 50 million by the end of 1998. By 1990, 70 to 75 million home computers will be in use — or viewed in different terms, two thirds of all households in the United States will have at least one home computer.

The projected popularity of home computers may be likened to that of black and white televisions. Within 15 years of their 1945 introduction, black and white TV sets could be found in nearly every American household. So far, personal computers have followed a similar entry pattern.

Within the total home computer industry, computers used for productivity applications — "serious" applications — will be the strongest growth segment. The high-end home market could equal 2 million units by the end of 1984. The Apple //c, being the first specifically designed serious home computer, should satisfy much of this growing market.

Apple expects that two-thirds of the //c computers sold will be purchased for use in the home, and that the remaining one-third will be split almost evenly between schools and businesses. The //c is so easy to transport, however, that chances are good it will be interchanged among the three environments and even taken to non-traditional settings such as motor vehicles and vacation sites.

The Apple II family accounts for more than one-half of all personal computers used in kindergarten through 12th grades. Because the //e and //c can run almost all of the same software, the many children already familiar with the //e will have a head start at operating the //c.

The Apple //e will continue to be the most cost effective basic Apple computer for most schools. With the //e at school and a //c at home, children can carry software back and forth between the two. Apple expects the //c to have an impact on the educational market by providing the same capabilities at home as the //e does at school.

The Apple //c, although simple enough for children to use, will be equally valuable to adults. Much of the software available, even programs that fall within the category of home education, covers the kinds of topics and information — such as business math and typing — that adults need or want to know.

As in education, the established presence of the //e and its enormous software bases in businesses will make the //c a valuable addition to the home and office. People have long demanded the best quality equipment for their businesses; the compact and affordable //c makes comparable quality available for the home as well.

Generally, families and individuals who wish to purchase computers must do so within their budgets. The Apple //c brings good news to these potential customers in the form of a suggested retail price of $1,295, which includes everything a new owner needs to connect a //c to a television set and begin using it.

The major competitor for the //c is IBM's PCjr — IBM's compact personal computer that falls into a similar price range as the //c. However, the //c offers far more capabilities than the PCjr, and Apple believes that the //c will emerge as the only transportable computer for serious home computing.

The Apple //c uses nearly identical software as the //e, giving the small

Not only can students learn and play on the //c, parents can use the computer for a wide variety of productivity applications such as word processing programs for writing letters as well as financial packages for planning taxes and investments and figuring home budgets.

computer access to the most extensive software base available today for serious home computing. The PCjr shares a much lower compatibility with its "parent" computer, the IBM PC, which in turn has fewer home computing software programs available than does Apple. The PCjr also lacks the //c's fully professional keyboard, a shortcoming that limits the number of serious applications that it can run.

The Apple //c

The Apple //c has a different look from its cousins in the Apple II family. Its design and features, which Apple will use on all its future products, culminate 2½ years' work by engineers and designers from Apple and from Frog Design, an award-winning West German firm.

Apple solicited proposals from industrial firms around the world to present a unified theme for Apple's computers, monitors, printers and other accessories. Apple's goal was a new line of computers with a stylish look that would blend handsomely in home and office decors. The result has been dubbed *Snow White*.

Hardware

The most noticeable feature of the Apple //c is its size. The main computer body — which includes the keyboard, printed-circuit board and built-in 5¼" floppy disk drive — weighs 7½ pounds and takes up about as much desk space as a looseleaf notebook. It can be set up on a desk, counter top, coffee table or floor, or the user can rest it comfortably on his lap.

To begin using the Apple //c, a user need only attach the cables included in the carton and connect a display screen. The screen could be a television set, its own monitor, or another Apple-compatible monitor.

The specially designed full-function keyboard features fast-action keys that depress with a comfortable tactile feel and non-metallic sound. The flip of a switch converts the standard keyboard to an alternative configuration — known as Dvorak mode — that more and more people find faster and easier to use.

The handle for the transportable Apple //c folds up to lie flush with the main body when not in use. It can also serve as a support to tilt the computer and keyboard toward the user. With the handle folded, no parts protrude

from the main computer body, giving it a smooth, streamlined appearance.

Plug-in-sockets — as opposed to add-on cards — line the back of the computer to accomodate at any one time a display screen, printer, modem, "mouse" pointer, joystick or paddles and a second floppy disk drive. Above each socket is an *icon* — a picture — that represents the function of the socket and corresponds to matching icons on the cables themselves. Each connector is configured so that it fits into its correct socket only, to prevent users from inadvertantly harming the computer.

Everything inside the //c has been miniaturized and specially engineered to fit as compactly as possible. Apple engineers reduced the number of chips in the //c from 110 (in the Apple //e) to 40, while at the same time doubling standard RAM memory to 128k.

Headphones and a volume control, along with the computer's built-in speaker permit the user to hear the five-octave sound range available for music, games and other programs.

Standard Apple graphics are a part of the package: 16-color low-resolution (40 by 48), six-color high resolution (280 by 192), and black and white ultra-high resolution (560 by 192) for maximum detail. In the future, this mode will support 16-color graphics.

Software

Hardware designs provide only the external body needed to operate a computer. Software adds the internal workings that determine what the computer can do. By choosing the 5¼" floppy for the Apple //c, Apple ensures an impressive amount of software at the disposal of the //c. The computer's features also make it easy for software developers to write future //c programs.

Its Apple II heritage gives the //c a head start on applications software. More than 10,000 programs have been written for Apple II computers, and more than 90% of the currently available programs will run on the //c.

Apple has put together a collection of 21 new and best-selling programs by Apple and third-party software developers. The four software packages developed by Apple have been enhanced specifically for the //c and consist of: *AppleWorks*, an integrated word processing, spread-sheet analysis and data-base management package; *Apple Logo //*, a graphics-oriented introduction to computer programming; *Apple Access //*, which uses an Apple-compatible modem to let the //c communicate with other computers, and the *Apple Education Classics*, a single disk that combines *Elementary*, *My Dear Apple* and *The Shell Games*.

In addition, the computer is pack-

Apple offers a new series of peripheral products designed to complement the //c including a thermal transfer printer called the Scribe that prints in several colors and black, a mouse pointing device, a monochrome ultra high resolution monitor and tilting stand, a second disk drive and a carrying case. In addition, the existing Apple modems, joystick, hand controllers and Imagewriter dot matrix printer work with the //c.

aged with six tutorial programs on floppy disks to introduce users to serious home computing. They contain everything a novice needs to know to operate the computer as well as information that familiarizes a more experienced user with specific features of the //c.

Accessories

Apple //c accessories that can be plugged into the back of the computer include the Scribe printer, ImageWriter printers and color plotter; //c monitor; mouse pointing device; joystick and hand controllers; second disk drive and extra power pack. In addition, a flat display screen is scheduled to be available in the fall of 1984.

The Scribe printer is the first color printer to use a new printing method called *thermal-transfer printing*, which works without special paper. It can print in six colors — magenta, cyan, yellow, green, orange and purple — plus black, on plain paper or transparencies.

In thermal-transfer printing, the ribbon works similarly to a typewriter ribbon, except that it is coated with special ink. The Scribe's heat-transfer process produces near letter-quality color images on ordinary paper. It operates at two speeds — letter mode at 50 characters per second and draft mode at 80 characters per second.

The //c monitor was designed to complement the //c computer in both color scheme and size. It weighs 11 pounds and, like the main computer body, is compact and has a handle to make it easy to carry. The matching stand permits the monitor's 9-inch screen to be angled to suit the viewer.

The AppleMouse //c pointing device, which also conforms to the Snow White design, comes with graphics software called *MousePaint*, and plugs into a rear-apron socket.

Apple plans to offer a flat panel display screen by the fall of 1984. The LCD (liquid crystal display) display is capable of 80 columns by 24 lines and displays all three Apple //c graphics mode options: low-, high- and ultra-high resolution. The addition of this display screen will make the Apple //c even more transportable, with the computer and flat panel both fitting into a light-weight carrying case.

In addition to the flat display screen, Apple will continue to add products to the Apple II family. As more people make computers part of their everyday lives, Apple will keep designing hardware and software solutions to fulfill expanding needs.

MagiGraphics

Roger Wagner

MagiGraphics is the Apple's Apprentice column that's meant to help teach you a little about creating your own computer graphics. In the last issue, we introduced the idea of screen coordinates, and screen motion.

Screen coordinates are the numbers assigned to each point that can possibly be drawn on the screen in the graphics mode. For low resolution graphics, the screen is 40 points, or *pixels*, wide by 40 pixels high. Any given point is identified by a number pair that indicates how many units horizontally from the left edge of the screen the point is, and how many units down from the top of the screen. Thus the upper left corner is numbered (0,0) and the lower right corner would be numbered (39,39). (You might remember from last time also that a lot of things in computers are numbered kind of funny, and this is no exception. They start with *0* and count to *39* for a total of 40 units!)

Motion is created by erasing a dot, then re-drawing in a different position

Motion is created on the screen by erasing an existing dot or shape on the screen, and then re-drawing the same shape or dot in a slightly different position.

All this was put together into a program called *RACER 1* that was listed in the last issue, but is reproduced here to refresh your memory:

To explain how it works, let's first outline all the important aspects that will be used in the program:

1. The program is in low resolution graphics. This means that our coordinate system will be a 40 by 40 unit screen.
2. The keyboard can be continuously read by the BASIC statement: **KEY = PEEK(-16384)**.

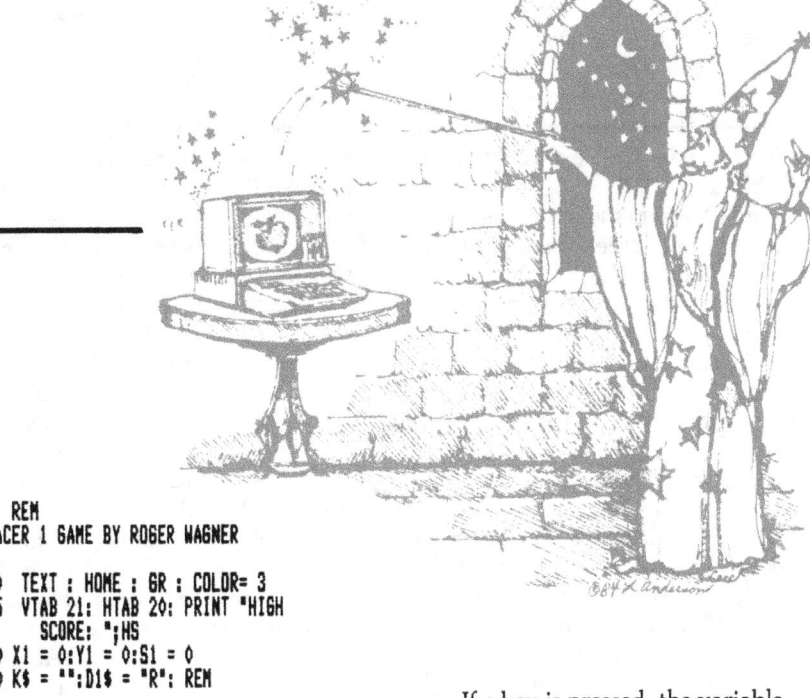

```
5 REM
RACER 1 GAME BY ROGER WAGNER

10  TEXT : HOME : GR : COLOR= 3
15  VTAB 21: HTAB 20: PRINT "HIGH
       SCORE: ";HS
20  X1 = 0:Y1 = 0:S1 = 0
30  K$ = "":D1$ = "R": REM


100 REM
MAIN SCAN LOOP

105 KEY = PEEK ( - 16384): IF KE
       Y > 127 THEN POKE - 16368,
       0:K$ = CHR$ (KEY - 128)
110 IF K$ = CHR$ (27) THEN RUN

115 IF K$ = "I" THEN D1$ = "U"
120 IF K$ = "M" THEN D1$ = "D"
125 IF K$ = "J" THEN D1$ = "L"
130 IF K$ = "K" THEN D1$ = "R"
135 IF D1$ = "U" THEN Y1 = Y1 -
       1: IF Y1 < 0 THEN Y1 = 0
140 IF D1$ = "D" THEN Y1 = Y1 +
       1: IF Y1 > 39 THEN Y1 = 39
145 IF D1$ = "L" THEN X1 = X1 -
       1: IF X1 < 0 THEN X1 = 0
150 IF D1$ = "R" THEN X1 = X1 +
       1: IF X1 > 39 THEN X1 = 39: REM


300 REM
DRAW PLAYER #1

305 IF SCRN( X1,Y1) < > 0 THEN
       COLOR= 15: PLOT X1,Y1: VTAB
       22: PRINT CHR$ (7);"CRASH!"
       : GOTO 600
310 PLOT X1,Y1
315 S1 = S1 + 1: VTAB 21: PRINT "
       SCORE: ";S1
500 GOTO 100: REM


600 REM
ANOTHER GAME?

605 IF S1 > HS THEN HS = S1
610 PRINT "ANOTHER GAME? (Y/N)";

615 HTAB 20: GET A$
620 IF A$ = "Y" THEN 10
630 IF A$ = "N" THEN END
640 GOTO 615
```

If a key is pressed, the variable KEY will have a value greater than 127. If KEY has a value less than 127, no key is being pressed.

3. Whenever you have finished reading a *pressed* key using principle number 2 above, you should "clear" the computer's memory of that keypress by using this statement: **POKE –16368,0.**
4. After a keypress, The value of KEY can be converted into a normal Applesoft string variable by subtracting 128 from the value, and then using Applesoft's CHR$ command as in: **K$ = CHR$(KEY–128)**
5. We will store the current location (called a *coordinate*) of our "racer" in two Applesoft variables, X1 and Y1. X1 will be the current horizontal position, and Y1 will store the vertical position.
6. The racer will be animated by continually changing X1 or Y1 in an Applesoft program loop. Each time the program goes through a loop, X1 or Y1 will be changed, and the racer re-drawn in the new position. The old racer position will not be erased, and this old image will create the "trail" that the racer will leave.

7. The program will use a special Applesoft command called SCRN, that tells the programmer what color a given dot on the screen is, and at the same time whether a dot is even drawn at a certain spot.

Now, for the explanation of RACER 1!

Line 10 sets up the screen display by clearing the screen, entering the graphics mode, and setting the COLOR to be drawn in to 3, which corresponds to purple. Line 15 prints the high score from the last game.

Lines 20 and 30 set the variables that we'll be using to either 0 for the number variables (X1, Y1, S1), or a null or empty string for the string variable K$, and "R" for D1$.

S1 is the variable that will be used as a counter for the score. K$ is a string variable that stores the value for the directional key that is pressed, and D1$ will store one of the letters U, D, L or R (for up, down, left and right) for the direction of the racer.

Line 100 begins the main program loop that will check the keyboard for a direction control key, change the direction of the racer, if necessary, and then erase and re-draw the racer in the new position.

Line 105 checks the keyboard and sets K$ equal to the character that was pressed. If the ESCAPE key is pressed, then line 110 re-starts the game.

Lines 115 through 130 use the direction key pressed (I,J,K or M), and set the program direction variable D1$ to U,D,L or R accordingly.

Lines 135 through 150 then use the direction variable D1$ to change either X1 or Y1 by 1 to create the effect of motion. If the racer's coordinates (X1,Y1) change, then you get the illusion of motion each time the racer is re-drawn.

You'll notice that each of the lines in 135 through 150 check to see that X1 and Y1 have not been changed to a value less than zero, or greater than 39. This is to prevent an ILLEGAL QUANTITY ERROR in the program (later on lines 300 up) from trying to plot a point which would be off the screen.

Line 305 checks to see if the racer has collided with a trail already drawn on the screen. It does this by checking for a SCRN value of greater than 0. Since 0 represents the black background of the screen, any value greater than 0 tells us that something's already been drawn at the spot where we want to draw the racer.

If no crash is detected, then line 310 just draws the new position. Line 315 adds one point to the current score and prints the new score on the screen.

Line 500 then repeats this loop more or less indefinitely until a crash occurs. When a crash finally does happen, lines 600 through 640 asks the user whether another game is wanted.

Long Life Games

Last time, we posed the question of how to get the maximum number of points during a game of RACER 1. If you drive around the screen more or less at random, you will make it virtually impossible to reach certain portions of the screen by "boxing off" areas.

(Continued on page 19)

```
5   REM

RACER 2 GAME BY ROGER WAGNER

10  TEXT : HOME : GR
20  X1 = 0:Y1 = 0:X2 = 39:Y2 = 39
30  K$ = "":D1$ = "R":D2$ = "L": REM


100 REM
MAIN SCAN LOOP

105 KEY =  PEEK ( - 16384): IF KE
    Y > 127 THEN  POKE  - 16368,
    0:K$ =  CHR$ (KEY - 128)
110 IF K$ =  CHR$ (27) THEN  RUN

115 IF K$ = "I" THEN D1$ = "U"
120 IF K$ = "M" THEN D1$ = "D"
125 IF K$ = "J" THEN D1$ = "L"
130 IF K$ = "K" THEN D1$ = "R"
135 IF D1$ = "U" THEN Y1 = Y1 -
    1: IF Y1 < 0 THEN Y1 = 0
140 IF D1$ = "D" THEN Y1 = Y1 +
    1: IF Y1 > 39 THEN Y1 = 39
145 IF D1$ = "L" THEN X1 = X1 -
    1: IF X1 < 0 THEN X1 = 0
150 IF D1$ = "R" THEN X1 = X1 +
    1: IF X1 > 39 THEN X1 = 39: REM


200 REM
PLAYER 2 SCAN LOOP

205 KEY =  PEEK ( - 16384): IF KE
    Y > 127 THEN  POKE  - 16368,
    0:K$ =  CHR$ (KEY - 128)
215 IF K$ = "W" THEN D2$ = "U"
220 IF K$ = "Z" THEN D2$ = "D"
225 IF K$ = "A" THEN D2$ = "L"
230 IF K$ = "S" THEN D2$ = "R"
```

```
235 IF D2$ = "U" THEN Y2 = Y2 -
    1: IF Y2 < 0 THEN Y2 = 0
240 IF D2$ = "D" THEN Y2 = Y2 +
    1: IF Y2 > 39 THEN Y2 = 39
245 IF D2$ = "L" THEN X2 = X2 -
    1: IF X2 < 0 THEN X2 = 0
250 IF D2$ = "R" THEN X2 = X2 +
    1: IF X2 > 39 THEN X2 = 39: REM


300 REM
DRAW PLAYER #1

305 IF  SCRN( X1,Y1) <  > 0 THEN
    COLOR= 15: PLOT X1,Y1: VTAB
    22: PRINT  CHR$ (7);"PLAYER
    #2 WINS!": GOTO 600
307 COLOR= 2
310 PLOT X1,Y1: REM


400 REM
DRAW PLAYER #2

405 IF  SCRN( X2,Y2) <  > 0 THEN
    COLOR= 15: PLOT X2,Y2: VTAB
    22: PRINT  CHR$ (7);"PLAYER
    #1 WINS!": GOTO 600
407 COLOR= 12
410 PLOT X2,Y2
500 GOTO 100: REM


600 REM
ANOTHER GAME?

610 PRINT "ANOTHER GAME? (Y/N)";

615 HTAB 20: GET A$
620 IF A$ = "Y" THEN 10
630 IF A$ = "N" THEN  END
640 GOTO 615
```

A Bumbler's Guide to Debugging:

Bumbling Through BASIC

Val J. Golding

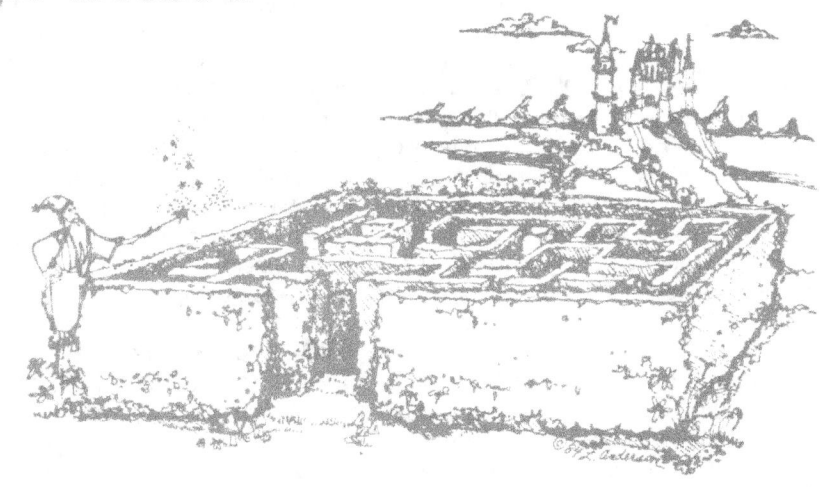

STOP! That's one of the things we're going to write about this time. As we write this in late April, we have spent the largest part of the last two weeks writing a text formatting program to help us see what our stories will look like when they are set in type, and how many column inches they will run. Lots of the problems we ran into at some time may plague you. Here are a few of our solutions.

Amazing Methods

Programming is like running a maze. There are many, many paths. Some lead to dead ends, where we must go back and retrace our steps: find out where we lost our way. Other paths are alternates. They may branch from the main and eventually return. But along the way, you are liable to find problems that wouldn't have been found on the main path. Conversely, you may find shortcuts or alternate solutions, just as

in an adventure game, a needed key may be found in some obscure passageway.

In March, we attended the ninth annual West Coast Computer Faire. Show hours were from 10:30 am to 6 pm, and in the meantime, we had time on our hands, so we wrote up about 15 scratch pad pages of a flow chart for our program-to-be. Going by the book, you should write flow charts for everything you do. Hogwash! Flow charts are for the birds. *But...* there are also times

... there are times when flowcharts are indispensable

when they are indispensable, and they do help get your logic flowing in the right direction.

As it turned out, and as often happens, our flow charts were very necessary and very wrong. When we got back home, we sat down and started typing in the program. Remember now, last time how we told you to use descriptive variable names? Yeah, well we used them, used them in a program no one but ourselves would probably ever see. And more than once they saved our neck. That you better believe. We'd like to give you some examples of those names. Notice how really long they are, but remember that a "cruncher" type program can strip them out later, for execution efficiency.

ALTFAWNT$
CHARACTER$
COMMND$
CRPERPICA
CURRENTCHARS
FYLNAME$
INCHES
INPT$
LEAD
LINES
MAXCPL
OLDPOYNTS
OUTPUT$
POYNTS
SBSCRIPT$
SPACES
SUPSCRIPT$
TBPSN
TCHARS
TFLAG
TPOYNTS
TTLCHARS

```
10   REM

INPUT ANYTHING ROUTINE

PETER MEYER AND OTHERS

100  HEX$ = "300:20 E3 DF A2 0 20
     75 FD 86 FD 20 39 D5 A5 FD 2
     0 52 E4 A2 0 A0 2 20 E2 E5 A
     0 0 A5 FD 91 83 C8 A5 6F 91
     83 C8 A5 70 91 83 60 N 3F5:4
     C 0 3 N D9C6G"
110  FOR I = 1 TO  LEN (HEX$): POKE
     511 + I, ASC ( MID$ (HEX$,I)
     ) + 128: NEXT : POKE 72,0: CALL
      - 144
200  REM

SYNTAX: & A$ OR & A$(I) TO INPUT
COMMAS, COLONS, QUOTES, ETC.
```

Thats about half of them, but you get the idea... In a 60 sector program, those names sure helped us find our way around.

You might ask why we didn't call INPT$ INPUT$, or why we didn't call ALTFAWNT$ ALTFONT$, and the answer is easy... watch out for the reserved word gremlin. Applesoft would have parsed (what does that mean?) ALTFONT$ as **ALTF ON T$** and given us a syntax error. Similarly, INPUT$ would not have been acceptable to Applesoft.

Modularize?

Absolutely. If there was one thing we could tell you that would help improve program readability, logic and flow, it is modularization. And boy does it ever help at debug time! You know *exactly where to go* to start tracing your problem. We use GPLE (Beagle Bros.) for our editor. It's super. In terms of program readability, it lets you force a [Ctrl-M] (carriage return) into a program line. This makes for readable REM's like nothing else. Here's an example of one REM that heads one of the several modules in our program:

9000 REM

INITIALIZE MOST USED VARIABLES

9010 INPT$ = "":OUTPUT$ = "":ESCAPE$ = CHR$ (27):CURRENTCHARS = 0:TTLCHRS = 0:LINENUM = 0

See how the carriage returns in the REM cause it to stand out? Very helpful in scanning a long listing. And line 9010 brings something else to mind. By assigning dummy values to your most-used variables at the beginning of the program, Applesoft will spend less time searching through the variable table for them. Particularly important in a program like this which makes extensive use of GET statements, which are slower than all get-out. (*How slow are they?*). They are *so* slow you have to get out and drive stakes to make sure you're still moving.

GET's should be avoided at all costs, other than as occasional menu

selection strings. If you are using GETs to read commas, colons and quotes from a disk file, then use an *input anything* routine. One is included here. So why are we using GET's? Because in our case, we have to check every single character that is read from disk, looking for some two dozen or so characters that require special handling. Is there any other way in our case? Yes, if we had the time, the whole input and search routine could be written in much faster assembly language. Ah well... maybe sometime...

STOP and TRACE: Two of Your Closest Friends

We learned a lot writing this program. Always you have to plan for the unplanned, the rare case. Such are the

You have to plan for the unplanned

facts of debugging. The rare case is what will trip you up every time. When you think the program is finished, and can't find any more errors — no way! We'll cite an actual f'rinstance. The typesetting code to right justify a short line is ;R . The semicolon was chosen because in normal use, it is rarely followed by another character. But look at the sample program listing in Mike Thyng's story. He uses the variable R in a PRINT statement that is concatenated (joined) by semicolons, and sure enough, it tripped us up. We had to go back and add a trap for this special case.

A lot of times, debugging is trapping — error trapping — through the use of helpful commands like STOP and TRACE, special counters inserted in the program solely for debugging, and careful examination of the program variables.

In our case, the program has a variable named LINE that counts each line of text that is output to the printer. We needed to halt the program at the point when a line that was far too long was output. We knew it was around line 18 or 19, so our statement read:

402 IF LINE = 18 THEN STOP

In a related instance, we wanted to know if and when a particular flag was being set (it shouldn't have been), so we trapped it with:

404 IF HT THEN STOP

That one did it for us, supplied us with the clue we need to fix the program. HT was being set when it should not have been, so then we went off to check the two modules that use the variable HT to find out what went wrong, and of course found the problem.

STOP is a neat debugging tool because it not not only halts program execution, just like END, but it also *displays the line number where execution was halted*. This can be very valuable when you don't know where in your program something is going awry. You just start out by making an educated guess, and place a STOP statement somewhere early in the program. When the program stops, you check all variables for their proper values, and if all is well, you move the STOP statement a little further along in the program, and repeat the process.

You should not overlook all of the neat debugging tools you have avail-

You should not overlook all of the neat debugging tools...

able at the time you have stopped the program. Not only can you display the *value* of each variable, you can test strings for length, value and content, using the LEN, VAL and PRINT (shorthand "?") commands. From the keyboard, you can do just about anything a program can do. For example, if you suspect there are control characters in a string, you can't simply print the string, because control characters do not display, but you can type from the keyboard:

FOR I = 1 TO LEN(ZZ$):?ASC (MID$ (ZZ$,I,1))" "; : NEXT

This will print the ASCII value for each character in the string. There are oodles of other tricks just like that, if you stop and think about the many commands Applesoft has set aside for your use.

STOP can also come in handy in checking out the menu selection portion of a program. By placing a STOP at the beginning of each module that can be selected from a menu, you can instantly find out if your keypress sends you to the proper line number.

TRACE is our other valuable command. TRACE can be used very nicely in conjunction with IF statements or, like STOP, placed in strategic points in your program. Its greatest utility is in a complex program where the logic and flow are difficult to follow. In a multi-statement program line, TRACE will display the line number once for *each statement within a program line*.

TRACE requires several words of caution. If you don't want to wait all day watching it in operation during a wait loop (**FOR I = 1 TO 10000 : NEXT**), then you better think about where in your program you place it. Likewise, when you interrupt program execution, you should *always* as a first step enter **NO TRACE** from the keyboard. Otherwise, the next time you start your program, it will still be in effect. It is not cancelled by the RUN command.

DOS was developed without consideration for the TRACE command, and special handling is required to use TRACE during disk read or write operations. Usually, a program will define D$ (the DOS string) as:

100 D$ = CHR$ (4)

If the TRACE command is in effect, you will find that DOS commands are ignored, and instead printed to the screen. This is because DOS requires a carriage return immediately preceding the [Ctrl-D] (D$), and TRACE will print a line number at the beginning of a line, thus negating the required carriage return. (This problem has been corrected in ProDOS.) There is fortunately, a simple solution. Temporarily *only*, re-define D$ as:

100 D$ = CHR$ (13) + CHR$ (4)

CHR$ (13) is a carriage return, and supplies the one taken away by TRACE. There is one proviso, however, and this is why we said to re-define D$ on a temporary basis only: Depending on the nature of your disk data files, you may read or write incorrect data, or foul it up beyond recovery. This is why

---

. . . it is always a good practice to keep at least one back-up. . .

---

it is *always* a good practice to keep at least one back-up disk during program development and debugging.

Back to Bumbling

If you're still with us, then we can tell you our program followed to the letter almost all the rules of bumbling. We followed our flow charts, typed them in, and ran the program. Of course, it ran correctly the first time (who's kidding who). But the procedures we outlined above did allow us to easily get to the heart of each problem, and then bumble our way through by trying various solutions and temporary patches on a hit-or-miss basis. But when we made a patch, and it worked, it helped us to see where our logic had gone wrong in the first place, and this in turn led to more correct (and proper) solutions. It also helped point out how a program must take into consideration each possible case. The more cases you consider before writing the code, the less debugging you will do in the long run.

Next time around, we'll try and offer some pertinent comments on menu writing, input checking, and when you should and should not use GETs or keyboard reads. We hope you'll be here with us, and we also encourage your comments and suggestions for future material.

Transylvania:

Shortcut to Adventure

Cassidy/Katz/Lynn/Waisman

Shortcut to Adventure is a series of excerpts from the first and subsequent volumes of "A Shortcut Through Adventureland," by **Jack Cassidy, Pete Katz, Richard Owen Lynn** *and* **Sergio Waisman.** *It was reviewed in the April Apple's Apprentice, and is copyright © 1984 by Datamost™, Inc., and is used by permission. We extend our thanks to Dave Gordon, president of Datamost, for his generosity.*

Introduction

Two things are important when you play an adventure game. One is that you find the game puzzles both interesting and challenging. The other is that you don't get stuck and give up.

The authors of the adventures have taken care of the first item. All of the games we feature are packed full of inventive puzzles that are a real joy to figure out.

We are here to keep you from getting frustrated. You must decide how much you want to use this material, but we recommend one thing — *try to solve each puzzle yourself before looking up the answer!* Don't just follow through the answers as you play, because if you do, you will miss out on a lot of fun.

We have tried our best to make everything accurate and to the point. However, we may have missed something here or there. If so, we apologize. Unfortunately, we are unable to individually answer any questions about the games, but if you want to suggest improvements, you can send a letter to us via Datamost.

Finally, we'd like to make a remark about pirated games. There are many pirated versions of adventure games floating around. We've seen a lot of them, and it often *appears* to be fine as you start to play. However, you may run into trouble at some crucial point in the game where it won't work right.

Another common problem is that you are unable to save the game, and you have to go back to the start any time you are killed. To be safe, avoid pirated games.

Map Notes

North is at the top of the map.
Each box □ represents one room or location. An empty box means there is nothing special to do here. A dotted line ... marks a passage that requires problem solving.
The letter **U** or **D** signifies that the passage goes up or down.

Transylvania™

Transylvania is a hi-res adventure game from Penguin. We think it has some of the best graphics around, and a good adventure to match. It is fast moving, mainly because of a menacing werewolf and a hungry vampire which chase you around. It is quite satisfying to get rid of these evil creatures who dog your footsteps and frustrate you at every turn.

General Hints

When you see the werewolf on the screen, you can do one of two things: run away or kill him. We recommend you kill him at the first opportunity with the silver bullet from #6 and the revolver from #8. Otherwise, he will follow you almost everywhere, making the game nearly impossible.

The werewolf won't follow you into the castle, but Dracula resides there, so it isn't safe either. He acts just like the werewolf, and we recommend you kill him right away with the cross. You could keep him away with a garlic bud from #3, but you would never get the chance to kill him (see #9 and #11).

Procedures

1. This is the start. After #12, come back here and pour the acid. Then follow instructions.

2. This note has a helpful hint.

3. The garlic bud will protect you from the vampire at #9. However, you want to kill, not avoid, Dracula. Do not take the garlic.

4. Pull the antler to reveal a secret room. (#5)

5. You need this cloak for #16. If you look at the cloak, you will find a pick to use at #13. When you are done, pull the antler to go back to #4.

6. Go to the wagon; you will see a coffin. Inside are a silver bullet (to use at #8) and three mice (use at #12). If the mice get away, catch them the next time you see them.

7. A cross is supposed to get rid of vampires. Use it at #9. After #17, come back here. Then move the gravestone, unlock the grate with the shiny key, and go down to #18.

8. This pistol can be loaded with the bullet from #6. Load it now, then shoot the werewolf when you see him.

9. Once inside the castle, you will encounter Dracula at random, unless you have the garlic from #3. When you see him, show him the cross from #7 to destroy him.

10. The flypaper is needed at #13.

11. When the vampire is dead (see #9), you will be able to open the coffin and get the ring (to use at #16).

12. Drop the mice to get rid of the cat. Take the acid to pour on the stump at #1. The broom will take you on a wild ride to #15 if you ride it — one time only. Now go back to #1 with the acid.

13. To get here from #1, knock on the stump. To go back to #1, try to take the book. If you read the book without taking it, you will get some information to use at #20. Get some flies here with the flypaper from #10. You will use them at #15. To get to #14, unlock the door with the pick from #5.

14. Look at the crystal ball to learn what to do at #16.

15. Give the flies from #13 to the frog. His information is for #17. The sailboat will be used after #20.

16. Wearing the cloak from #5 and the ring from #11, wave your hand. A few turns later, you will see a shooting star (regardless of where you are). When you see it, come back here and try to enter the saucer. You will get a black box to be used at #20.

17. Say the word you learned at #15 (ijnid) to get the key for #7. See #7 for the procedure to get to #18.

18. This magic elixir is used at #20.

19. Go up the ladder to #20.

20. Move the vines to reveal a sarcophagus. To open it, press the button on the box from #16. Then follow the procedure described at #13 (i.e., wave elixir, pour it, clap hands). Take Sabrina, go to #15, and sail the boat to victory.

Transylvania is a registered trademark of Penguin Software, Inc.

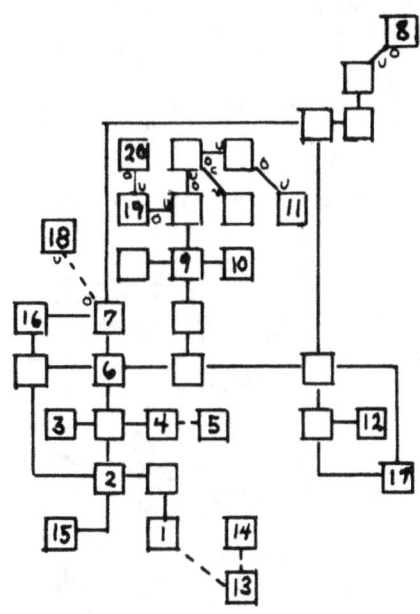

MagiGraphics *(From page 14)*

Since this is essentially a game of making the screen area last as long as possible, the question then becomes how to most efficiently fill the area that you have available.

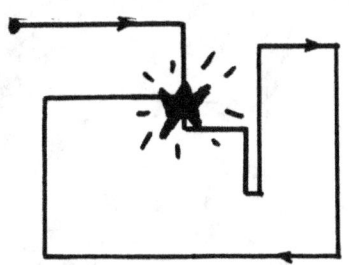

The answer is to sequentially fill the screen, either by a line-by-line pattern, or by a spiral-in pattern like these:

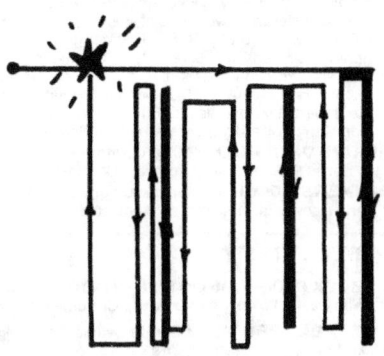

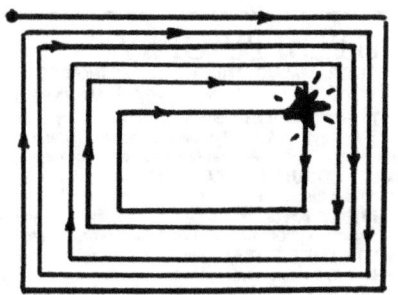

Two Player Version of the Racer

This program is virtually identical to the first listing, except that lines have been added (and a few others changed or deleted) to allow the program to keep track of *two* coordinate pairs, (X1,Y1) and (X2,Y2).

The main differences are as follows. Line 20 now includes X2 and Y2, and these are set equal to 39,39 to put the second racer in the lower right corner at the start.

Lines 200 through 250 parallel the logic used in lines 100 through 150 in their checking for a directional keypress for racer number 2.

Lines 400 through 410 duplicate the drawing function on lines 300 through 310 for player number 2.

For speed purposes, no score or high score is kept in this game. In many animated programs, you will find that there is usually a speed trade-off in the number of features or functions that are present in the program. Each time you ask the computer to do another calculation or draw or print more information on the screen, the program will run a little slower than without that function.

Thus, when you write your own programs, you will have to weigh the advantages of adding a given feature to your programs versus the slowing down effect that feature will have on your program.

As an added challenge, you might want to try converting this program to high resolution graphics. The main changes that have to be made are the GR, PLOT, SCRN, and COLOR commands, and the overall scaling of the screen (280 by 192 for Hi-Res versus 40 by 40 for Lo-Res).

Have fun, and we'll be looking for you next issue!

Apple® Programming Utilities

☐ GPLE™ (Supports DOS 3.3 and ProDOS™)
GLOBAL PROGRAM LINE EDITOR by NEIL KONZEN
$49.95: Includes Peeks/Pokes Chart & Tip Book #7

THE NUMBER 1 APPLE PROGRAM LINE EDITOR
GPLE lets you edit 40- or 80-column Applesoft program lines *FAST* without awkward cursor-tracing or "Escape editing". Compatible with Double-Take's 2 way scrolling.

INSERT & DELETE: GPLE works like an in-memory word processor for Applesoft program lines. Simply jump the cursor to the change-point and insert or delete text. No need to trace to the end of a line before hitting Return.

GLOBAL SEARCH & REPLACE: Find any word or variable in your programs, *FAST*. For example, find all lines containing a GOSUB, or all occurrences of variable XY. REPLACE ANY VARIABLE or word with any other. For example, change all X's to ABC's, or all "Horses" to "Cows".

DEFINABLE ESC FUNCTIONS: Define ESC plus any key to perform any task. For example, **ESC-1** can catalog drive 1, or **ESC-N** could type an entire phrase or subroutine. *Anything* you want, *whenever* you want.

GPLE DOS MOVER: Move DOS 3.3 & GPLE above main memory for an EXTRA 10K of programming space.

PLUS APPLE TIP BOOK #7: Learn more about your Apple! Includes all-new useful GPLE tips and tricks.

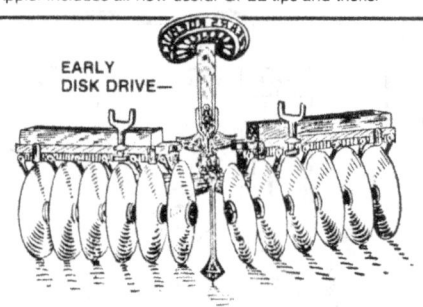

EARLY DISK DRIVE→

☐ BEAGLE BASIC™ (REQ. 64K)
APPLESOFT ENHANCER by MARK SIMONSEN
$34.95: Includes Peeks/Pokes Chart & Tip Book #6

RENAME ANY APPLESOFT COMMAND or Error Message to anything you want. For program clarification, encryption/protection or even foreign translation. Example:

10 POUR X=1 TO 3: ECRIVEZ "BONJOUR": ENSUITE
RAM Applesoft is *better* Applesoft! Beagle Basic replaces those obsolete cassette commands (SHLOAD, etc.), with powerful new commands that you can USE—
ELSE follows Applesoft If-Then statements, like this:
IF X=2 THEN PRINT "YES": **ELSE** PRINT "NO"

HSCRN reads the color of a hi-res dot for collision testing. **SWAP** exchanges variable values. **TONE** writes music without messy Pokes or Calls. **SCRL** scrolls text in *either* direction. **TXT2** lets Text Page 2 act exactly like Page 1...

GOTO AND GOSUB may precede variables, as in "GOSUB FIX" or "GOTO 4+X". Escape-mode indicated by a special ESCAPE CURSOR. Replace those awkward Graphics screen-switch pokes with one-word commands. Change your ctrl-G Beep to any tone you want. **INVERSE REM STATEMENTS** too! GPLE/Double-Take compatible.

☐ DOS BOSS™
DOS 3.3 EDITOR by BERT KERSEY & JACK CASSIDY
$24.00: Includes Peeks/Pokes Chart & Tip Book #2

RENAME DOS COMMANDS and Error Messages— DOS 3.3's "Catalog" can be "Cat"; DOS's cryptic "Syntax Error" can be "Oops" or almost *anything* you want it to be.

PROTECT YOUR PROGRAMS. Unauthorized Save-attempts can produce "Not Copyable" message, or *any* message. **List-Prevention** and other useful Apple tips and tricks. Plus one-key program-execution from catalog.

CUSTOMIZE DOS. Change Disk Volume headings to your message or title. Omit or alter catalog file codes. Fascinating documentation, tips & educational experiments.

ANYONE USING YOUR DISKS (booted or not) will be forced to use DOS formatted the way YOU designed it.

☐ DOUBLE-TAKE™ (DOS 3.3 and ProDOS™)
2-WAY SCROLL/MULTI-UTILITY by MARK SIMONSEN
$34.95: Includes Peeks/Pokes Chart & Tips Chart #1

2-WAY SCROLLING: Listings & Disk Catalogs scroll Up *and* Down, making file names and program lines faster to find and easier to access. Change Catalog or List scroll-direction with Apple's Arrow keys. Machine Language and Hex/Ascii dumps scroll two-ways too. All features are GPLE compatible and support 80-column display.

BETTER LIST FORMAT: Each Applesoft program statement lists on a new line for *FAST* program tracing & de-bugging (see sample below). Printer-compatible in any column-width—Great for archive printouts.

A$="DOGFOOD" ◄ **VARIABLE-DISPLAY:** prints
X=3.14159   all of a program's strings and vari-
Y=255   ables with their current values.

A$: 100 200 250 ◄ **CROSS-REFERENCE:** Sorts
X: 10 20 3000   & displays line numbers where
Y: 10 40 55 60   each variable & string appears.

AUTO-LINE-NUMBER, instant Hex/Dec Converter, better Renumber/Append, Program Stats, Eliminate/Redefine Cursor, Free Space-On-Disk... All GPLE/Pronto compatible.

```
]LIST
10 HGR2
  : FOR Y=0 TO 191
  : POKE 228, C
  : C=C+1/9-256*(C=255)
20 REM "Double-Take
   optionally lists each
   Applesoft program
   statement on a new
   line, making pro-
   gram code much
   easier to read."
30 HPLOT 0,Y TO 279,Y
  : NEXT Y
  : POKE 2053,58
  : GOTO 10
```

2-WAY VIDEO SCROLLING

High-Speed DOS

☐ PRONTO-DOS™
HIGH-SPEED DOS/DOS-MOVER by TOM WEISHAAR
$29.50: Includes Peeks & Pokes Chart

TRIPLES THE SPEED of disk access and frees 10,000 bytes of extra programmable memory by moving DOS 3.3.

Function	Normal	Pronto
BLOAD HI-RES IMAGE	10 sec.	3 sec.
LOAD 60-SECTOR PROGRAM	16 sec.	4 sec.
SAVE 60-SECTOR PROGRAM	24 sec.	9 sec.

(Text-files no change) **Bload language cards** at *triple speed*. Create bootable high-speed disks with the normal INIT command. Compatible with *all* commands, GPLE, Double-Take, DOS Boss, DiskQuik & most unprotected programs.

MOVE DOS 3.3 above main memory to free *10,000 bytes* of memory for your programs (64K required to move DOS).

15 EXTRA SECTORS per disk. Catalog Free-Space is displayed on the screen every time you Catalog a disk.

NEW TYPE-COMMAND ("TYPE filename") prints the contents of any Text File on-screen or to your printer.

☐ DISKQUIK™ (Requires IIe with 128K)
DISK EMULATOR by HARRY BRUCE & GENE HITE
$29.50: Includes Peeks & Pokes Chart
Requires Apple IIc or IIe with EXTENDED 80-col card)

ACTS LIKE A DISK DRIVE in Slot 3, but super-fast and silent! Enjoy many of the benefits of another drive at 1/10th the cost. Catalog with "CATALOG, S3" command. Access all kind of files in RAM with normal DOS commands.

SILENT AND FAST: Since no moving parts are involved, DiskQuik operates at super-high speeds. See to believe! Your Apple IIe's Extended 80-column Card (required) holds about half the amount of data as a 5¼" floppy!

MANY USES: For example, load often-used files like FID into RAM when you boot up, so they are always available when you need them. Copy files from RAM onto disk and vice versa, just as if a disk drive were connected to slot #3.

COMPATIBLE with all normal DOS procedures.

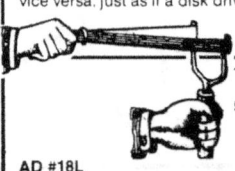

```
1234  TEXT: HOME: NORMAL:
      PRINT CHRS(21)
5678  R=INT(RND(1)*10): N(R)=
      N(R)+1: VTAB R+9: HTAB
  40: PRINT CHRS (124); SPC
      (N(R)); CHRS(R+65); :
      IF PEEK(36) THEN 5678
```

AD #18L

Multi-Utilities

☐ UTILITY CITY™
21 PROGRAMMING UTILITIES by BERT KERSEY
$29.50: Includes Peeks/Pokes Chart & Tip Book #3

LIST FORMATTER prints each Applesoft program statement on a new line. For-Next Loops are indented with printer Page Breaks. A great Applesoft program de-bugger.

MULTI-COLUMN CATALOGS to your printer, with or without sector and file codes. Organize your disk library.

INVISIBLE AND TRICK catalog File Names. Put invisible functioning commands in Applesoft programs too.

21 UTILITIES TOTAL, including auto-post Run-number & Date in programs, alphabetize/store info on disk, convert dec to hex or Int to FP, protect and append programs, dump 40-column text to printer. And More.

LEARN PROGRAMMING TRICKS: LIST-able programs and informative documentation. Includes Tip Book #3—Hours of good reading and Applesoft experiments.

Beagle Bros
Micro Software Inc.

3990 OLD TOWN AVENUE, SUITE 102C
SAN DIEGO, CA 92110 / 619-296-6400

Attention Applers: Most Apple dealers and software stores have Beagle Bros products on their shelves. If you can't find the disk you want, bug the manager—he can have *any* of our products in his store for you within a couple of days.

FREE APPLE COMMAND CHART: Each SILICON SALAD and TIP DISK #1 comes with an 11x17 poster of all Applesoft, Integer & DOS Commands with Descriptions.

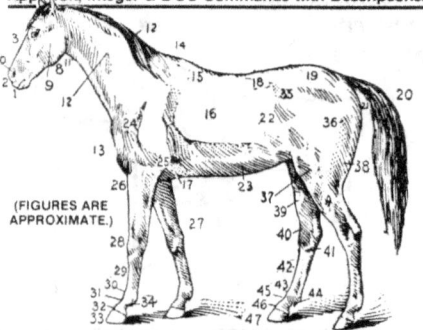

(FIGURES ARE APPROXIMATE.)

☐ SILICON SALAD™
WITH TIP DISK #2 by BERT KERSEY & MARK SIMONSEN
$24.95: With Peeks/Pokes Chart & Apple Command Chart

MANY MINI-UTILITIES: Program Splitter makes room for hi-res pix in large Applesoft programs, **Disk Scanner** finds bad disk sectors, **Key-Clicker** adds subtle sound as you type, **DOS-Killer** adds two tracks of space to your disks, **2-Track Cat** allows up to 210 DOS 3.3 file names per disk, **Text Imprinter** converts text-screen text into hi-res text, **Onerr Tell Me** prints the appropriate error message but continues program execution, **Text Screen Formatter** formats and converts text layouts into Print statements... plus much more Apple wizardry from the boys at Beagle Bros.

MORE TIPS ON DISK: Over 100 programs from Beagle Bros Tip Books 5, 6 and 7; *and* from Tip Chart #1.

TWO-LINERS TOO: From our customers around the world—and elsewhere. New tricks for your old Apple!

☐ TIP DISK #1™
100 TIP BOOK PROGRAMS ON DISK by BERT KERSEY
$20.00: With Peeks/Pokes Chart & Apple Command Chart

100 LISTABLE PROGRAMS from Beagle Tip Books 1-4. Make your Apple do things it's never done! All 100 programs are LISTable and changeable for experimentation. Two-Liners too, plus a free *Apple Command Chart*.

Logo Lingo

Jeff Sandys

Habla usted Espanol? Sprechen sie Deutsch? Many people can speak more that one language. Can you? People use languages to express ideas to other people. Languages are universal, any idea you can say in English can be translated into any other language.

Your Apple computer can also speak more than one language. Its native tongue is BASIC. There are two dialects, Integer and Applesoft. With the proper disk, your Apple can understand Pascal, Assembly, Forth, C, LISP or Logo languages. And just like human languages, any idea expressed in one language can be translated to any other language.

Like human languages, Logo is made up of words. Words in Logo act like verbs and nouns. Sentences are made from these words according to syntax rules. For computers, these rules are more rigid than for spoken languages. Logo will tell you when it doesn't understand your sentence.

Sentences in Logo are called *instructions.* Each instruction starts with a command. In English a command is a verb, the subject of the verb is an understood "you." For example an Army drill instructor might shout, "Attention." He doesn't need to say who, he is talking to you. In an adventure game you simply say "Look" or "Go North." You don't have to say who when you enter these commands. Some Logo commands are:

CLEARSCREEN
HOME
HIDETURTLE
CATALOG.

Many Logo commands refer to objects. Objects are the nouns in Logo or in English. For example the drill instructor might say, "Climb the wall." In this command "wall" is the object of the verb "climb." Objects are used as inputs to Logo's commands. Here are some Logo commands with inputs:

FORWARD 50
RIGHT 90
PRINT "HELLO
SAVE "PROGRAM.

Operations are another type of Logo verb. In English they would be called *gerunds.* Our drill instructor might say "Start digging a hole." The word "digging" is a gerund, "dig" is a verb, but "digging a hole" is acting like a noun for the verb "start." Yet as a verb, "digging" has the object "hole." Operations in Logo output an object that can be used as the input for a command. Here are some examples:

PRINT HEADING
SETX RANDOM 100
PRINT FIRST [ONE TWO THREE].

Logo's nouns are called objects. There are two types of objects in Logo, words and lists. A word is made up of characters. Some valid words are: "FOO, "R2D2, "DOG, and "$27.95. The quote tells Logo that the characters form a word. Numbers are a special type of word, they don't need a quote. For example FORWARD 100 is the same as FORWARD "100. Logo keeps a list of all the words that it knows. This is called the contents list and you can see it with:

PRINT .CONTENTS

Lists are objects made up of words and lists. Some valid lists are: [FOO R2D2 DOG $27.95] and [EGGS BACON [ORANGE JUICE]]. Lists are punctuated with square brackets. Also notice that the words in a list do not need a quote. A list can also be one word, like: [HELLO] and [27]. The nil list is an empty list and it looks like this: []. Logo has many commands and operations that work on lists.

Objects can be given a name. The command MAKE is used to assign a name to an object. Some examples are:

MAKE "FOO 27
MAKE "DOG "SPOT
MAKE "GROCERIES [EGGS BACON [ORANGE JUICE]]

By putting dots (: a semicolon) on a name we can get the object that is attached to that name. If we instruct Logo to PRINT :FOO it will print 27. Dots,

quotes and brackets tell Logo that these are objects (nouns). Words without punctuation are commands or operations (verbs).

Just as you can name an object, you can also define your own commands and operations. This is easily done with the word TO. These definitions are called procedures. We write a Logo program by writing procedures that work together. This is why Logo is called a procedural language. Listed below is a short program that draws a picture. Try to identify the commands and operations and their inputs or objects. Each procedure name is in a different language. Can you name them?

We have covered a lot of ground in a short space. Let us review the syntax rules that we have mentioned:

- *An instruction starts with a command.*
- *A command doesn't have an output.*
- *Some commands have inputs.*
- *An operation outputs an object.*
- *Some operations have inputs.*
- *An object is a word or a list.*
- *A quote means, use as a word.*
- *Numbers are self-quoting words.*
- *A square bracket means, use as a list.*
- *An object can have a name.*
- *A semicolon means, use the object named.*
- *A procedure is a command or operation.*
- *A word without punctuation is a procedure.*

This is the end of the hard stuff, the syntax rules will become natural as you use Logo. In Logo Lingo we will talk about languages, mathematics, problem solving, and turtles as we learn to write Logo programs. If you have questions or comments about Logo, send them to the address below. If you want a reply, you must include a self-addressed stamped envelope.

Logo Lingo
P.O. Box 30668
Seattle, WA 98103

Program on page 26

The Sourceror's Apprentice

Mike Newton

Hello again! This month we'll start out by talking about those strange creatures, the Hexels. As I mentioned before, Hexels have eight fingers on each hand, for a total of sixteen on both hands. Because they have a different number of fingers than we do, they count differently than we do.

We have ten fingers and we count 1, 2, 3, 4, 5, 6, 7, 8, 9, 10. Notice that the first number with two numerals is the tenth number. This is because we have ten fingers, and it is easy to count in multiples of ten. We call this the *decimal* number system, or *Base 10*. The 16-fingered Hexels, unlike us, count 1, 2, 3, 4, 5, 6, 7, 8, 9, A, B, C, D, E, F, 10. Strange, isn't it? Notice that the first number with two numerals is the sixteenth number, since they have 16 fingers.

Most people who have to talk to Hexels use this number system, called *hexadecimal*, or *Base 16*. Likewise, most assembly language programmers use hexadecimal numbers when writing assembly language programs. Most machine language and Apple hardware manuals list all numbers and addresses in hexadecimal. It is a good idea to begin getting familiar with hexadecimal numbers. *Figure 1* shows a partial list of hexadecimal numbers and their equivalent decimal numbers.

Most editor/assemblers allow you to use decimal, hexadecimal, binary and octal numbers. We will use hexadecimal numbers more and more as we begin exploring the vast expanse of the Apple. You will probably notice in the illustration that all of the hexadecimal numbers are preceded by a dollar sign

...hexadecimal numbers are preceded by a dollar sign

[$]. This is to let you know the numbers are hexadecimal numbers, and not decimal numbers.

Remember last time we talked about the mail storage room in the dungeon, and compared it to electronic memory in the Apple. We even drew a diagram to help explain the similarities between the mail room and the Apple's memory. You might like to go back to the April issue of *The Apple's Apprentice* and re-read it.

Letters sitting in the mail boxes can either be read, moved or written on. Likewise, numbers residing in memory can either be read from, moved, or written on. To move a number from one location in memory to another, you would merely read it at the location it is currently at, and write it at the loca-

tion you wish to move it to. Notice that at this point there are two copies of the original number. If you wished to erase the number from the original memory cell, you could write another number, such as zero, at the first location.

Every one of the mailboxes has its own box number, called also an address. Just like the mailman puts the mail that is addressed to you in the mailbox with your unique address, each mailbox in the castle dungeon has a unique address. And just as each mailbox has its own address, so each location in the Apple's memory has its own address.

Each location in memory holds a hexadecimal value called a byte

Each location in memory holds a hexadecimal value called a *byte*. Exactly

Figure 1

Hexadecimal	Decimal
$ 00	0
$ 01	1
$ 02	2
$ 03	3
$ 04	4
$ 05	5
$ 06	6
$ 07	7
$ 08	8
$ 09	9
$ 0A	10
$ 0B	11
$ 0C	12
$ 0D	13
$ 0E	14
$ 0F	15
$ 10	16
$ 20	32
$ 40	64
$ 80	128
$ C0	192
$ 100	256
$ 200	512
$ 300	768
$ 400	1024
$ 800	2048
$ 1000	4096
$ 2000	8192
$ 4000	16384
$ 8000	32768
$ C000	49152
$ FFFF	65535

Figure 2

BINARY #		DEC	HEX
00000000	=	0	$00
00000001	=	1	$01
00000010	=	2	$02
00000011	=	3	$03
00000100	=	4	$04
00001000	=	8	$08
00010000	=	16	$10
00100000	=	32	$20
01000000	=	64	$40
10000000	=	128	$80
11111111	=	255	$FF

one byte, no more, no less. A byte is a number between 0 and 255 [decimal] or 0 to $FF [hexadecimal]. Why the 255 limit? The reason for this lies at the foundation of the structure of the microprocessor, and involves a bit of mathematics. If you want to learn about this, read the next two paragraphs. If you don't want to know, or can't handle too much math, skip the next two paragraphs. Keep in mind, though, that to be a real assembly language programmer you will eventually need to know this information, so you'll have to read it sooner or later. Some of it is rather tough to understand.

A *bit* [**bi**nary dig**it**] can be one of two values, 0 or 1. This is much like a being that can count only on two fingers. *Figure 2* is a partial list of some binary numbers and the decimal and hexadecimal numbers that they equal. The BASIC program listed here will let you do your own conversions from binary numbers or bit patterns to decimal and hex numbers.

The 6502 is what is known as an eight bit processor. This means that it can work on only eight bits at a time. As you may have heard before, a byte is made of eight bits. The largest number that can be represented by a single byte is 255 [$FF]. How did we get this number? We get it by raising 2 to the 8th power [2^8]. (Actually the result of this exponential number is 256, but zero takes away one of the possible

values, leaving 255 for all other positive numbers.) This tells us the maximum value that a binary number with eight digits can represent.

Most microprocessors use addresses that are twice as long as its basic data length. Since the 6502 is an eight bit processor, it uses sixteen bit addresses (requiring two bytes for representation). What is the largest address that the 6502 can use? We can figure this out by raising two to the sixteenth power [2^{16}]. This number is 65536. In hexadecimal, it is $10000, one more than the $FFFF the Apple can count to. Notice that $FFFF is the largest value that a four digit hexadecimal number can have. The more that you use hexadecimal, the more you will appreciate its value for assembly language programming.

Let's talk now about registers, those in the mail room, and those in the 6502 (the Apple's microprocessor). The simplest operation that can be done on a register is to store the number written in the register to a location in memory, or read the value of a location in memory into a register. The accumulator is a special register that is used for arithmetic, so, as you can see, registers are used mainly for reading, writing and arithmetic. The registers could even be thought of as very special memory locations within the 6502 itself. Later on we'll use the registers to do some really neat programs.

The Hexel's mail storage room contains 65536 different mailboxes. Every

mailbox is the same, with room for only one letter at a time. The mail room is divided into many different sections, however. The section that is nearest to the door (and therefore very fast and easy to get to) is a special section used for express mail. The good King Buckingham has reserved this section for any mail that needs to be processed rapidly. It is called the Z Page section because there is a very reliable page boy named Zee who delivers the mail here.

The mail room has another section called the Stack, which is also close to the door (but not as close as the Z Page). The King also reserves this for his own use. There are many other special sections in the mail room, but we'll discuss them later.

Getting back to computers, the Apple is simply a gigantic memory box with a microprocessor that reads values from certain memory locations and writes values to other memory locations. Everything on the Apple is controlled or altered by getting values from or putting values in certain sections of memory.

Whenever you're in Applesoft Basic, for example, and looking at a screen of text characters, you're really seeing in a different form, the values of bytes in a section of memory called text page number one, or more commonly, just the *text page*. There are many special sections of memory that serve special functions such as this. The Hi-Res pages, where high resolution

```
10   REM

BIT PATTERN CONVERTER

     VAL J GOLDING

100  HOME : PRINT "ENTER 0'S OR 1
     'S FOR ALL 8 BITS, LEFT    TO
        RIGHT... ENTER MSB FIRST": PRINT
110  PRINT "BIT NBR -> 76543210
         DEC HEX"
120  PRINT : HTAB 12: PRINT "";:B
     IT = 0:MLT = 128
130  FOR PSN = 1 TO 8:CHR =  PEEK
      (PSN + 1418): POKE 1418 + PS
     N,CHR - 128
140  GET BIT$(PSN): IF (BIT$(PSN)
     ) <  > "0" AND BIT$(PSN) <  >
     "1" THEN 140
150 BIT(PSN) =  VAL (BIT$(PSN))
160  HTAB PSN + 11: PRINT BIT$(PS
     N);
170 BIT = BIT + (BIT(PSN) * MLT):
     MLT = MLT / 2
180  POKE 1418 + PSN,CHR: NEXT : PRINT
     " = ";

190  IF BIT < 100 THEN  PRINT " "
     ;: IF BIT < 10 THEN  PRINT "
      ";
200  PRINT BIT" $";
210  POKE 26,165: POKE 27,25: POKE
      28,76: POKE 29,218: POKE 30,
     253: POKE 25,BIT: CALL 26
220 SAVVTB =  PEEK (37): VTAB 23:
      PRINT : PRINT "PRESS ESC TO
     EXIT, ANY KEY TO CONTINUE "
     ;: GET Z$: ON Z$ =  CHR$ (27
     ) GOTO 230: VTAB SAVVTB + 1:
      GOTO 120
230  END
300  REM
```

This program prints the decimal
and hex values of an eight-bit
pattern input by the user.

```
400   REM
```

Lines 130 and 180 show how to
POKE directly to the screen.
Line 190 right justifies output.
Figure out how line 210 converts
decimal to hex.

graphics are displayed, are actually just giant chunks of memory. Low resolution graphics (often called Lo-Res graphics) reside on the text pages. Only one type of display, text, Lo-Res or Hi-Res, can be displayed at one time, except for a "mixed" mode, which allows four lines of text on a graphic screen. After being told which of the three display modes to show on the screen, the video display circuitry will get the values from the special section of memory that the display page resides in.

One section of memory is quite different from all of the others, because data can not really be stored there, nor can these locations be read from. Instead, this section contains what we call *soft switches*, which in a lot of ways

. . . soft switches work like electric light switches

work just like the electric light switches on your wall at home. When you "store" data in these locations, it actually turns a "switch" in the Apple on or off. The soft switches control things like selecting graphics or text mode. These soft switches and other special nearby locations enable your program to control various aspects of the hardware.

Another section of memory contains the actual machine language program called Applesoft. As we've learned before, the only language the computer really understands is machine language. By writing a special program in machine language, the computer is made to seem like it "knows" Applesoft.

There are many little segmentations and special uses for different sections of memory. A chart that shows you what each section of memory is used for is called a memory map. In the future, we'll see memory maps of the Apple's inner realm.

Speaking of realms, the King is beginning of hear stories of Apples now. A few wandering minstrels who have been to the Silicon Valley are bringing word to Fairhill Castle of these electronic wonders. Most people don't know what to make of it yet, supposing that the minstrels have invented these stories because they've run out of things to sing about. After all, have many songs about dragons and battles and maidens in distress could you bear hearing?

One of these days, one of them might actually bring an Apple with him, trying to enlighten and entertain the primitive folk here. The poor lad will probably be accused of witchcraft and be sent to the dungeons. I'll take care him if that happens. It's really a shame that so many people are scared of things that are new and mysterious to them. Sometimes they feel threatened by the good minstrels, just because they come bringing strange news from far off lands. Many is the minstrel I've saved from punishment. That's why I took over running the dungeon.

Here comes *Haloholahiho*. He's a Hexel. These Hexels have really strange names. Some of their names are longer than they are. He just told me that a group of flat-footed, pointy-eared *Dunglebaries* have escaped from their section in the fifth level of the dungeon. Those Dunglebaries are so troublesome!

They're really tiny creatures, about the size of your feet. They like to escape to the town at night, when everyone is asleep and eat all of the alarm clocks they can find. No one wakes up for work or school until late, and the whole town gets off schedule by at least an hour. Then, after they've eaten all of the alarm clocks, they hide in bath tubs and chew on dirty socks. If I don't catch them, the town will be in chaos! I look forward to seeing you soon! Keep up the good work, apprentice, so you don't have to do all the absurd things I do!

At the ripe age of 18, Mike Newton is a self-taught writer and computer programmer, currently residing in southern California. He is currently finishing a technical book on assembly language graphics for Broderbund Software, and is starting to work on a book about programming the Apple Macintosh in assembly language.

Newton has not yet received a college education, but plans on attending the University of California over the next few years. His favorite books are Lord of the Rings *and* Illusions, *and his favorite authors include* Godel, Escher, *and* Bach. *His musical interests run to* Pink Floyd *and* YES.

He enjoys programming in assembly language the most, and prefers the Motorola MCS68000 for a microprocessor. He looks forward to a long and prosperous relationship with the Macintosh, and with the Apple's Apprentice.

LOGO PROGRAM *(From page 23)*

```
TO PROGRAM
HOME CS TESTA
FD 80 OIDO
LT 120 FD 22 NEUS
FD 40 VISAGE
OWGHER HT
END

TO TESTA
CHETYRE 80 60
END

TO OIDO
LT 90
TRZY 15
LT 180 FD 60 LT 60
TRZY 15
END

TO NEUS
LT 90
CHETYRE 40 16
END

TO VISAGE
RT 30 TRZY 16 FD 16
LT 60 TRZY 40
END

TO OWGHER
PU SETX 5 SETY 60 SETH 90 PD
TRZY 12 PU FD 38 PD TRZY 12
END

TO CHETYRE :A :B
REPEAT 2 [FD :A RT 90 FD :B RT
                    90]
END

TO TRZY :N
REPEAT 3 [FD :N RT 120]
END
```

Thief
Val J. Golding

Like day turning to night,
the September change
    somewhere 'round the eighth
a fallish touch.

    Subliminally, just a bite,
an autumn nip
    bright sun-filled days
somehow less warm.

    Night colors encroach
stealthily
    from each hour a moment stolen:
shadows so long.

Spells and Potions

George Spelbin

Welcome back to Fairhill Castle. Step into the apothecary with me, and I'll hand out some of my best spells, for just the cost of this magazine! I remember back when I myself was but a mere apprentice, writing my first programs, and I couldn't figure out how to print a long message to the screen without having it scroll away.

Now if you know how long your text will be, it's a pretty easy matter to figure out how many lines you can print before you scroll the top line away, but what if you have text of varying lengths? That's what I want to tell you about.

In the last issue, *The Wizard* wrote a little bit about location 37. There's nothing mysterious about this location, it's one of many the monitor uses in its normal operations. One of the things the monitor must do is always keep track of the screen line that is being printed to, so even if *you* don't know where you're at, the monitor does, and it uses location 37 for this bit of hocus–pocus.

In the monitor program, location 37 is called CV, which stands for *cursor vertical*. If you are writing an adventure game that selects data to be printed to the screen from among a group of data, you certainly want the player to be able to read the complete screen. The easiest thing to do is have all your print statements in the form of strings that can be printed at the appropriate time. If your program knows how many strings to print at any given time, you can do it in a FOR/NEXT loop and check CV (37) each time through the loop. A few program lines to do that might look like this:

```
300 FOR PLOOP = 1 TO
    NUMSTRINGS
310 IF PEEK(37) > 16 THEN
    PRINT : PRINT "ANY KEY TO
    CONTINUE" : CALL -756 :
    HOME
320 PRINT OUT$(PLOOP)
330 NEXT PLOOP
```

The **CALL -756** is a kind of dummy input. It does nothing except wait for a keypress. You could just as well use **GET Z$, INPUT Z$,** or **WAIT -16384,128.** All have the effect of pausing the display until you do something. Of course, when you PEEK at 37, you could check for a greater or lesser screen line number.

Sometimes you want to be able to use part of a program — like a favorite subroutine — in another program. In fact, some people will keep a whole disk of subroutines that they can use in other programs.

One way to save a subroutine for future use is to write it to a text file. As a text file you can use the EXEC command to bring it into your new program. Page 160 of the DOS manual explains a little about the EXEC command. Right now, I'm going to give you a short program that will create an EXEC type of text file that you can use to "capture" a program, or a part of a program.

```
How to capture a program in a
text file in three easy lessons

2 Q$ =  CHR$ (34):D$ =  CHR$ (13)
    + CHR$ (4): PRINT D$"OPENC
    APFILE"D$"WRITECAPFILE"
3  PRINT " 63999 D$=CHR$(13)+CHR$
    (4):?D$"Q$"OPENLISTFILE"Q$"D
    $"Q$"WRITELISTFILE"Q$":POKE3
    3,33:LIST-63998:?D$"Q$"CLOSE
    "Q$":TEXT:END
4  PRINT  CHR$ (4)"CLOSE"
```

Now when you want to capture a program, just make sure you have in memory only that part you want to save. You can get rid of unwanted lines with the DEL command, or by typing the line number. Now type "EXEC CAPFILE" and the disk drive will come on and you will see a few Applesoft prompts (]) on the screen while the disk is running. If you list the program now, you will see there is a new line, number 63999. All you do is type "RUN 63999" and the disk drive will start up again, and write your program to a text file named "LISTFILE".

In the future, when you want to add this file to a program, just type "EXEC LISTFILE" and the saved lines will be added to your program, just like line 63999 was. After LISTFILE is created, you might want to rename it. Wouldn't do to have two of them y'know. And watch out also for duplicate line numbers.

In the program above, Q$ represents a quote mark ["] and is a way to use quotes within quotes. Sometime I'll tell you about that, too, but the day grows short and I have many chores yet to do.

Quick Adder

Batteries gone dead on your calculator? Or keys sticking? (Ours do.) Sometimes you wonder if buying a new calculator every few months is worth it.

You have an Apple, why not use it? In fact you can write simple two and three line programs in a few seconds. Here's one that's only two lines long, and will add any group of figures for you. It uses just two variables, NUM for the number to be input, and TL for the total. Whenever you want to subtract, just use a minus sign before you type the number, and whenever you want a total, input a zero for your number. OK, gang?

```
100 INPUT NUM
110 TL = TL + NUM : ON NUM
    <> 0 GOTO 100 : PRINT TL
```

Cross Words

Don't be angry, let's not have words . . .
Unless, of course, they are cross words . . .

Hints

You should read the *Apple's Apprentice* carefully. Many of the answers appear in the stories. Watch out for puns and word plays. For example, the clue "job" might mean "tasc" (the compiler). When you think you have an answer but are not sure, look it up in a dictionary or a BASIC manual.

Answers appear on page 40. Good luck!

Across

5. Connect it to an Apple
6. Where the wizard lives
8. Editor
9. Type of register
12. Stumble
13. . . . else
15. R2D2
18. The program stops here
19. Game name
22. Walk, don't . . .
23. What a loop is called
27. Dad
29. Donna
32. Eastern teacher
33. A pile
34. Fairhill
36. Check the program
37. Separates statements
38. Binary digit
39. Automatic option
40. What the Wizard does
43. Module or section
44. Mountains
45. Number system

Down

1. Drugstore
2. Stephen
3. Do it often
4. I follows it
7. Comment
8. Silicon
10. What you read
11. Telecommunications protocol
14. Antonym for daze
16. Always do it
17. Aries
20. Permanent memory
21. Less than three
23. Dark and damp
24. Not the head honcho
25. Eight-fingered
26. Negative logic
28. The good king
30. What you press often
31. Made of parchment
32. A BASIC JMP
35. Collect or put together
41. Opposite of PEEK
42. Assignment statement

Daze of the Knights

Arise, ye varlets, arise to the challenge. With these taunting words, we bring to you the first pair of *Daze of the Knights* contests. These are very special contests. They are designed to bring you hours of fun and challenge, while at the same time pointing out some of the powerful things your Apple can do when you know enough of its internals to do amusing things.

There will be all sorts of prizes. There will be points awarded for correct solutions, and a grand winner, based on points, at some time in the near future. There will be individual prizes of subscriptions and software. These are details we are still working out as we go to press, and they will be announced in the next issue. There will be general contest rules that apply to all contests, and there will be specific rules which apply to each individual contest.

We want to hear from you: we want to know how you like the contests; we also welcome your contest submissions. Most of all, we want you to enjoy the *Apple's Apprentice* and have fun learning about computing. Comes now the rules (and not too heavy, either).

General Rules
* Be sure to include your name, address and *age* with each entry.
* Duplicate prizes will be awarded to each of two age groups: under 15 and 15 and older.
* In the event of a tie, the earliest post-marked entry will receive the prize.
* Winner's names will be published in the *Apple's Apprentice* and added to our "honor roll"
* No more than one entry to one contest may be enclosed in the same envelope.
* Envelopes must be marked on the outside with the number and/or name of the contest, and addressed to:
  Apple's Apprentice
  P.O. Box 582-AA
  Santee, CA 92071

Contest No. 1
This is a trick program, but it will run. Tell us how you got it to run, and send along any listings to prove your claim.

Contest No. 2
This program will run as listed. Show your skill by reducing it to its essentials, i.e., remove the cloak of hocus-pocus, and send us the *shortest* program listing you can make from it that will still execute.

Extra Special...
If you can write a good explanation that can be understood by others and help them learn about the Apple, we will consider it for publication! And now, it's time to get to work. Good luck!

DAZE OF THE KNIGHTS

CONTEST NO. 1 : KEN KASHMAREK

```
5 NEXT = 1:END = 10:ON = 2
9  FOR STEP = NEXT TO END STEP ON

15  PRINT STEP
20  NEXT STEP

]RUN
1
3
5
7
9
```

DAZE OF THE KNIGHTS

CONTEST NO. 2 : VAL J GOLDING

```
113  GOSUB 45221:WINNER =  PEEK (
     989) -  PEEK (992):TRICK =   PEEK
     (2050):GUESS = TRICK - WINNE
     R:LAM =  PEEK ( - 12031)
699  FLASH : PRINT : PRINT " SPEE
     D IS NOT MY FORTE ": NORMAL
     : PRINT
1111 HAHA$ = FOO$ + ":D 44 49 53
     4B 20 56 4F 4C 55 4D 45 20 3
     2 35 34 D D 2A 42 20 30 30 3
     2 20 41 50 50 4C 45 27 53 D
     20 52 20 30 30 34 20 41 50 5
     0 52 45 4E 54 49 43 45 D 2A
     41 20 30 30 33 20 49 53 20 4
     6 4F 52 N D9C66": GOSUB 5555
     5
2345 HAHA$ = APPLE$ + ":D 20 54 2
     0 30 30 33 20 4B 49 44 53 20
     4F 46 D 2A 53 20 30 30 37 2
     0 41 4C 4C 20 41 47 45 53 D
     0 N D9C66": GOSUB 55555
6789 TURN =  PEEK ( - 16151):TSKT
     SK =  PEEK ( - 7221): FOR CN
     TEST = WINNER TO GUESS:LFT$ =
     LFT$ +  CHR$ ( PEEK (( - 856
     )) - (WINNER + WINNER) * (LA
     M / (GUESS - 4))):RIGT$ = RI
     GT$ +  CHR$ ( PEEK (63809)):
     : NEXT CNTEST
15336 D$ =   CHR$ (4):: POKE TSKTS
      K, PEEK (58530): POKE TSKTSK
      + WINNER, PEEK ( - 6435):::
      ::: POKE TSKTSK + (WINNER +
      WINNER), PEEK (61601) +  PEEK
      ( - 3890): POKE TSKTSK + (GU
      ESS - (WINNER * 4)),( PEEK (
      - 1755))
20007 HAHA$ = "6:A0 3 A9 0 4C C6
      D9 N 66 N D9C66": GOSUB 5555
      5
31415  CALL  VAL (GOLDING$): PRINT
       D$"CATALOG"LFT$RIGT$
32767  CALL APPRENTICE +  PEEK ( -
       GUESS)
44444  POKE 49384,GUESS: CALL 100
       2: END
45221  GOLDING$ = "64600":FOO$ =   STR$
       ( PEEK ( - 1302) *  PEEK ( -
       115)):APPLE$ =  STR$ ( VAL (
       FOO$) +  PEEK (63553)): RETURN

55555  FOR CNTEST = WINNER TO  LEN
       (HAHA$): POKE ( PEEK ( - 114
       02)) * WINNER * ( PEEK (1023
       ) +  PEEK ( - 10941)) - WINN
       ER + CNTEST, ASC ( MID$ (HAH
       A$,CNTEST)) + ( PEEK (54597)
       +  PEEK ( - 10941)): NEXT C
       NTEST: POKE LAM,ERR: CALL 65
       392: RETURN
65535  REM
```

THE APPLE'S APPRENTICE

Ask the Wizard

the Wizard of Fairhill Castle

Dear Wizard:

Please forgive a dumb question, I'm still brand new to computing. I've written a program on my Apple //e that turns on 80-columns, but when I go to read the disk, my commands just print on the screen. Help!!!

That's not dumb, it's something that happens to a lot of beginners. Fortunately, the answer is easy. If you had tried to turn your printer on, most likely the same thing would have happened.

Any Apple peripheral is turned on with a *PR#* command. PR#n, by itself is a BASIC command which in the process of turning your peripheral (80-column card or printer) on, resets all "I/O hooks," which has the effect of turning off DOS. However, DOS has its equivalent command, and the only difference is that you precede it with a "PRINT D$" or "PRINT CHR$ (4)." A program line would look like this:

620 PRINT CHR$(4)"PR#3"

Or, if you continue to use the BASIC form of the command, then follow up with a CALL 1002, which will restore DOS.

Dear Wizard:

I really enjoyed your first issue of Apple's Apprentice. Could you type in the following listing exactly as shown, and tell me why each time A$ is printed, it is printed differently. And what happened to the < and > signs the second time A$ was printed?

```
10   A$ = "1234567890ABCDEFG
     HIJKLMNOPQRSTUVWXYZ?
     +<>#$%&*"
15   TEXT
20   HOME
25   POKE 32,2
30   PRINT A$
35   VTAB 4
40   PRINT A$
45   TEXT
50   VTAB 7
55   PRINT A$
```

Let's answer your second question first by adding a line to your program as follows:

```
42   PRINT CHR$( PEEK (1449))" "
     CHR$( PEEK (1450))
```

What do you suppose will be printed on the screen now? Exactly right, your two missing characters!

How did they get from the screen to locations 1449 and 1450? Take a look at figure 1, on page 16 of the *Apple] [Reference Manual* right now, and see if you can figure it out before you read on.

What, back already? So now you've probably guessed *what* happened, but how about the *why*? Well, let's look at the total picture. The second time you printed A$, you did so on screen line four, and just before that, you POKEd 32 with a 2. That had the effect of resetting your left margin two places to the right. *But,* you never told Apple you wanted to change the length of your text line, which is normally 40 characters, so the poor monitor tried to do exactly what you told it to: print 40 characters in consecutive memory locations, and the 39th and 40th positions, in this case, are not on the text screen!

You see, the monitor only issues a carriage return after you have printed 40 characters on a screen line. The monitor always checks location 33 to find out the column number at which you want a carriage return executed, so whenever you change location 32, you must also change location 33. The total of the two values at each location should always equal 40. Now try adding the following line to your program and RUN it again:

27   POKE33,38

I think you've found the answer if you understand that location 33 serves as a right window *only* when location 32 is zero, otherwise it is used to determine how many characters to print per line.

Lastly, your very first question as to why the first time A$ was printed, it didn't start at column two, since you had just POKEd 32 with a 2. The contents of location 32 (known as WNDLFT) are only checked by the monitor on the next scroll operation, clear-to-end-of-page operation, or carriage return output. To make your POKE take effect, add to your program either of the two following lines:

28   VTAB 2

29   PRINT

Thanks for writing, and remember, no question is too tough or too easy for the Wizard of Fairhill Castle.

Opening Your Apple Crate:

What to Do Till the Wizard Comes

Val J. Golding

You've just brought your new Apple Computer home — maybe it's a //e, or perhaps a //c (no matter), anyway, you're unpacking the box, scrambling for the information that tells you which way the cable from the disk drive goes on the controller card (yes, a goof *can* blow a chip), and now you're ready to go, so what's the next step, read the manuals?

There are things the manual fails to tell you . . .

That's a real good idea, but forget it for now. There are lots of things the manual fails to tell you that can *save you from disaster*. That's why we're here. Remember we just said how easy it is to blow a chip? That's right. So before you do another single thing, *stop*. Get a good flashlight or a bright portable light, and examine your handiwork minutely. Look at every single peripheral card you've plugged in, every cable connection you've made. Look at them from the front, the back, the sides. Make sure every single pin on the card (or cable) is plugged correctly into its corresponding socket (or plug). When you're sure this is the case, then make sure the card is *firmly* seated in the slot. Push down on the card, first from one end, then from the other. Rock it gently back and forth. If it's well seated, there should be little play. That's step number one.

Now you're ready to see if it flies. Are you going to put a diskette in the drive, turn the power on and off we go (perhaps to the wild blue yonder of never–never land). No, you are not. Here's step number two: Forget about putting a disk in the drive. Plug your Apple into an AC power outlet (forget about power strips, surge protectors, etc., for the moment), reach around to the rear of your Apple and *quickly* flip the power switch up *and back down* again. In that split second, you should have heard a beep sound from the Apple's speaker. If so, all is well, and you can proceed to the following steps.

If there was no beep, then you have a problem, and the quick flip of the power switch may have saved you many dollars and/or service problems.

. . . if there was no beep, you have a problem

Here is what you do next: Remove *all* peripheral cards and connecting cables. Try the quick power switch test again. No beep? Oh-oh. Stop. Go see your dealer. It beeped? Good. Put one peripheral card in the machine and try again. Each time you get a beep, it means the card or cable is plugged in correctly. You should now be able to go ahead step by step and either locate the faulty component (if there was one), or be assured your connections are correct to this point.

Currently, two disk operating systems are supplied with each Apple //c or Apple //e, DOS 3.3 and Pro-DOS. In typical Apple fashion, no manuals for DOS 3.3 (which has been around a few years) are supplied. Pro-DOS was introduced in early 1984, and is a far superior operating system. At the same time, it is more complex and less easy to learn. We would suggest for the time being at least, that you get a copy of the DOS 3.3 manual from your dealer. When you have mastered DOS 3.3, conversion will be simple, almost all DOS 3.3 commands are also available in ProDOS, along with some new ones.

Either operating system can be pretty unforgiving when you have made an error like deleting a file you wanted to retain. The cardinal rule is: *back up everything in sight*. Start with the

. . . back up everything in sight

system masters that come with your Apple. Once you have made back–ups of the system masters, *never use them again*. store them in a safe place as insurance against a future failure.

Both operating systems have copy programs that allow you to make copies of diskettes. "FILER" on the Pro-

DOS master diskette will copy only ProDOS or Apple /// SOS disks. "COPYA" on the DOS 3.3 system master will copy DOS 3.3, ProDOS, SOS, Pascal, and CP/M diskettes in about half of the time. Using either copy program, it is not necessary beforehand to *format* or *init* your diskettes. The copy programs do this for you. More about this later.

Both of the Apple copy programs are reasonably *user-friendly* or *self-prompting*. This means they are pretty good at taking your hand and printing *prompts* (messages that describe what is expected of you next) on the screen. A good self-prompting program will often anticipate what your answer will be, and print the *default* choice in *inverse* mode on the screen, which means if you accept the default, all you need to do is press the [RETURN] key. If not, then you correct the prompt by typing your own number or response. By the way, inverse means a certain character or characters on your video monitor are displayed black on white, the opposite of what you usually see.

Now let's make our back–ups. Put your DOS 3.3 master diskette (it is labeled "disk][SYSTEM MASTER DISKETTE" in the drive, and turn the power on. The disk drive will probably whir and clank and groan for a few seconds (this is entirely normal), and then you will see "DOS VERSION 3.3 08/25/80 APPLE II PLUS OR ROM-CARD SYSTEM MASTER (LOADING INTEGER INTO LANGUAGE CARD)" on your screen. Press [RETURN], then type "RUN COPYA." If your Apple has lower case, make sure the caps lock key is *on*. Now press [RETURN] again and the disk drive will come on for a few seconds, and you will see the copy program heading on your screen. The rest is easy. The copy program is pretty smart. It already knows whether you have one or two disk drives, and will set up its prompts accordingly. If you have two drives, it will expect the master (the disk to be copied from) to be in drive one, and the *slave* or *target* diskette (a blank) to be in drive two.

All you do is press a few keys and (assuming the default setting) it will display the following messages as it starts the copy process:

READING (from drive one)
FORMATTING (on drive two
WRITING (on drive two)

Then it will go back and repeat the reads and writes until the entire diskette has been copied. That's all there is to it, except you should now take the newly-copied duplicate out of drive two, place it in drive one, and *boot* it by turning the power off and back on. If you get the same display that you did when you booted your master a few minutes ago, then it's a reasonable (but not absolute) assumption that you have a good copy. Now put your master away, and use the copy hereafter to bring the system up.

If you insist on using ProDOS to copy your ProDOS master, the procedure is similar. When you boot, you will see a display which indicates the ProDOS version and date, then clears the screen and prints out the result of a *slot search*, which means that ProDOS has "looked" inside your Apple, and knows what kinds of peripherals you have installed.

The ProDOS equivalent of COPYA is called FILER

The ProDOS equivalent of COPYA is called FILER, except that it has several additional functions. ProDOS has a "smart" RUN command, which supplements the DOS 3.3 RUN, BRUN and EXEC commands by using a dash "—", so to access the FILER, type "—FILER" and press [RETURN]. You will see a "menu" of four choices:

? — TUTOR
V — VOLUME COMMANDS
D — CONFIGURATION
        DEFAULTS
Q — QUIT

We are interested only in the "volume" commands, so type "V," and you will be presented with a second menu delineating the specific volume commands. Of the eight listed commands, only two have any significance at the moment:

F — FORMAT A VOLUME and
C — COPY A VOLUME

Press the "C" for copy, and you will see a screen display similar to the of the COPYA program in DOS 3.3. The default handling is the same, but one additional option has been included: volume name. In ProDOS, volumes (or diskettes) are named, rather than numbered, thus there is no limitation on the number of unique volumes as in DOS 3.3. ProDOS will offer as a default the same volume name as the diskette to be copied, but you may change it if you wish. Beyond this point, ProDOS will copy in a manner almost identical to COPYA.

Now to the last stage. You have already backed-up your DOS 3.3 and ProDOS masters: what more can we do? How about some blank diskettes, ready to use? Usually you do not want to save programs or files to a master disk. Among other things, they are near capacity, anyway, so we should prepare some blank diskettes, ready to receive our data. A new diskette, fresh out of its cellophane wrapper; it must first be prepared by a process called formatting. This is a procedure where the disk operating systems write zeroes and other data to each track and sector on the diskette. Formatting varies somewhat between DOS 3.3 and ProDOS, although the end result is much the same. We will describe each.

Each DOS 3.3 diskette is encoded with the name of a *greeting* program. This will be the BASIC program that will be executed when the diskette is booted. Convention dictates naming this program "HELLO", but there is no such requirement; you may name it whatever you wish.

INIT is the command to format a diskette

Under DOS 3.3, the command to format a diskette is "INIT". It requires you to supply a filename for the greeting program, usually "HELLO". The *syntax* to format a diskette is: "INIT HELLO", followed by [RETURN]. Slot and drive *parameters* are optional, and may be added using a comma *delimiter*. Your command line would now read: "INIT HELLO, S6, D1". If you have a BASIC program in memory at the time you issue the INIT command, it will be saved to the new diskette as your greeting program. It is not necessary to have the greeting program in memory;

it may be added at any time, so long as it is saved to the disk under the original name. In fact, in some cases, it may be preferable to have no program saved at the time of initialization. You may clear any program out of memory prior to formatting by typing "FP" or "NEW".

When DOS 3.3 initializes a diskette, it also copies the DOS *image* to the disk, so that each INITed disk has a copy of the operating system on it, and may be booted directly. About 127,000 *bytes* (or characters) remain for your use. This is not true of ProDOS; you must specifically copy the operating system to your newly formatted disk to be able to boot on it.

ProDOS does not automatically place a copy of the operating system on a diskette

ProDOS differs from DOS 3.3 in that it does not automatically place a copy of the operating system on a newly formatted diskette. This has the advantage of leaving you with some 140,000 bytes of data storage, and the disadvantage of requiring you to copy the two operating system modules, PRODOS and BASIC.SYSTEM on your own to the new disk. The FILER program, sub-system FILE COMMANDS allows you to do this. However, if you have only one disk drive, FILER inanely refuses to let you copy individual files from one diskette to another, thus instead you must "COPY" the disk and delete off any unwanted files.

Under ProDOS, the program you boot to *must* be named "STARTUP", whereas under DOS 3.3, the name of the greeting program was optional. However, ProDOS *does* allow the greeting program to be either a BASIC program, a binary program, or an EXEC file.

To format a ProDOS diskette, you go to the FILER with "—FILER", and select "V" (for volume commands). From the sub-menu, select "F" (format a volume). The usual questions as to slot and drive are asked, and in addition, you are asked to supply a volume name. The default for this option is "/BLANK00/", and you may utilize this if you like, since a volume rename feature is available to you at any time.

(Continued on page 34)

YE OLDE GAME SHOP

Val J. Golding, prop.

Ah, welcome, welcome back, my young friends, please do come in and rest yourselves. I am well pleased to see you have returned. Your youthful exuberance is a delight to see.

So much time has passed since your last visit, my newest games are already gathering dust. But come, bring those stools from the corner over — and mind the cobwebs — so that I may tell you about my newest games and books...

Chivalry is the Name of the Game

Chivalry is a board game. A board game on a computer, you say? Yes, a board game and more. It is an arcade game... no, it's a number of arcade games, a board game, and an adventure game, all rolled into one. Your quest is to rescue the King from the clutches of the Black Knight, who holds him prisoner in the castle of the Black Knight.

Up to four may play, starting at a common position on the game board, which has illustrations that match exactly the visuals of the video screen. Along the various roads to the Black Knight's castle, you encounter obstacles such as the Troll's bridge, where you must dodge the Troll's club in order to cross. For this and the other diversions, you may use either paddles or keyboard. When you have successfully passed, the computer will throw the dice or spin a wheel for your next move.

Should you fail to pass, you will be instructed as to where to move next, but you can be assured it will not be toward your goal. Some of the arcade "gamettes" are simple and require little skill to get by; others are almost equal to the best around. As you can see, reaching the castle is in itself no easy job. When you you finally do arrive at the castle of the Black Knight, you must scale the castle wall, while at the same time avoid the rocks being hurled at you by the Black Knight.

The graphics are great, the off-pitch music tolerable. In addition to the 18" x 18" playing board, you get a poster, warranty registration card, and a 16-page, heavy stock, illustrated instruction manual, making the whole package worth the higher-than-average price.

Chivalry
Weekly Reader Family Software
245 Long Hill Road
Middleton, CT 06457
$49.95
Replacement (after 90 days) $10.00

Of Such Stuff are Superheroes Made...

Superhero is sort of a typical or average adventure game. Note that average does *not* mean mediocre, just good solid adventure. As you travel using the usual N, S, E, W, etc. commands, new scenes — created with Pelczarski's excellent *Graphics Magician* — appear, and you can find and add various objects to your inventory that may aid you at a later time.

Like many good adventure games, Superhero is deceptive. Our first impression was that there was little here of appeal, but when you find yourself trapped in a location with no apparent way out, that's a "gotcha," and that means creators Peter Sivo, Keith Ohlfs, Greg Piper and Ted Griggs got us, because we ran out of time and had to quit.

"Superguy" and "SuperThor" are only two of the collection of superheroes one can become, and because we stupidly trapped ourselves, we didn't have the time to find out how to save the world from the evil forces of Scorpio. Since we don't like to leave things undone, no doubt we'll be back to play some more.

The diskette is two-sided with a somewhat confusing boot procedure where the label, or front, side of the disk is called side two, and the back, side one. There are some 200 Hi-Res scenes on the disk. We saw perhaps 40. The documentation is skimpy, but in this case, it is not a drawback — it just means you must discover many of the command verbs on your own. If you are tired of games where you are stuck with the character you have created, this may be just the ticket.

Superhero
Kopp Systems
11128 Sutherland Ave.
Cupertino, CA 95014
$29.95
Replacement free up to 30 days

Far Out!

Sundog: Frozen Legacy™ is by far the most sophisticated space/adventure game we've come across in many a moon. It is played with joystick only, and uses the mouse/icon concept, with the joystick functioning as the mouse. All choices are made using the joystick to move the cursor to the appropriate icon, then pushing the button to select. Additionally, the joystick is used to move the player on foot, aboard the spaceship, or in one of the more than 50 cities on 18 different planets scattered among 12 star systems.

This game is only for the bold and daring adventurer. It would seem a necessity to keep a notebook devoted to it, so far-reaching are its options and complexities. Vice-President Bruce Webster of FTL Games is to be congratulated for the thoroughness of planning and engineering the program design and, with Wayne Holder, the creative concept.

On shipboard there are at least a dozen physical locations the player can go to, and there are more within the self-propelled space pod. Aboard ship there are also close to a dozen Zoomaction™ windows to display vital status information: pilotage, tactical, navigation, engineering, etc. Each window is partioned into four or five areas and includes a status menu, which is of course selected using the joystick. Similarly, while on foot in the different cities, Zoomaction windows are used for banking transactions, conversations with traders and shopkeepers.

So far, we have covered only a few of the many adventure possibilities. The player must always be on the alert for pirates, thieves and other baddies, and must be prepared to enter into combat, either hand-to-hand or ship-to-ship. Should you be so unlucky as to get killed, a game feature allows you to restart the game from the point of the last save, an important feature for a game that can last for many hours.

The flip side of the disk is a utilities package which allows you to hold up to eight in-progress games, endow your characters with attributes, abort an old game or start a new one.

The 20-page illustrated manual offers plenty in the way of hints and instruction. It includes a three-page science-fiction story which brings you to the point that you come aboard the Sundog, which you have just inherited from your uncle who died under mysterious circumstances. You know nothing about starships, and must start from scratch. Your quest aboard the Sundog includes three tasks — also inherited from your uncle under terms of a contract he had signed to aid in building a colony which you must locate, along with the cryogenically-frozen colonists, scattered in warehouses on various planets.

This is a game that can literally go on for months. To play it well requires considerable study, planning and understanding. It is not for the casual game-player. Captain Kirk would enjoy it; you will too. It's a bargain for the price.

Sundog: Frozen Legacy
FTL Games
Suite F — 7907 Ostrow
San Diego, CA 92111
$40.00
Replacements $6.00 after 90 days

. . . and Books to Boot

Two pretty decent books have come our way of late: "34 More Tested, Ready-To-Run Game Programs in BASIC," by Delton T. Horn, Tab Books, Inc., P.O. Box 40, Blue Summit, PA 17214, 224 pages, $9.25 and "Tim Hartnell's Giant Book of Computer Games," Ballantine Books, 201 East 50th Street, New York, NY 10022, 390 pages, $7.95.

34 more. . . is the fourth printing of a book originally published in 1981. But newness doesn't always count. Each program is listed in "standard" BASIC and TRS-80 Basic, plus a summary of variables and, most helpful to the computer student, a flow chart and a sample run. One neat feature is a full easy-to-read index, set in an extremely clear typeface, but the best feature of all is an appendix that describes in non-computerese each of the standard BASIC commands. You don't need to know programming to type in these programs.

The Giant Book is similar. The listings are in "standard" BASIC only, but a brief conversion table to other BASICs is furnished, along with a glossary of terms. Again, sample runs are furnished, and in addition, a few words to a few paragraphs describe each program.

If you're a game fanatic, you'll probably want both these volumes; they represent a good "game-per-buck" value.

Passing Parade

Some-Games-That-Look-Good-But-We've-Run-Out-Of-Space-Dept.:

From Datamost:

$29.95 each, arcade:

Super Bunny. Paddles or keyboard. The magic carrot does the job. Comes with a comic book.

Ardy (the aardvark). Joystick or keyboard. Frustrating and addictive. Gobs of fun.

From Penguin:

$29.95 each, arcade:

Bouncing Kamungas. Joystick or Keyboard. They fall from the sky and destroy your newly planted crops. It's a "can't quit."

The Spy strikes Back. The familiar spy in a museum setting. With the many rooms and elevators, almost like an adventure. Typically Penguin good.

From Origin Systems:

$34.95, arcade-adventure:

Caverns of Callisto. Joystick. Recover parts stolen from your spaceship and hidden in the caverns. Watch out for creatures. Point scores. Haven't played this one yet, but looks good. Author is "Chuckles" who wrote jawbreaker, one of our all-time favorites.

———

Once more the sun bows low and looks for its hiding place among the peaks of the Far Mountains. It is time now to bid you farewell and wish you a pleasant journey home. I hope soon you will pass our way again, so that we may sit and exchange news or your world and mine. And now, my friends, my belly complains of my lack of attention. . .

What To Do (From page 32)

It is a good idea, particularly in ProDOS, to have formatted disks made up ahead of time. Under standard DOS 3.3, you may format a disk at any time, but under ProDOS, because you need to run a separate program, you may find that inconvenient. If you don't have more than one package of blank diskettes on hand, you probably should pick some up from your dealer. You'll be surprised at how fast they can go.

Diskettes are relatively inexpensive. You may be able to find a box of 10 for less than $20.00. Diskettes are like many other products. As a general rule, you get what you pay for, thus a higher price usually (but not always) is an indication of superior quality. Apple diskettes have a relatively high data density per surface area, so diskettes certified as "double density" often turn out to be less error prone than single density diskettes. But don't let this limit your purchases. There are many applications for which single density is adequate, particularly if you religiously make back-ups. And even the finest quality diskettes occasionally have surface imperfections which can eventually lead to a crash. Again, the cardinal rule: *back it up!*

---

first of a breed:

The Apple I

Elsewhere in this issue is a story on the newest product from Apple Computer, Inc., the Apple //c, an innovative and truly portable machine, mostly compatible with earlier Apples. Following the introduction   is a brief history of the Apple][, itself, in 1977 a pioneer, the first ready-to-plug-in-and-run computer. We should not, however, overlook *the* original, the *Apple I* which started the whole parade.

The Apple I was designed and built in 1976 by *Steven Jobs* and *Stephen Wozniak*, and assembled in a garage,   an operation quite common for that period. 200 Apple I's were built, and 175 sold at approximately $650. What made the Apple I different from all other computers of its time, is that all components, from the 6502 microprocessor to the RAM chips and cassette port, were all built on a single circuit board — the world's first single-board microcomputer.

It had one peripheral slot — for the cassette recorder — and came with 4K of RAM. Another 4K was optional, as was the cassette tape of *Game Basic*, a 2K BASIC which loaded from $E000–$EFFF. A later version of this BASIC would be known as "Integer Basic," and would be supplied with Apple]['s yet to be built. A 256–byte monitor ROM was supplied with the Apple I, but the user was expected to furnish a keyboard, cabinet and power supply.

The story of its development at meetings of the Homebrew Computer Club by Woz and Jobs has been told in print many times, and will not be repeated here. More importantly, the Apple I was the direct ancestor of today's Apple //e, and much of its basic design is still in use. Today, original Apple I's in good condition sell for thousands of dollars.

Take a look below, now, at "Grandfather Apple".

The $650 Apple

Basic Hints for Beginners:
Window On BASIC

Ralph Swerdlow, md

Did you know that *windows* are big news in computers this year? Oh, I know that we all have windows in our houses, some large and others small, but these are not the windows we will look at.

Many of the newer computer software and hardware products are being developed around the concept of windows. What this means is that the computer's screen or T.V. monitor can show several different text panels and/or commands in various parts of the display. Some of this new technology requires the use of a *mouse* to move the cursor across the screen.

Most Apples do not as yet have a mouse, but we are still able to create the effect of windows by some simple programming techniques using BASIC (Applesoft). Here is an easy program to show you how to do this. It is fun to watch how it works, and it might impress someone to show that computers can do interesting things as well as being practical. Let us look at it:

Line 10 is a REMark statement. You should always place some identification of the programs you write (or copy from a magazine) here, because it is easy to forget when you wrote the program or where it came from. A brief note will prove to be very valuable at some future date when you wish to review some of the programs you will accumulate as you use a computer.

Line 20 clears the screen after the **TEXT** command sets the screen to normal width. It is a good practice to always start a program with the **TEXT** and **HOME** commands, because you will be starting fresh each time. The last program that ran may not have done this.

Line 30 sets the cursor to vertical position 8, and line 40 prints "DEAR MOTHER" to the screen. If you wish to change this line to any other name (for example that of a friend), feel free to do so. Line 50 moves the cursor to row 12 and line 60 prints some instructions to users so they know what to do next. Lines 70 to 100 continue the process of moving the cursor to a specific row and printing instructions to be followed.

Some people are able to read faster than others, so we would like to stop the program at this point to allow them to read what has been printed on the screen. Line 110 does exactly this.

The GET command causes our Apple to pause

The **GET** command causes our Apple to pause until any key is hit. In other words, the computer waits for some input from the user. **GET** requires a string function, so I have set up a dummy string variable called "C$." Think of C$ as representing "CONTINUE"! Another command that will do the same thing is **CALL –756.** You could also try **WAIT –16384,128.**

After any key is pressed, the program continues with line 120 which sets the computer to function at a slower than normal speed. Normal is **SPEED = 255,** and we will see this command used later in the program.

Line 130 begins a loop increasing "N" from 1 to 11. While this loop is being performed, line 140 causes a line feed to be executed. **CALL –912** is a command that directs the computer to an address in ROM that contains a machine language routine which moves each text line of the screen up one row. See page 130 of *The Basic Programming Reference Manual* for more details of various calls that are available to the Apple programmer. Line 150 prints CHR$(7) which is the bell character. Try this as an experiment. Type **PRINT CHR$(7)** and a RETURN, and the Apple's bell will sound. This is an example of a command that can be issued from within a program or as an immediate command, by merely typing it and hitting RETURN for it to function.

But we need to delay the line feed just a bit, and line 160 does this by starting a timing loop; first the variable T is given the value of one and increased to 100 by the **FOR–NEXT** command.

Note that this entire delay loop can be written in one line of the program. For a longer delay, increase the upper value of T and for a decreased delay, reduce the final value of T. Think of T as representing "TIME"!

Lines 180 and 190 reset the computer's output speed to normal and wait for a key to be pressed. Line 200 creates a string consisting of a blank space. Note the space between the quotation marks. Whenever S$ is printed, a space will result. Think of S as meaning "SPACE".

But how about printing in reverse, a white space on a black background. This is easy to do by using the **IN-VERSE** command as in line 210. Now let us create a loop that prints a negative space across the entire screen. The next few lines do exactly this, by creating *two* loops, one for the vertical position of the cursor starting at row 1 and increasing VTAB to 23 and the second part of the loop moving the cursor across columns starting at column 0 (the left most portion of a row) and increasing HTAB to 39 (the right side of the screen). S$ is now printed at VTAB V and HTAB H, and because S$ was an inverse space, the entire screen will change to white. This process takes a short but definite time to be completed. In some future article, I will show you how to do the same thing using machine language, which for all practical purposes, seems to do this task instantly!

Line 270 returns the screen output to normal. You should know by now what line 280 does.

Now, let us make an even longer blank space. Line 290 does this. Again notice the number of spaces between the quotation marks. When E$ (for Empty string) is printed, a blank space equal to the number of spaces between the quotes will be printed. This will be used to create our window, black on a white background!

Line 300 to 340 do this. Note the location of the VTABs and HTABs. These may be changed by you to create any effect you desire. Lines 350 to 410 should be obvious by now. You may of course prefer to print any other text, rather than what I have elected to do. If you change the length of the text to be printed, you will have to recalculate the width of the window you make by altering the dimensions of E$, and the HTAB position of where you want to print the text in the window. You will have to do this by trial and error until it is right, but this is good experience in learning how to format text to the screen.

Lines 420 to 500 create another window on the screen and print another message. Can you guess where it will be by just looking at the program?

Now let us create an even longer blank line, as in line 520. There are 40 spaces between the quotation marks, exactly the width of the screen. If we print S$, we will print a totally blank line across the face of our monitor.

Lets slow the speed of the video display in line 530, establish a loop to clear the top half of the screen in lines 530 to 580, and also sound the bell while this occurs. The screen is cleared by printing a blank row, namely S$.

Now lets clear the bottom half of the screen, starting at row 23 and working our way up to row 12. Lines 590 to

620 do this, but because I became tired of hearing the bell sound, I left out the **PRINT CHR$(7)** in this portion of the program. Line 630 resets the computer to normal speed.

After the program has run its course, the next lines enable you to insert another disk in the same drive that you booted your Apple from, and have any other program available to for you to use. If you don't change disks, the one that is currently in Drive 6, Slot 1 will be booted. Note how this is done. First the screen is cleared by the **HOME** command, and the output is set to **FLASH** to call your attention to what is to happen next. Then at VTAB 12 and HTAB 4 a message is printed.

Applesoft requires commands that are directed to DOS to be printed normally, therefore line 710 does this, and line 730 prints a **CHR$(4)**, which is a *CONTROL-D* and then the DOS command *"PR#6"*, booting the disk in drive 1.

If you do not wish your program to boot a disk, replace line 650 with:

650 END

and the program will end here.

To save this program to a disk, first boot the disk, and then copy the program as given, and then save it by typing "SAVE WINDOWS" and, of course, a return. Now whenever you wish to run it, you will be able to do so.

Experiment with different VTAB and HTAB settings in your loops, and different values in the **SPEED** commands to have the program perform at the speed you like best. The time delay in line 160 can also be modified to suit.

This program demonstrates several useful programming techniques that will enable you to place text where you want, to call a ROM sub-routine, to cause the computer to pause and wait for a key stroke from the user, and to use loops for delay purposes. By studying it carefully, you will have gained some valuable tricks to use in your future computing.

```
10   REM

     "WINDOWS"          BY
     RALPH H. SWERDLOW, M.D.

          4/25/84

20   HOME
30   VTAB 8
40   PRINT "DEAR MOTHER : "
50   VTAB 12
60   PRINT "WHENEVER NOTHING SEEMS
     TO BE HAPPENING,"
70   VTAB 14
80   PRINT "PLEASE HIT THE RETURN
     KEY TO CONTINUE"
90   VTAB 20
100  PRINT "NOW HIT RETURN....."
110  GET C$
120  SPEED= 50
130  FOR N = 1 TO 11
140  CALL  - 912
150  PRINT CHR$ (7)
160  FOR T = 1 TO 100: NEXT T
170  NEXT N
180  SPEED= 255
190  GET C$
200  S$ = " "
210  INVERSE
220  FOR V = 1 TO 23
230  FOR H = 0 TO 39
240  VTAB V
250  PRINT S$;
260  NEXT H,V
270  NORMAL
280  GET C$
290  E$ = "          "
300  FOR V = 3 TO 10
310  VTAB V
320  HTAB 5
330  PRINT E$
340  NEXT

350  GET C$
360  VTAB 5
370  HTAB 8
380  PRINT "HI THERE"
390  VTAB 7: HTAB 8
400  PRINT "DEAR MOM"
410  GET C$
420  FOR V = 16 TO 20
430  VTAB V
440  HTAB 20
450  PRINT E$
460  NEXT V
470  GET C$
480  HTAB 24
490  VTAB 18
500  PRINT "WELCOME"
510  GET C$
520  S$ = "                                        "

530  SPEED= 150
540  FOR V = 1 TO 12
550  VTAB V
560  PRINT CHR$ (7)
570  PRINT S$
580  NEXT V
590  FOR V = 23 TO 12 STEP  - 1
600  VTAB V
610  PRINT S$
620  NEXT V
630  SPEED= 255
640  GET C$
650  HOME
660  FLASH
670  VTAB 12: HTAB 4
680  PRINT "INSERT YOUR DISK IN D
     RIVE #1"
690  VTAB 14: HTAB 10
700  PRINT "AND HIT RETURN KEY"
710  NORMAL
720  GET C$
730  PRINT : PRINT  CHR$ (4);"PR#
     6"
```

Apple //c Accessories

Apple Computer has introduced a series of accessory products for use with the new transportable Apple //c — the company's serious home computer which was announced in April at the company's *Apple // Forever* product exposition in San Francisco's Mosconi Center. The optional add–ons — all styled with the same look — enhance the //c's capabilities.

A multi–color high quality printer based on new thermal transfer technology, a high resolution monochrome monitor and stand, a "mouse" pointing device, an external disk drive, an external power pack and a carrying case have all been specifically designed for the //c. The new computer and its accessories are the first Apple products designed in the new "Snow White" style, which consists of fine–grained textures, rounded corners and an ivory color. All future Apple products will adopt this look.

In addition, the existing Apple modems, joystick, hand controllers, Imagewriter printers and color plotter work with the //c.

The accessories plug into icon–labeled sockets in the back of the //c, thus eliminating the need for add–on cards. Each of the products extends the //c's functions. For example, the new Scribe thermal–transfer printer lets users print letters, manuscripts, mailing lists, spread sheets, graphics and more, in either six colors or in black. The modem, available in either 300–baud or 1200–baud models, connects computers in distant locations through telephone lines.

Printer Offers Professional Quality, Low Price

The Scribe printer — using new technology — prints professional–quality text and graphics faster than any other printer in its price category.

In draft mode, a lower–resolution text, it can print 80 characters per second and in the higher–resolution letter mode, Scribe prints 50 characters per second. Shifting between the two speeds can be done by merely flicking a switch or by issuing a software command. Graphics print just as quickly: an 8–inch by 7.5 inch graphic image takes less than four minutes.

Styled to coordinate with the Snow White Look, the small (16–inch by 12–inches), lightweight (13 pounds) and quiet printer offers varied type styles as well as underlining. The printer produces superscripts and subscripts used in technical notation. Text and high–resolution graphics can be combined on a single page.

The scribe prints using either a black or a three–color — magenta, cyan and yellow — ribbon. Mixing these colors, the printer can also produce green, orange and purple. The ribbon cassettes are easily interchangeable.

The Scribe printer can be used with any Apple computer that has a standard RS–232 interface.

Monitor Crafted to Coordinate With //c

Those //c users who want higher resolution graphics or 80 instead of 40 columns will need to purchase a monitor instead of hooking up the //c to a TV. The 11–pound Apple Monitor //c provides professional display performance at an affordable price.

A 9–inch screen provides a low–glare, green phosphor display that reduces eye strain and fatigue. A matching stand allows the monitor to be positioned at any angle a user desires. Like the //c, the monitor comes with a handle for transportability.

Newly Designed Mouse

The AppleMouse //c pointing device is similar to the mouse used with the Lisa and Macintosh computers, except that it conforms to the Snow White design guidelines. It comes with a free–form graphics program called *Mouse-Paint* and a MousePaint product–training disk. Additionally, it plugs into a socket in the back of the //c and does not require an add–on card.

Of the more than 10,000 Apple II family software programs available, a growing number use the mouse as a cursor–control device. It provides people with an easy way to interact with the computer.

Second Disk Drive Adds Storage

Besides the internal disk drive built into the //c, a matching external disk drive, call the Disk //c, can be added to save more information or to copy disks. The 5¼" half–height drive has a 140–kilobyte capacity.

Apple II-Family Accessories Compatible

The high–quality Imagewriter dot–matrix printer, both the 300– and 1200–baud modems, the Apple joystick, hand controllers and color plotter are existing Apple II–family accessories that run on the //c.

Price

Scribe printer	$299.00
Monitor //c	$199.00
Monitor stand	$ 39.00
AppleMouse //c	$ 99.00
Disk //c	$329.00
Imagewriter printer	$595.00
300–baud modem	$225.00
1200–baud modem	$495.00
Joystick	$ 59.95
Hand controllers	$ 34.95
Extra power pack	$ 39.00
Color plotter	$779.00
Carrying case	$ 39.00

Line of //c Software Featured

Apple Computer recently announced the availability of 21 newly developed or enhanced software packages for the new Apple //c. These packages were selected to offer the //c user a variety of serious application programs that are useful in the come and that can take advantage of the //c's special design features. The software packages are described in Apple's *Software Sampler* brochure.

Software Takes Advantage of //c Features

The 21 products have been designed to take advantage of one or more of the //c's features.

For example, since the //c comes with 128 kbytes of RAM memory, programs written for it can be more complex, easier to learn and can store more information than previous versions.

Another //c feature developers have taken advantage of is the mouse. Some of the enhanced programs incorporate this cursor–control tool, which makes interacting with the computer more natural. Still other products use the //c's ultra–high resolution (560 by 192 pixels) graphics mode.

Developers have agreed to restrict these enhancements to Apple versions of the software products for six months.

Other Developers Upgrading

A large number of other enhanced and new products are being developed by the almost 100 hardware and software developers that were provided with the //c developer guidelines before the //c's release. The resulting products will be marked with red and yellow "Works on the Apple //c" identification stickers.

Thousands of Programs Available

To help customers determine which of the Apple //e programs will work on the //c, Apple is conducting compatibility tests and publishing an updated list of the findings every two months. This list will be distributed to all authorized Apple //c dealers.

Incompatibility stems from a software developer's either incorporating a copy protection mechanism or using reserved memory locations not recommended by Apple. Also any program that requires the CP/M operating system will not run on the //c.

Apple expects software developers to ensure compatibility by offering new //c-specific versions of their packages. More than 90% of the currently available software will run on the //c.

Availability

All 21 products are now available at computer retail stores.

The following is a list of the 21 featured software packages for the Apple //c:

Productivity

1. Apple Access //— Apple Computer Inc.
2. Appleworks— Apple Computer Inc.
3. Bank Street Writer— Broderbund, Inc.
4. Compuserve Consumer Information Service— Compuserve Corp.
5. Dollars and Sense— Monogram/Tronix Publishing Inc.
6. Dow Jones Investor's Workshop— Dow Jones & Co. Inc.
7. Financial Cookbook— Electronic Arts
8. Multiplan— Microsoft Corp.
9. Personal Tax Planner— Aardvark/McGraw-Hill
10. PFS:File and PFS:Report— Software Publishing Corp.

Home Education

11. Apple Logo //— Apple Computer Inc.
12. Crypto Cube— Designware Inc
13. Fact and Fiction Toolkit— Scholastic Wizware
14. Grandma's House— Spinnaker Software
15. Mastering the SAT— CBS Software Inc
16. MasterType— Scarborough Systems
17. Rocky's Boots— The Learning Company
18. Stickybear Shapes— Xerox Educational Publications
19. The Apple Education Classics — Apple Computer Inc.

Entertainment

20. How About a Nice Game of Chess!— Odesta Corp.
21. Apple Computer Inc.axxon— Datasoft Inc.

Dynacomp Expands Software Line

DYNACOMP, Inc. 1427 Monroe Avenue, Rochester, NY 14618 is continuing to rapidly expand its line of quality software products in the fields of business, education, games, engineering, personal finance and science. Some of the most recent additions include:

Genesis, the Adventure Creator

Until now, if you wanted to write an adventure game, you needed lots of time and considerable programming skill. Such a task requires you not only to create a world — the fun part — but to write routines to keep track of everything taking place in it — the drudgery. Now, however, there is Genesis. You design your world, Genesis programs it.

Genesis has two parts. The creator allows you to create and edit your adventures. The player allows you to play any adventure you have created.

Apple][plus or //e, 48k RAM, disk drive, $39.95

Talking Typewriter

This package combines Apple's graphics and sound capabilities to teach the alphabet, numbers, and the keyboard layout to young children, ages 3 to 8. The player must press the correct key to launch a missile towards a moving target. There are two prompts for the key. The first is a High–Res display of the keyboard with a key "lit up." The second is the spoken name of the key! No special hardware is required for this speech ability. Requires 48k. $19.95

Dominoes

The origin of Dominoes dates back before 1000 BC. The rules are simple and the game is fun to play. It is an easy game for children, but difficult for champions.

The traditional game of Dominoes is played with four people forming two teams. In the Apple version, the computer takes the place of your partner and opponents. Three levels of play are available.

The package comes with a 28–page manual which describes the game and strategies. The program uses graphics to simulate the playing table. 48k, $29.95

The Unofficial I Hate Computer Book is a computer hater's guide to 76 anti–computer cartoons that offer a tongue–in–chip look at the every day evils of home, personal and big computers.

Introduced are page after page of tattered terminals, mauled monitors, chopped chips, and pulverized peripherals.

Author John Barry is an editor at *Info World* and cartoonist Richard Tennant has appeared in a number of computer publications.

Paperback, 80 pages, 8½ by 5¼, $4.95. Hayden Books, 10 Mulholland Drive, Hasbrouck Heights, NJ 07604.

You must escape the "Institute," but the key to that escape exists only in your dreams!

The Institute, created by veteran adventure writer Jyym Pearson, is a psychological drama. In true Freudian fashion, the clues to your escape can only be found through a series of four dreams, induced by a mysterious red powder.

In the Institute, you may find yourself in a prehistoric jungle, or aboard a doomed Titanic. Whatever the adventure, watch closely — each dream provides you with information and items you will need to escape!

The Institute, 64k Apple, $29.95. Screenplay, PO Box 3558, Chapel Hill, NC 27514.

Solution to puzzle on page 28

MICROCHIPS

by Robert Cavey

sᴏᴜᴛʜᴡᴇsᴛᴇʀɴ ᴅᴀᴛᴀ sʏsᴛᴇᴍs™

CHANGES ITS NAME TO

Roger Wagner Publishing, Inc.

With my name on the software, you have my personal guarantee of uncompromising quality, ease of use, and reliability in both product and support.

—*Roger Wagner, President*

THINGS TO DO TODAY!

Get: 1) Word Processor (easy to use, less than 100.00)
2) Typing Program (the kids can use it too)
3) Books to help with writing and word processing

WORD PROCESSORS
Homeword 69.95
Bank Street Writer 69.95

Books?
Writing 5.00
WP Style 10.00

TYPING PROGRAMS
Master Type 39.95
Type Attack 39.95
Typing Tutor 39.95

PLAN #2
Bank Street 69.95
Type Attack 39.95
No Books
109.90

PLAN #3
Homeword 69.95
Typing Tutor 24.95
Books 15.00
109.90

PLAN #1
Homeword 69.95
Master Type 39.95
Books 15.00
124.90

PLAN #4 — the Write Choice

The Correspondent	Included
Tut's Typer	Included
Word Processing Style Manual	Included
Elements of Style	Included
The Analyst	Included
Unlocked and copyable	

44.95

Everything we need!
All new from Roger Wagner

The **Personal** Word Processing System designed for the home or classroom.

With all the tools you need, including a full-featured word processor, a HiRes typing tutor, classic guides on writing style and suggested formats for letters, reports, outlines, etc.!

IT'S SIMPLY...

THE WRITE CHOICE!

Apple II, II+, IIe or IIc

See your local Apple Dealer or contact us for details

Current Correspondent Owners please contact us for update information

RogerWagner
PUBLISHING, INC.

10761 Woodside Avenue • Suite E • P.O. Box 582 • Santee, CA 92071 • 619/562-3670

REPORTER
artsci

N E W S & I N F O R M A T I O N

Volume One

Number Three

ARTSCI announces INTERMATRIX'S *Computerphone for APPLE Macintosh*

The INTERMATRIX **Computer***phone* creates an entirely new aspect to telephone voice communications.

Lawyers, Salesmen and anyone who uses a telephone will improve their work performance and save long distance charges.

Software is provided to manage and dial hundreds of phone numbers. The system provides a wide range of phone and billing services:

- Long distance charges can be calculated for each call.
- Consultation rate charges are provided.
- A printed Phone Log is updated after each call complete with length of the call and all billing totals.
- Tone Dialing is provided for long distance services like SPRINT, MCI and other long distance services.
- A Calendar is provided.
- Pull-down Menus are used for frequently dialed numbers.

$199.95.

- A Phone Book window is provided to view all available names.
- Last Number Re-dial.
- Hourly/Minute Beep Signal while calling.
- MAC eight-page Note Pad is available.

The **Computer***phone* can be used as a stand-alone telephone without Macintosh control. **Computer***phone* base will allow you to use any handset of your choice: Speaker Phones, Remote Phones, Office Phones, or the one provided with the system.

Installation is a snap. You simply plug the **Computer***phone* into your Macintosh speaker jack, and into your phone line.

Custom Phone systems may use the **Computer***phone* using the adapter provided by the phone company.

Computerphone is a trademark of Intermatrix.

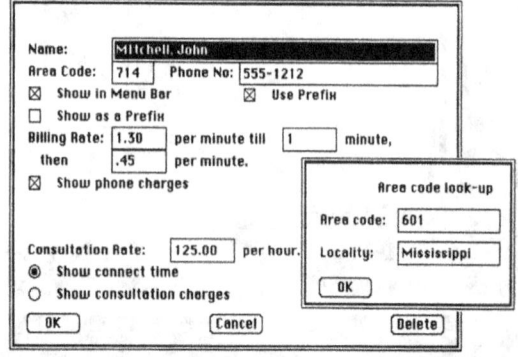

Macintosh is a trademark of APPLE Computer, Inc.

ARTSCI, INC.
5547 Satsuma Avenue
North Hollywood, CA 91601
818/985-2922

Volume I, No. 3

August, 1984

the Apple's Apprentice

Learning about Apples

$2.50 [$3.25 Canada]

fantasy: it's fun learning
. . . the Apple's Apprentice way!

Pretty, Pretty Pictures:
- ## MagiGraphics

Thyng's of Interest
- ## READ, DATA, RESTORE

- ## GAMES

- ## CONTESTS

- ## PROGRAMS

- ## HINTS

- ## FUN!

The Apple magazine for kids of all ages

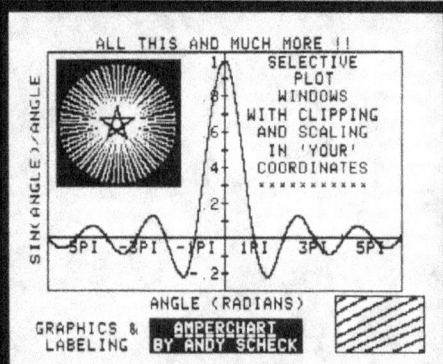
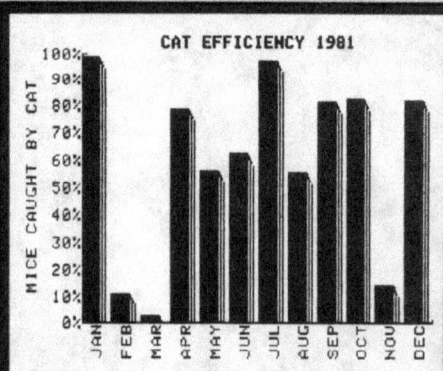

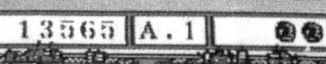

Take a bite...

...of Apple Orchard!

Your Apple will love you for subscribing to APPLE ORCHARD Magazine, the premier magazine for Apple owners!

APPLE ORCHARD has all the information you need for your Apple. Our hardware and software reviews are done by professional computer people. Our NEW PRODUCT section is the largest in a monthly publication. In addition, there are articles that let you know what people are doing in business, finance, education and at home. We make sure that our utilities, diagnostics, and programming tools are easy to use.

You and your premier computer deserve the best. Subscribe today and save 36% over the newsstand price. Why not give a gift to a deserving Apple owner?

Volume I, No. 3

August, 1984

The Apple's Apprentice is published by:

Emerald City Publishing, Inc.
P.O. Box 582-AA, Santee, CA
92071, (619) 562-7785. Entire
Contents copyright © 1984 by
Emerald City Publishing, Inc.

Roger Wagner, publisher
Val J. Golding, editor

Donna Sexton
    Advertising Director
Pamela Lambert
    Circulation Manager
Linda Anderson
    Illustrator
Margot and Al Tommervik
    Godparents

Subscriptions: $24/12 issues,
$46/24 issues

Advertiser's Index

The Apple Magazine
For Kids of all ages

Table of Contents

From the Tower

the Apprentice Wizard

Welcome. We're glad to see you have joined us again. We're always happy to see our old readers back, along with the new ones. For the benefit of the new readers, a word or three on what **Apple's Apprentice** is all about.

The Apprentice is a different breed of Apple magazine. It is for kids, but in addition, for kids of all ages. Or, as we like to say, "for kids from 8 to 80." Mainly it's a place where you can drop your hat, put your feet up on a chair, relax and **learn** about Apple Computers in an informative, fun way.

A lot of magazines **say** they cater to beginners; we **do**. You don't have to know much at all about Apples to read and enjoy the Apprentice and learn about them from stories written in a loose, breezy style that don't push you into the high-tech world on page two. What's more, as we progress, we will regress. That is, somewhere along the way we'll pause and review or rewrite some of our earlier beginner's material.

Best of all, you don't have to learn about Apples at all if you really don't want; you can enjoy the game reviews, the comics, puzzles and contests or look in the **Crystal Ball** to see what the newest in peripherals and software is. On the other hand, you might like to wander through (and maybe even get involved in) stories like Joe Holt's fantasy **The Duncan Letters**. You might even find out that programming can be fun. Graphics is accounted for as well, with **Magigraphics:** Pretty, Pretty Pictures. Talented author David Sparks tells you all you ever wanted to know about Spirographs, and cycloids, as well.

For those who want to learn programming, we offer several delicious flavors, all easy to take. This month we introduce **Uncle Bill's Column**, filled with gems of humor and handy hints. **Thyng's of Interest** also premieres this time, with author Michael Thyng telling the truth, the whole truth and nothing but the truth on how to use DATA, READ, and RESTORE commands. Ralph Swerdlow has come up with a way to simulate the IF/THEN/ELSE statement in **Spells and Potions**, and if you really want to get into it, **The Sourceror's Apprentice** will take you teenagers and adults by the hand and gently guide you into the realm of assembly language programming.

By the way, speaking of the Sourceror's Apprentice, author Mike Newton included a little chart of ASCII screen display characters to go with his story. It's mighty small, you'll admit, and if we could have made our printer print even smaller, we would have. Why? So we would have an opportunity to tell you about our ASCII wall chart. In addition to the data in the small chart, we've added a brief explanation of why ASCII is different in Applesoft than in the monitor. How can you get it? That's the easy part. It's all yours, postpaid, for just $1.50 (deduct 25% for multiple copies). Send to:

ASCII Chart
P.O. Box 582-AA
Santee, CA 92071

A funny thing happened to us on the way to San Diego . . . Many of you may know us as the former editor of **Call -A.P.P.L.E.** and in fact may have read the story on "Val's Basement," along with its photographs, in the June issue. The long and short of it is that literally a ton of documentation, disks, programs and books was packed into our decrepit VW beetle, probably a rare example of programs in a bug, rather than the other way to.

Oh well . . .

Last on the agenda (well, almost). Reader participation. **The Apple's Apprentice** can only be **your** magazine with your help and participation. We have three features specifically for that purpose: **Back Talk** (letters, round table discussions, etc.), **Ask the Wizard** (The Wizard of Fairhill Castle answers all programming questions, none too easy, none too hard), and **Daze of the Knights** (witty contests to tax your wits and programming skills). So let's hear from you guys and gals out there, and that includes comments on what you'd like to see in **The Apple's Apprentice**, as well.

Almost as a postscript, don't forget you can receive 12 fun-packed issues of **The Apple's Apprentice** for just $24.00; that's only $2.00 per issue. Note that we said 12 **issues**. That's because we started in April, then skipped a month, but every subscriber can be assured of receiving their full subscription and their money's worth. Now it is past the witching hour, so until next time, we'll leave you with this thought: **On a clear disk, you can seek forever.**

READ, DATA and RESTORE:
Thyng's of Interest

Michael Thyng

One feature of Applesoft that is commonly under–utilized is the DATA statement. The DATA statement is one of the common methods of entering working data into a computer program. Its advantage is that you can count on the same data time after time. Its disadvantage is that it is only sequentially accessible. Lets look at its structure, then try out some examples.

You prepare the data you're going to use by keying in a line number, the command word DATA, followed by the actual data you want to use. The data does not have to be in any particular order to meet the Applesoft requirements. So you enter it in the order for your specific programming needs. For numeric data, a typical line of code looks like:

200 DATA 34,16,73,106,4

I chose line 200 for my DATA statement. I could have chosen line 5, or line 62000. I can put the data in the beginning, middle or end of the program. I can use any of the valid line numbers that any other Applesoft command can use. It doesn't matter. Your program will find the data. The only thing you really should do every time you use DATA statements, is to bunch them together so they are easier to find.

Anything that's easy to find is faster to modify if and when that becomes necessary.

DATA statements may be placed anywhere in the program

You can have more than one DATA statement. In fact, you can have a program of almost all DATA statements. The only limit I have ever found is that you are limited by the amount of memory in your computer. For most applications this means you will never run out of DATA space. Let's look at variations of line 200 that are its equivalent. Instead of writing line 200 as it is, we could have substituted:

300 DATA 34,16
310 DATA 73,106
320 DATA 4

Or, we could have put each piece of data in a separate DATA statement as in:

410 DATA 34
420 DATA 16
430 DATA 73
440 DATA 106
450 DATA 4

As you can see, you can mix and match the data you are keeping in DATA statements in any logical way you see fit. Also, note that I just used 5 data elements in my line 200 DATA statement. You could use 10 or 20 or more. In fact, the only limit imposed on you is the 238 character entry limit of an Applesoft programming line.

Okay, now we've got the data stored. But you can't work with it just yet. You have to have a way to access it. You access the data by using a READ command. The READ command looks like this:

700 READ R

When the computer is running a program which encounters our line 700, it will immediately do a search for a DATA statement. Actually, it will look for the first DATA statement in your program. The first DATA statement in your program is, of course, the one with the lowest line number. DATA statements may be placed anywhere in the program, but tradition usually places them at the end. In some ways, DATA statements are like REM statements in that the Applesoft interpreter will completely ignore them, except when it is executing a READ.

I've been consistent to use the same data and in the same order in our ex-

---

---

amples, so we shouldn't have much confusion. The first piece of data that is read into R is 34. From this point on, numeric variable R has 34 as its value. Why did I choose R as the numeric variable? Only because it will be more meaningful in the examples I will use in this article. I was free to use any numeric variable that follows the syntactic rules of Applesoft.

Now we're going to use the value of R in a formula to calculate something. For this case, let's figure out the area of a circle. The formula is PI times the radius of the circle squared. In Applesoft, it would look like:

```
800   PI = 3.1415926
900   A = PI * R * R
1000  PRINT "RADIUS ";R;" AREA
      ";A
```

What you will see output is: **RADIUS 34 AREA 3631.68105** — That used our first numeric value in the DATA statement. Suppose we run the program again. What value will be used this time? Did you say 16? Wrong! The answer is 34. Run it and see. The reason is that each time you run the program, a certain pointer inside the computer points to the first value following the first DATA statement in any program. How do you get to the data elements past the first one? You need to execute the READ command again.

By the way, I have been interchanging the words command and statement. Generally, they are interchangeable, but statement seems passive, as DATA statements are, and command seems active, as READ commands are. Now, back.

To get the program to READ again, we just have to GOTO line 700 again. We'll add line 1100 to our program.

```
1100 GOTO 700
```

At this point you should have a program with one set of data in it. Depending on which option you chose to hold your data, you should have something like I have below. I chose yet another variation in the ways to keep data in DATA statements to further emphasize the flexibility of options you could use.

```
200   DATA 34
220   DATA 16,3,106
240   DATA 4
700   READ R
800   PI = 3.1415926
900   A = PI * R * R
1000  PRINT "RADIUS ";R;" AREA
      ";A
1100  GOTO 700
```

RUN the program. Now you get all five numeric values out as well as the areas calculated for all five. Congratulations. But the kudos are short lived. You also get an **?OUT OF DATA ERROR IN 700** message. This means your program tried to read more data than there was available. Let's see how reading again and again accesses different data. Each time you READ data, you get the data element that the pointer I talked about earlier is pointing at. When the computer executes the READ statement the first time, the pointer points at 34. It points at 34 because it is the first data element in the first DATA statement. As soon as it does the READ, the pointer moves to the next data element. That way, it is always ready to READ the most currently available piece of data. So after the computer has done three READs, the pointer is pointing at the fourth piece of data. In our example, it points at 106.

What happens if you try to READ more data than is in the program?

What happens if you do more READing than you have data? That's what we did. We tried to read six times, but we only had five data elements. After five READs, the pointer had adjusted itself to point at the sixth piece of data. But there is no sixth piece of data. That in itself is okay. It's only when we try to READ a sixth time that we encounter a problem. Obviously, if we try to read data and there is no data, something has to be faulty. I mean computers are supposed to be logical devices. (Aren't they??) Some people might attempt a band–aid type solution to this situation by using an ONERR GOTO. This is a poor programming practice. (You will see this done even in commercially available programs, but what can I say.) No, the correct solution to the problem is to find the last piece of data and either bring the program to a logical conclusion or go on to another place in the program. We can accomplish this in at least two ways.

The first way is to know what the exact value is of the last data element in your list of data. Then test for that value and, in our example, end the program. Our last data element is 9. We would test for that with an IF statement. The logical place would be just before the GOTO. We want to have read all the data, have done all the calculations, and have displayed all the output. Then when we test, we are going to prevent the computer from going back to do another READ.

1020 IF R = 4 THEN END

This way presents a problem if our last data element ever changes. You see, if the fifth data element is 8, and we are testing for 4, then the computer won't end, and we'll go back to read a sixth data element, run out of data, and the program will break in 700 again.

. . .add a special last data element

The second way, and a way I always use, and highly recommend, is to add a special last data element. This last data element must be a value that is never going to be found in the working data. I usually use 99999. In all applications with which I've worked, I've never come across 99999 as a legitimate piece of working data. If, in your appli-

Solution to puzzle on page 29

cation, you found that 99999 might be valid data, you would just choose a final value that wouldn't be. To use this method, pull out line 1020 and enter:

720 IF R = 99999 THEN END

Why did we have to move the IF? Line 1020 tested the data *after* we had used it. What we need with the code data is to test *before* we use it. With line 720, our program reads the data and before any piece of data can be used, it is checked for the value 99999.

One of the uses for the concept of the DATA statement is in something called edit checking. Suppose you wrote a program to enter the data to pay bills by check. You would probably have a need to enter the payee's name, today's date, the amount of the check, and some expense account number. You probably have certain expense account numbers that are valid for your company or home. You only want to input valid expense account numbers. But people make mistakes, so you know that from time to time, someone is going to key in data that "just ain't right." Now comes the DATA statement's use. All the values in the DATA statement are exactly your expense account numbers — except the last one, which is

99999. After each input for an expense account, you read the valid expense account numbers from DATA statements, and compare them against the expense account number that was input. If the first one doesn't match, you read again and keep reading until you find a match or until you reach 99999. If you reach 99999, and you know you have every valid account number stored in DATA statements, then it means the expense number entered through the INPUT statement was wrong, and should be re-entered.

A portion of the code to enter and check expense account numbers would look like this:

```
100  INPUT "ENTER EXPENSE
     NUMBER (9999) ";EX
300  READ X
500  IF X = 99999 THEN PRINT
     "NO FIND":GOTO 100
600  IF X = EX THEN 1000
700  GOTO 300
800  DATA 1018,1020,1030,1050
810  DATA 3000,3010,3030,3070
820  DATA 4002,4020,4050,4060
890  DATA 99999
1000 REM CONTINUE ON WITH
     THE PROGRAM
2000 PRINT "FOUND ";X
2020 FOR DE = 1 TO 1200:NEXT
     DE
2100 GOTO 100
```

To check this out, why don't you run it and enter valid account number 3010. You should see it displayed with the message: **FOUND 3010**. Now try 4050. It works too. Just one more. Try 1020. It's on our list. Oops, what happened? We got a message **NO FIND**. That suggests that we got to the end of our data. Well, we did. Remember the internal pointer? Where was it after we found 4050? It was pointing at 4060. When we input 1020, the program read 4060. The pointer advanced to 99999. When the program discovered that 4060 and 1020 didn't match, it went back to read another value. The only value left was 99999.

Wouldn't it be nice if we could manipulate the pointer so we could look at the same set of data more than once? Guess what — we can. There is a command called RESTORE. This causes that pointer (no, you can't ignore it) to place itself in the same position it had just after you typed RUN. That means we can read the data from the beginning anytime just by using

---

...we can READ data from the beginning by using RESTORE...

```
]LIST

10   REM

MULTI-USE DATA STATEMENT DEMO

     MICHAEL THYNG

100  DATA DAYS
110  DATA SUNDAY,MONDAY
120  DATA TUESDAY,WEDNESDAY
130  DATA THURSDAY,FRIDAY
140  DATA SATURDAY
150  DATA END
200  DATA PASSWORDS
210  DATA LEO,JOHN,LOUISE
220  DATA EVERETT,ARLEAN,JOAN
230  DATA END
300  DATA MEDICAL
310  DATA EB25-X,T3-00SL.34,DD25
320  DATA W99,W89,W96,W12,W14
330  DATA M10,M20,M30,M40,M60
350  DATA END
400  DATA EXPENSES
410  DATA 1018,PAYROLL
420  DATA 1020,OFFICE EXPENSE
430  DATA 2000,RENT
440  DATA 2500,VEHICLE FUEL
450  DATA 3000,WELDING
460  DATA 5000,COFFEE
470  DATA 7800,LEGAL EXPENSE
490  DATA END
1000 REM
PASSWORD INPUT AREA

1100 INPUT "ENTER PASSWORD ";P$
1200 RESTORE
1300 READ PC$: REM
LOOK FOR "PASSWORD"
1400 IF PC$ <  > "PASSWORDS" THEN
     1300
1500 READ PC$
1600 IF PC$ = "END" THEN  PRINT
     "INVALID USER ACCESSING SYST
     EM.": PRINT "SUMMON HELP": END

1700 IF P$ <  > PC$ THEN 1500
1900 REM
NOW SYSTEM HAS VALID USER

2000 REM
DAY INPUT AREA

2100 INPUT "ENTER DAY OF WEEK ";
     W$
2200 RESTORE
```

RESTORE. Let's put it in the program. First let's try it in line 400.

400 RESTORE

Running the program again, we'll start our test trying to find 3010. Something different happens. It looks like the program went away and forgot us. It didn't stop doing things. As a matter of fact, it is doing a lot of things — the same things over and over. It is reading the first data element 1018. That automatically causes the pointer to point at 1020. Then in line 400 we restore the pointer to 1018. There is no match of 99999 or 1018, so program control goes back to line 200 to read another value. The pointer is currently pointing at 1018. Every time we read, we get 1018. We can't have the RESTORE in line 400. We could have it in line 200 instead. This is the right location for RESTORE. This is the most basic use of the DATA statement.

We just read one variable at a time with our READ statement. If we were going to use DATA to store X and Y coordinates for some application, we could read them with a line like this:

2300 READ X, Y

It will require that your data be considered as pairs of values. Each time you do a read, you are accessing the next two numbers. Don't forget that the last data, 99999, also needs a second 99999. If you don't do that, X would get a value and Y would cause an out of data error.

The data statement can also be used with alphanumeric data. The only major change, if you can call it major, is to change the variable to a string variable. If we went back to the expense account number example, with modifications, we could access the number and the description of the number. The data would look like this:

```
1000 DATA 1018,PAYROLL
1100 DATA 1020,OFFICE
     EXPENSES
1200 DATA 1030,RENT
1900 DATA 99999,99999
```

To read this data, the READ statement would need to be modified to look like:

12000 READ ACCT,DESC$

I'd like to show you a trick that I learned. I had a need to use the DATA statement for more than one type of data. That is, we used it for expense account numbers here. Well I had a need to check about four different things and had to find a way to read each set of data differently. I wanted to check the days of the week against a DATA table (that's what we've been making). I wanted to check expense account numbers. I had to check out who was operating the system against a list of those who were acceptable, and I had to check a list of special medical codes that were susceptible to entry errors. The problem was (is) that the days of the week, the passwords, and the medical codes just require one alphanumeric entry and the expense accounts require two entries — a numeric and an alphanumeric. Besides that, there is also the problem of telling the computer which group of data is which.

Where do the passwords end and the medical codes begin? What I did is label each set of data with yet another entry. At the beginning of the days of the week, I put in an entry of "DAYS." Just before the passwords, I put in "PASSWORDS". Before the medical data I used "MEDICAL," and before the expenses, "EXPENSES". To use this setup, I had to have a few lines of code that just check for the four code words. But after I have detected the code word for which I'm looking, I can branch right to the proper read routine to access the data. I think this program will show you how it works.

```
2300   READ WC$: REM
LOOK FOR "DAYS"
2400   IF WC$ < > "DAYS" THEN 230
       0
2500   READ WC$
2600   IF WC$ = "END" THEN  PRINT
       : PRINT "WRONG DAY": PRINT :
       GOTO 2100
2700   IF W$ < > WC$ THEN 2500
2800   REM
DAY OF THE WEEK

2900   REM
NOW SYSTEM HAS VALID
DAY OF THE WEEK
3000   REM
MEDICAL CODE INPUT AREA

3100   INPUT "ENTER MEDICAL CODE "
       ;M$
3200   RESTORE
3300   READ MC$: REM
LOOK FOR "MEDICAL"
3400   IF MC$ < > "MEDICAL" THEN
       3300
3500   READ MC$
3600   IF MC$ = "END" THEN  PRINT
       : PRINT "WRONG CODE": PRINT

       : GOTO 3100
3700   IF M$ < > MC$ THEN 3500
3900   REM
NOW SYSTEM HAS VALID MEDICAL CODE

4000   REM
EXPENSE ACCT INPUT AREA

4100   INPUT "ENTER EXPENSE ACCT "
       ;A
4200   RESTORE
4300   READ AC$: REM
LOOK FOR  "EXPENSES"
4320   REM
NOTICE ONLY THE ALPHANUMERIC
READ FOR AC$
4400   IF AC$ < > "EXPENSES" THEN
       4300
4500   READ AC,AC$
4600   IF AC$ = "END" THEN  PRINT
       : PRINT "WRONG CODE": PRINT
       : GOTO 4100
4700   IF A < > AC THEN 4500
4900   REM
NOW SYSTEM HAS VALID EXPENSE DATA

5000   REM
REST OF THE PROGRAM GOES HERE.
```

Pretty, Pretty Pictures:
MagiGraphics

David Sparks

Cousin Ricky appeared to have it better than I did. At least I thought so while we were growing up. His sandbox had a roof. No matter what house he moved into, his backyards were wonderfully large, wooded, and sometimes steeply sloped. I was always glad to go for a visit. Ricky's room contained lots of the most amazing toys. And of all the toys, one in particular drew me back and back again: his Spirograph.

Do you know what a Spirograph is? A box full of plastic circles with gear teeth inside and out and pencil holes in the rim. You thumbtack one circle to a piece of paper. Engage its teeth with those of a second, unattached circle. Put a pencil point through one of the holes in the movable circle. Go around and around as long as you like, making the most amazing patterns.

You could put a tiny circle inside a bigger one and make patterns in the middle. You could make patterns outside a circle. You could do both. You could draw one pattern, then another over the top of it. You could have different colors. You used up all the paper the grown-ups allowed long before you ran out of ideas. In an age without video games, these splendid figures set the light dancing in my childhood eyes.

Grown-ups, it is well known, cannot tolerate childlike enthusiasm very long. It makes them quite uncomfortable. It's bad enough when the enthusiast actually is a child, but let someone Big get caught up in the sheer joy of a thing? Oh dear! It just isn't done.

To play with Spirograph pictures, grown-ups have to call them something else. Something terribly dreary and Important-Sounding. Either that or something trendy and high-tech, perhaps hinting of robots or the Space Program. And definitely, something which can be done using a Computer. Something which sounds Terribly Difficult, if you please, but actually is quite simple.

We're only too happy to oblige. Say hello to *Epicycloids* and *Hypocycloids*. They are, respectively, the Spirograph pictures you draw outside the fixed circle, and inside. This concept is illustrated in the accompanying box.

Good tools already exist to turn your Apple into an electronic artist of astonishing capacity, so I'll just tell you what they are, and give you an example program showing how to use them.

In the February 1984 *Byte,* an article by Robert and Ted Sussman described a method for calculating computer plotting points of epicycloids and hypocycloids. Their work was adapted from Murray Spiegel's *Mathematical Handbook of Formulas and Tables,* McGraw-Hill Schaum's Outline Series, 1968. Their formulae, along with some definitions of various terms in this article, appear at the end of this article.

For the program listed here, I have converted the Sussman formulae into Applesoft Defined Functions, one of the little-known, little-used bits of "magic" your Apple can perform. With these particular functions, the program computes the way to draw spirographic pictures on your screen.

While you can use the program without needing to know about Apple Hi-Res graphics, let's discuss how the Hi-Res screen works. Apple Graphics consist of thousands of tiny dots. Hi-Res graphics give you control over each dot individually. You can make it be any one of four colors, plus white. Black is a color, too, which we use to "turn off" the dots. You set the color with the Applesoft command **HCOLOR=X** where X is a value from 0 through 7. See your Applesoft manual.

To "turn on" a dot you select the color then use the Applesoft command, **HPLOT X,Y** where X and Y are the *screen coordinates* of the dot. X values can range from 0 to 279. The lower the number, the nearer to the left edge of the screen. Y values can be from 0 to 191. The lower the number the nearer to the *top* of the screen. **HPLOT 0,0** would activate the dot in the upper left corner. **HPLOT 279,191** would affect the dot in the lower right.

Now, most of us have drawn graphs in math class at school, and the arrangement of the Hi-Res screen can be a bit vexing at first. We're used to the 0,0 location, also called the *origin,* being the lower left corner, not the

upper left. Why is the Apple different? For some very complex reasons, it was easier for the designers of the Apple to do it that way. They figured, hey, it's like a bicycle — looks complicated at first, but once you get the knack of using it, then it's easy and a lot of fun.

Let's talk about *aspect ratios*. When I first wrote this program, my pictures came out as ovals. For a while this was alright. Cousin Ricky's Spirograph never gave *him* ovals! But I felt there should be a way to control things, even to get that special oval known as a circle if I wanted it. There were two approaches, one to add complexity to the Defined Functions, the other to simply adjust the scaling on the screen. I chose the latter.

Your screen probably will be different from mine. Do this. In Line 4 make ASPECT = 1. In line 5 make A = 100000. In line 6 make B = 1. This will attempt to draw a circle on your screen. If it doesn't come out a circle, get a ruler. Divide the width of the image by the height. In line 3, type "SCIRCLE =" [the value you just calculated]. In line 4, type "ASPECT = SCIRCLE." RUN the program again, and this time you should have a circle.

If you have a printer, again set ASPECT = 1, RUN the program, and dump the resulting image to paper. Divide the width of the output by the height, and in line 3, add the statement "PCIRCLE = " [your calculated value].

In line 4, you can now set "ASPECT = PCIRCLE" when you want circular printouts, and "ASPECT = SCIRCLE" when you want circular screen images. Obviously, "ASPECT =" [anything else] will give you ovals. Different monitors and printers will require different aspect ratios, because of the way they space their dots.

What about patterns? The pattern you get depends upon the relative sizes of the "fixed" and "moving" circles. The variable "A" is given the diameter of the fixed circle, and "B" the diameter of the movable circle. Though I don't know how to prove it, my observation is that, adjusting the fraction A/B to the lowest integer values for both A and B, the number of points in the pattern will be A, and the number of revolutions required to complete the pattern will be B. Try different combinations and see what happens.

```
1   REM   CYCLOIDS BY DAVID SPARKS

2   TEXT : HOME : REM
    CLEAR THE SCREEN
3   PCIRCLE = 176.4 / 134:SCIRCLE =
      6.875 / 5.4375: REM
    ABOVE ARE ADJUSTMENTS FOR
    PRINTER AND SCREEN ASPECT
    RATIOS ON MY SYSTEM
4   ASPECT = SCIRCLE: REM
    SET TO DRAW CIRCULAR
    IMAGES ON SCREEN
5   A = 8: REM
    RADIUS OF "FIXED" CIRCLE
6   B = 3: REM
    RADIUS OF "MOVING" CIRCLE
7   EPICYCLOID = 1: REM
    MAKE THIS NON-ZERO IF
    YOU DO WANT AN EPICYCLOID,
    ZERO IF YOU DO NOT.
8   HYPOCYCLOID = 0: REM
    MAKE THIS NON-ZERO IF
    YOU DO WANT A HYPOCYCLOID,
    ZERO IF YOU DO NOT.
9   REM
    MAKE BOTH EPICYCLOID AND
    HYPOCYCLOID NON-ZERO
    FOR A COMBINATION PATTERN

10  DEF  FN XH(Q) = ((A - B) *  COS
       (Q) + B *  COS (Q * ((A - B)
       / B)) - XL) / (XR - XL) * 2
       79: REM    X FOR HYPOCYCLOID
15  DEF  FN XE(Q) = ((A + B) *  COS
       (Q) - B *  COS (Q * ((A + B)
       / B)) - XL) / (XR - XL) * 2
       79: REM    X FOR EPICYCLOID

20  DEF  FN YH(Q) = ((A - B) *  SIN
       (Q) - B *  SIN (Q * ((A - B)
       / B)) - YT) / (YB - YT) * 1
       91: REM Y FOR HYPOCYCLOID
25  DEF  FN YE(Q) = ((A + B) *  SIN
       (Q) - B *  SIN (Q * ((A + B)
       / B)) - YT) / (YB - YT) * 1
       91: REM Y FOR EPICYCLOID

30  IF EPICYCLOID THEN 100: REM
    BRANCH IF EPICYCLOID WANTED.
35  IF HYPOCYCLOID THEN 500: REM

    BRANCH IF HYPOCYCLOID WANTED
40  PRINT "YOU DIDN'T SELECT EITH
    ER PATTERN.": PRINT  CHR$ (7
    ): END : REM
    RING THE BELL AND STOP IF
    NEITHER PATTERN SELECTED.

100 REM         EPICYCLOID

110 HGR : POKE  - 16302,0:X = B *
      2 + A: REM
    SELECT AND CLEAR HI-RES SCREEN,
    SELECT FULL-SCREEN DISPLAY,
    CALCULATE SCALING PROPORTION
    FOR EPICYCLOID.

115 XL =  - X * ASPECT:XR = X * A
      SPECT:YB =  - X:YT = X: REM
      SCALING PARAMETERS

120 HCOLOR= 3: HPLOT  FN XE(0), FN
      YE(0): REM
      SELECT WHITE AS COLOR AND
      PLOT STARTING POINT.

130 :: FOR Q = 0 TO B * 8 *  ATN
      (1) STEP 8 *  ATN (1) / 360:
        REM PROPER NUMBER OF REVO-
    LUTIONS ONE DEGREE AT A TIME

140 HPLOT  TO  FN XE(Q), FN YE(Q
      ): REM NOTE HOW A CALL
    TO A DEFINED FUNCTION CAN BE USED
        ANYWHERE A REGULAR NUMERIC
    CONSTANT OR VARIABLE IS ALLOWED.

150 NEXT
200 ::: IF HYPOCYCLOID THEN 520::
        REM IF BOTH EPICYCLOID AND
    HYPOCYCLOID DESIRED, THEN BRANCH
    INTO HYPOCYCLOID MODULE PAST ITS
    INITIALIZING-SCALING INSTRUCTIONS

210 GOTO 700: REM

500 REM          HYPOCYCLOID

510 HGR : POKE  - 16302,0
512 X = (A * (A >  = B)) + ((2 *
      B - A) * (B > A)): REM  USE
    OF BOOLEAN LOGIC TO DETERMINE
    DIMENSIONS OF FIGURE
515 XL =  - X * ASPECT:XR = X * A
      SPECT:YB =  - X:YT = X: REM
      SCALING PARAMETERS
520 HCOLOR= 3: HPLOT  FN XH(0), FN
      YH(0)
530 FOR Q = 0 TO B * 8 *  ATN (1
      ) STEP 8 *  ATN (1) / 360
540 HPLOT  TO  FN XH(Q), FN YH(Q
      )
550 NEXT
590 GOTO 700: REM

700 REM             FIND OUT WHETHER
        PRINTOUT DESIRED

710 POKE  - 16301,0: REM SELECT
      MIXED TEXT AND GRAPHICS
720 VTAB 20: PRINT : REM MOVE TO
      TEXT WINDOW ON SCREEN
730 INPUT "DO YOU WANT A PRINTOU
      T? ";X$
735 POKE  - 16302,0: REM GO BACK
      TO FULL-SCREEN DISPLAY
740 IF  LEFT$ (X$,1) <  > "Y" THEN
      2000: REM
      GO TO PROGRAM ENDING SEQUENCE
        IF NO PRINTOUT DESIRED.

1000 REM         PRINT THE PICTURE

1003 REM
    PRINTER OUTPUT NOT REQUIRED TO
    RUN PROGRAM. SEE YOUR OWN SYSTEM
    MANUALS OR DEALER FOR HI-RES
    PRINTING INSTRUCTIONS ON YOUR
    SYSTEM, AND INSTALL CODE
    AT LINE 1010
1010 REM (HI-RES DUMP CODE HERE)
1020 PRINT  CHR$ (4);"PR#1": FOR
      Q = 1 TO 33: PRINT : NEXT : PRINT
      CHR$ (4);"PR#0": REM  PRINT
      ENOUGH BLANK LINES TO EJECT
      SHEET FROM PRINTER.
1030 GOTO 2000: REM

2000 REM PROGRAM END SEQUENCE
2010 END : REM
      MORE COULD BE DONE HERE,
      BUT WE'LL LEAVE THAT TO YOU.
```

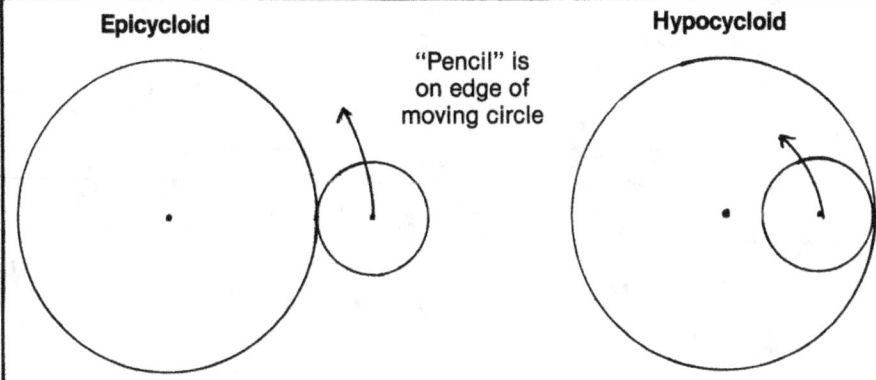

Epicycloid

Hypocycloid

"Pencil" is on edge of moving circle

Here are the Sussmans' *Parametric Equations* for the two types of curves:

Epicycloid

x =	(a+b)cos(Q) – b cos(gQ)
y =	(a+b)sin(Q) – b sin(gQ)

Hypocycloid

x =	(a–b)cos(Q) + b cos(hQ)
y =	(a–b)sin(Q) – b cos(hQ)

where

a =	radius of fixed circle
b =	radius of rolling circle
Q =	angle between the x-axis and the line connecting the two circles' centers, in radians
g =	(a+b)÷b
h =	(a–b)÷b

EPICYCLOID and HYPOCYCLOID, in the program, are *boolean* variables, or true–false tests. Any Applesoft numeric variable can be used as a boolean. Applesoft defines the value zero as "false," and any non–zero value as "true." This program uses non–zero, or "true" values to mean "draw one of these."

In the program as printed here, the variable EPICYCLOID is given a value (1) in line 7, and the variable HYPOCYCLOID is given the value zero in line 8. Line 30 begins, "IF EPICYCLOID . . ." Notice it doesn't say,

"IF EPICYCLOID = 1 . . ." This is an example of boolean, or true–false use of a variable. With EPICYCLOID = 1, the program will "branch" to line 100. Try changing the values in lines 7–8 and see if you can follow the boolean logic in lines 30, 35, and 200.

Epicycloids are curves "described" by a point on the circumference of a circle rolling freely, but without any slippage around the outside of the circumference of a second, fixed circle. Hypocycloids are a similar concept, except the rolling circle moves inside the circumference of the fixed circle:

Well, time passes, and children grow up. Cousin Ricky is now Richard, a hot–shot computer geology expert for a big oil company. He makes computers print 3–D color pictures of rocks three miles down. But I, I can produce Spirographs of many shapes. And this time, the toy belongs to me.

I've had a lot of fun with this. A young lady in my household loves to color the printouts. I've printed them on tracing paper, then used my darkroom enlarger to "blow up" the image onto the top of a cake. We traced the image

in icing and had a wonderful time. It's fascinating to just sit and watch them go. And I've only used **HCOLOR=3**, which is white. I've yet to try changing colors.

If you select both an epicycloid and a hypocycloid, the screen will be scaled for an epicycloid, the pattern will be drawn, then the hypocycloid will be produced inside it. With a bit of work, you might be able to get multiple, concentric patterns by proportionally adjusting both A and B.

As written, the program runs on an Apple II Plus, 64K, Epson MX–80 printer with Graphtrax 80, and a Mountain Hardware CPS Multifunction Card. It should run equally well on a 48K Apple. Graphics printout is obtained with The Routine Machine and Amperchart from Roger Wagner Publishing. Obviously, many graphics printer interface cards, such as the Dumpling GX, afford the ability to output Hi–Res images. There are also other software packages which can do the job.

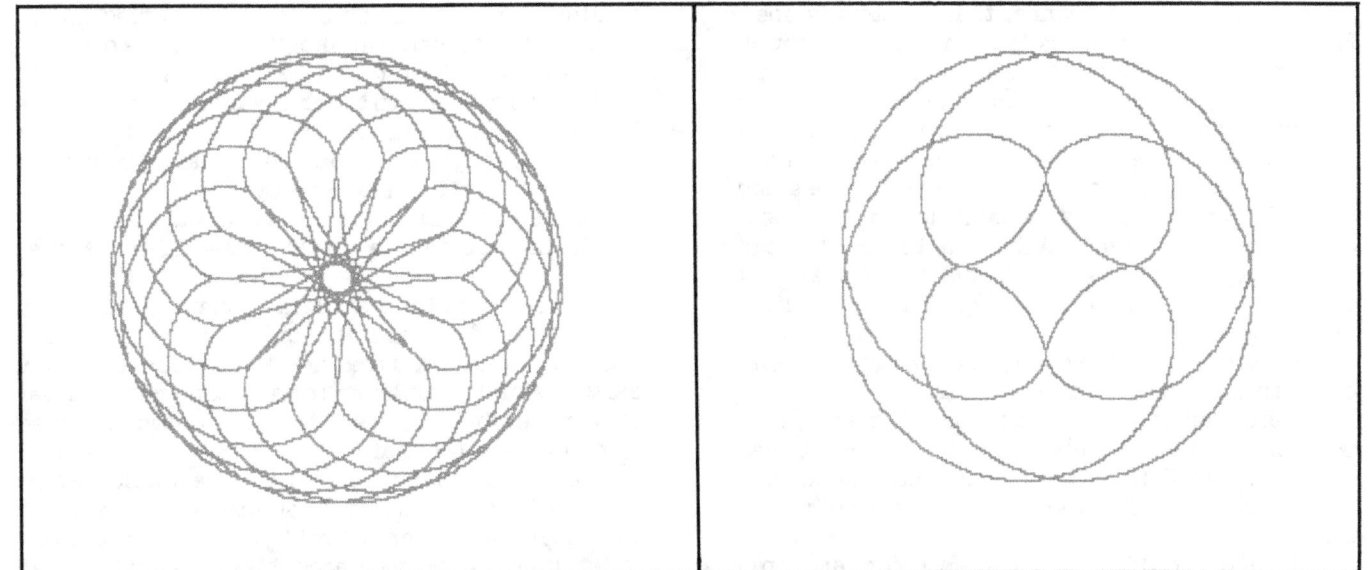

The Duncan Letters

Joe Holt/Laurie Wofford

Duncan my Friend!

Salutations again from Fairhill Castle! The Winter in all her fury has finally left us, leaving behind a white world, which is just now beginning to turn green. Soon, the King's horses will be running wild on the East Pastures outside these stone castle walls, happy to finally see the spring.

And they aren't the only ones! The warmth of a fire is one thing, but the warmth of the sun. . . ah! I think I'll go out and find me a nice spot upon the walkways around the top of the inner wall, then continue this letter. . .

Much better! After seeing the four walls of my quarters for so long, and only white outside my window, it's refreshing to gaze westward and see the familiar forests of Greenwood, stretching even as far as the Far Mountains. I can almost imagine your small village on the other side of those snowy peaks. . .

Which reminds me: When I'd sent you my last letter, and some weeks after had still not heard a word from you, I began to worry. Had the nomadic Wanderers raided your village? I shuddered at the thought. I decided to pay the Sorceror and his mail service a visit down in his dismal hole under the castle to find out if my letter had gotten delivered safely to you.

Of course, when I arrived in the Sorceror's chamber, he was busy tending to some new experiment. He was hunched over a table, staring into a small upright box. A glow from inside the box illuminated the Sorceror's face. Its flickering cast made him look even stranger than he already does. His right hand was resting on another, much smaller box, sitting on the table next to the other.

I politely interrupted him, and after excusing myself numerous times (it is unwise to upset a sorceror), asked if the mail had been delivered over the Far Mountains and to your village safely. He stood up, and after setting down what he later told me was a "mouse," informed me that the bad winter had taken its toll on his Hexels who deliver the mail, but yes, the mail had gotten through, although a little behind schedule.

My mind thus relieved, I began to wonder what on earth was inside that box of his.

I ventured to ask. "Excuse me, Sorceror, but, well, if it won't be intruding too much, I was wondering, well, if — what's inside that box on your table?" His response took me by surprise, to say the least.

"I knew I couldn't keep it a secret for very long!

Very well, then. There is Magic inside this box, Joseph. Inside this box is power. It is the world at your fingertips. Ah, but more than the world — it is anything you could ever imagine! This, Joseph, is a Magic Apple!"

A Magic Apple! One of the very kind which that traveling minstrel had spoken of! All the wonderful things the minstrel had claimed Apples could do, and how fantastic he'd claimed they were. . . and the Sorceror has had one all the time! I was taken aback, and I told him so.

He was upset. "What did you think I did my magic with? Newt's eyes and bat's wings?!?" Well, I must confess that your cousin's knowledge of magic is very limited. . . I was too embarassed to answer honestly.

"But, that doesn't look at **all** like an apple," I said cautiously. "It's square, and white, and **glows**!"

"Of course it doesn't look like an ordinary apple, because it isn't! You don't eat Magic Apples," the Sorceror replied.

"Thank goodness. I don't think that **that** apple would go down very easily. In fact, it doesn't look very edible at all." I stepped closer to the Magic Apple, and stared at it for a while. There were images on one side of the box, Duncan, glowing images! It was like bright candles placed behind a sheet of writing paper which someone had scribbled upon.

Then the sorceror spoke: "Well. . . go ahead."

"You mean I can touch it?" I asked.

"Of course you can **touch** it! I mean, you can take it back to your room and use it for a while. It's not difficult, and I'm sure you can quickly grasp it."

I was more than shocked by this unusual show of generosity. Think of it, Duncan: A Magic Apple! I would be able to use one of these Magic Apples myself!

The sorceror then explained that he had many other types of apples in his cubby hole to keep him busy for a while, and that he was anxious to see how easy it would be to learn for someone who'd never used one of these apples before. I suppose he picked a good person for that!

He talked at length about this particular Magic Apple, which he called a "Macintosh." He said that the wizard Woz, whom I told you about in the last letter, had originally created the Apple I, which was the first of the Magic Apples. Then, not content with giving the world one Magic Apple, he created another, named (cleverly enough) the Apple II. After a little help from a friend, he began to sell these Magic Apples, and soon they were in every imaginable marketplace.

Eventually, an entire proprietorship was formed because of the success of these Magic Apples. The sorceror said that his Hexels which got the apples from Silicon Valley told him that it is almost like a small city, peopled by an entire band of Wizards working together to create even better Magic Apples!

And that's what this Macintosh Magic Apple is. Although the wizard Woz had little to do with this particular apple, the sorceror said that it indeed is as wonderful as the original apples.

So, Duncan, that's how Macintoshes came about, and how I have in my room right now one of these Magic Apples.

After the sorceror explained all this, he carried the Macintosh up to my room (in a basket, so none of the other inhabitants here would see it; he doesn't want word of this to get out right now. I agree; I want to have it all to myself for a little while, at least!). He set it on my drawing table and started looking around on the walls for something. He said he was looking for an "electrical outlet." Did I ever tell you about these?

Well, I've always been suspicious of all that copper tubing the Sorceror ran throughout the castle last summer, even to strange places like the dungeon and the tower. Ever since he fell into the moat, I think his brain has been a little waterlogged. I recall I've told you about his peculiarities, have I not? Flying kites in thunderstorms, and muttering things about "electricity" and such (that pointed hat of his is surely cutting off the circulation to some vital area).

Anyway, this copper tubing, through which he claims his "electricity" flows, is used to fuel the Macintosh, or so he says. Between you and me, Duncan, I've placed my ear against the tubing many times, and I hear nothing flowing! But it's true. When I connect the Sorceror's Apple to the tubing, it tells me all sorts of things (some of which I don't yet understand, like "VIEW BY ICON"), but when I "pull the juice" (as the Sorceror is fond of saying), which is to say that I disconnect the Apple from the tubing, it suddenly goes quiet and the glow fades, and even my most urgent promptings are ignored by it.

The Sorceror has this to say about electricity and Magic Apples:

"Apples use electricity as power, and, through a most ingenious internal switching power supply, are able to transform 120 volt AC castle current to various DC voltages, such as $+5$, -12, ground, and so on, which, when applied to the various components within the Apple, integrated circuits being the majority . . . er, Joseph, where was I?"

What I think he's trying to say is that the electricity is like food for the Macintosh, just like or-

dinary apples are food for us, and without food, the Apple will die. This sounds all very simple now that I think back upon it, and even though the Sorceror has told me that Apples will "come back to life" when re-supplied with their electric food, I've yet to turn it off. We've only just been introduced, but I already feel as if the Macintosh is my friend. You can't just go around disconnecting your friends!

This is what I've been able to figure out about how Magic Apples are able to help me with my humble goings-on:

First, of course, is the fact that Apples simply cannot do anything without being connected to electricity. Try as you might, they just won't.

Second, Apples need to be told what to do, whether by me or by someone else. Usually when I "talk" to the Apple, I'm actually talking to it through the instructions of someone else. Hmmmm . . . now I'm starting to sound like the Sorceror . . .

That second thought is somewhat difficult to understand. I've got an idea which may explain it a little better:

Do this: next time your parents ask you to feed the unicorn, shout at the top of you lungs "I CERTAINLY WILL!" And next time they ask you if you've done your studies, spin three times in a circle and tell them (closing one eye) "YES I HAVE!" And before they even ask if you've washed behind your ears, when you see that "have you washed behind your ears" look on their faces, hop on one foot and whistle, then hop on the other foot and say "OF COURSE!".

Have you got that? Let's give it a try . . .

"Duncan my son, will you feed the unicorn?"
[you say:]
"I CERTAINLY WILL!"
"Duncan dearest, have you done your studies?"
[spin three times, close one eye:]
"YES I HAVE!"
"Duncan, oh Duncan, have you . . ."
[hop on one foot, whistle, hop on the other:]
"OF COURSE!"

And then if your parents ask you why you're acting so strangely, tell them your cousin Joseph told you to (then, when your parents look at you sideways, you'll know better than to do everything your cousin Joseph tells you to do!).

You see, just as I told you what to do when your parents ask you certain things, so has the wizard Woz and his friends told their Apples what to do if I ask it things. The Macintosh is unique, according to the sorceror, in that to use it, you hardly have to know anything about these instructions the Wizards gave it. Thank goodness for that!

Of course, Magic Apples don't have ears to wash behind or unicorns to feed, but they can do many useful things (or so the Sorceror tells me). All these things will have to wait until next time, because my hand has grown weary, and my mind is soon to follow. And so, Duncan, to tell you the truth, I want to go back to my quarters and play with the Macintosh!

It's very hard, not being able to tell anyone else

Continued on Page 26

Assembly Language for Teen-agers
The Sourceror's Apprentice

Mike Newton

Welcome back to Castle Fairhill, my apprentice! I know that your father, Sir Touhee, waits outside with your mount, to take you to the Tuldurry Knights Tournament, so we'll get right to your studies.

Wizards have all kinds of important tools and helpful items. Where would a wizard be without his staff? Up the stream without an oar, I'll warrant. There are a lot of other magic tools as well, like cloaks of invisibility, eyes of Newt, seeing stones, ancient scrolls of enchantments . . . well, you get the idea. Working magic without one's tools is extremely difficult, if not impossible.

Just as wizards have these special tools, programmers have many programming tools, commonly called *utilities*. Your editor/assembler is one of these tools, and the most important one to an assembly language programmer. Other tools include base conversion charts, debuggers, reference manuals and monitors. Life can be made much simpler with these programming utilities.

Every Apple computer contains a built-in *monitor*, hidden away amongst the Apple ROMs. Don't confuse this monitor with the *video monitor* that displays text and graphics and looks like a TV set. The monitor utility program allows you to "get into" the Apple memory. It has commands to store values in memory, inspect the values in memory, jump to a program in memory, and many other useful functions.

Let's get acquainted with the monitor. From Applesoft, type "CALL –151" and then press the RETURN key. You should now see an asterisk (*) at the far left side of the screen and a blinking cursor. The asterisk is the monitor *prompt*, and always indicates that you have "entered" the monitor. A prompt is a special character that is used to tell you which of the Apple's operating systems you are currently using.

The first monitor command that we will learn about is the "G" command. The "G" stands for "Go," and is more or less the machine language equivalent of the Applesoft command "GOTO." The monitor commands always come after the data that the command operates on or uses.

Among the subroutines in the Apple monitor ROM is a routine called "BELL." As you might guess, this routine beeps the speaker with the same annoying sound that occurs when your Applesoft program makes a ?SYNTAX ERROR. The BELL routine begins at memory location $FF3A — notice that this is a hexadecimal number (all numbers and addresses used in the monitor must be expressed in hexadecimal). To call this routine, and thus beep the speaker, you must type "FF3AG" from the monitor and then press the RETURN key. The monitor will then "GOTO" to FF3A, where the BELL routine starts. The BELL routine beeps the speaker and then returns to the monitor. If you're wondering why we suddenly dropped the dollar sign ($) in front of the hex numbers above, it is because when we are working in assembly language, all numbers and addresses are assumed to be hexadecimal.

Well, the BELL routine is none too exciting. In fact, individually, none of the routines in the monitor are very exciting, but then a lot of programming is sort of drab. However, taken as a whole, the Apple monitor is as fine a collection of utility routines as you might hope for. While they are all we have to work with for a while, there's power in them thar bytes. Live without excitement for a while longer, then see how using these unexiting subroutines can make things easy for you.

Let's call another unexciting monitor routine, "ERR." This routine, located at $FF2D, prints the word "ERR" on the screen and then calls the BELL routine, which of course beeps the speaker. To call the ERR routine, we enter "FF2DG" into the monitor.

Let's call just one more routine from the monitor ROM. This routine is the first one that you see when you turn on your Apple — that's right, this routine clears the screen, beeps the speaker and prints the word "Apple] [" at the top of the screen. It is located at memory address $FB60. To call it, we simply enter "FB60G," which says to the monitor, "go to the machine language routine starting at memory location FB60".

Let's learn another monitor command, the List command. As you might guess, this command is very much like the Applesoft LIST command. Instead of listing an Applesoft program, however, the List command *disassembles* a machine language program in memory. Disassembling is, of course, the exact opposite of assembling: a disassembler converts machine language binary numbers into readable assembly language *mnemonics*.

A mnemonic is a made-up word that is easy to memorize, because the characters stand for something we can understand. For example, the mnemonic "LDA" means **L**oa**D** the **A**ccumulator. The monitor includes a disassembler which disassembles the raw binary data in memory, and converts it into mnemonic *opcodes* and *operands*. Opcodes and operands are terms we will discuss a little later on.

Even though we haven't started learning the many assembly language mnemonics yet, let's use the List command to disassemble memory anyway, just for the practice. We'll disassemble the BELL routine, and see what the machine language commands to beep the speaker look like. To do this, we simply enter the address and follow it by the monitor command: "FF3AL".

You should see all kinds of letters and numbers on the screen that probably don't mean much to you. I'll briefly explain what these different things mean. At the far left of the screen are hexadecimal addresses, ranging from FF3A to FF59. The next set of numbers are the bytes that comprise the current machine language instruction. Instructions are made of from one to three bytes, depending on exactly what the instruction is. Following this group of machine language numbers is the disassembled assembly language *instruction*.

The first disassembled line should look like this:

FF3A—   A9 87   LDA #$87

This line means: starting at hexadecimal address $FF3A are the bytes $A9 and 87, which comprise the machine language instruction which is "LDA #$87" in assembly language. The "LDA" is the mnemonic *opcode*, and when converted to machine language, tells the computer *what* to do. The "#$87" is the *operand*. Once the computer knows what to do, it must be told what to do it *with*. This is the function of the operand. As an assembly language programmer, you'll probably use the disassembling feature of the Apple monitor quite a bit in debugging programs that have gone haywire.

Another monitor command that is used often is the command to store bytes in memory. Let's say, for instance, that we wished to store the value $11 at memory location $2000. To tell the monitor to do this, we would simply enter "2000: 11 [RETURN]." If we wished to store a series of numbers starting at an address, you merely specify the starting address, type the colon (:), and enter the series of hexadecimal numbers. Remember that each hexadecimal number must consist of two hexadecimal digits. The value $4, for instance, *must* be entered as 04. If we wished to store the values $AB C2 D1 1F starting at the address $3000, for instance, the monitor entry would be "3000: AB C2 D1 5F [RETURN]." Note that there is a space between each hexadecimal number.

If you wish to see the values of bytes stored in memory, you can use the dot (.) command. If you wished to inspect memory from $2000 to $20FF, for instance, you would enter "2000. 20FF [RETURN]." While this is a very simple command, it is used often to print the contents of memory. To inspect the contents of a single memory location, you can just enter the address of the location to be inspected. The monitor will reprint the hexadecimal address and follow it with the hexadecimal contents of that location.

Now that we've learned all these new commands, let's do something with them. Look at Table I. (An enlarged copy with additional details, and printed on cardstock, is available. An ad appears elsewhere in this issue.) Table I is a chart of the values of characters on the screen. A normal "A", one that is not inverse or flashing, for instance, has a value of $C1. The text screen is an area of memory which starts at $400 and ends at $7FF. Let's put some characters on the text screen. To do this, we can use the monitor colon (:) command to store a series of values on the screen.

From Applesoft, type "HOME [RETURN]" to clear the screen. Then type "CALL –151 [RETURN]" to enter the monitor. The screen display memory starts at address $400, and if we begin storing values there, they will appear on the top of the screen.

Let's put the word "MAGIC" on the screen. Referring to the ASCII code chart, we can see that this would be the values $CD C1 C7 C9 C3. To "PRINT" the word on the screen, we can type in the monitor command "400: CD C1 C7 C9 C3 [RETURN]," and as if by magic, the word "MAGIC" should now be at the top of the screen.

Have you ever wondered how the Applesoft "PRINT" command works? Well, now you know. It simply stores ASCII values to the memory area that is associated with the screen text display. That's all that most machine language programs do: store various values at various memory locations.

An understanding of the Apple II monitor is very important for an assembly language programmer. It is usually the only thing that there is to help you debug your machine language. There are all sorts of assembly/machine language aids available. The only tools that we will use together, however, are the monitor and the editor/assembler.

There are so many things that you need to know before you can program in assembly language that it has taken us a while to get as far as we have gotten. My master always told me that a journey of a thousand miles starts with a single step, and that is what we've been doing: taking those first short and simple steps. Being an assembly language wizard is truly an infinite journey: there is always a new exciting landscape on the horizon, some new unexplored land. Even an old wizard is always learning new things.

I bet you're really looking forward to the Tuldurry Knights Tournament. I remember seeing it as a boy. That iron mail shirt you're wearing, isn't that the official coat of mail of the Tournament? It's really rather strange how those Knights are boycotting the Tournament, isn't it? But what else should this year's host expect after boycotting the last Tournament himself? Aren't people strange, especially those Knight types? Always looking for something to quibble over! Have fun, and come back soon!

	Inverse				Flashing				Normal Ctrl		Normal				l/case	
	$00	$10	$20	$30	$40	$50	$60	$70	$80	$90	$A0	$B0	$C0	$D0	$E0	$F0
$0	@	P		0	@	P		0	@	P		0	@	P	`	p
$1	A	Q	!	1	A	Q	!	1	A	Q	!	1	A	Q	a	q
$2	B	R	"	2	B	R	"	2	B	R	"	2	B	R	b	r
$3	C	S	#	3	C	S	#	3	C	S	#	3	C	S	c	s
$4	D	T	$	4	D	T	$	4	D	T	$	4	D	T	d	t
$5	E	U	%	5	E	U	%	5	E	U	%	5	E	U	e	u
$6	F	V	&	6	F	V	&	6	F	V	&	6	F	V	f	v
$7	G	W	'	7	G	W	'	7	G	W	'	7	G	W	g	w
$8	H	X	(	8	H	X	(	8	H	X	(	8	H	X	h	x
$9	I	Y	)	9	I	Y	)	9	I	Y	)	9	I	Y	i	y
$A	J	Z	*	:	J	Z	*	:	J	Z	*	:	J	Z	j	z
$B	K	[	+	;	K	[	+	;	K	[	+	;	K	[	k	{
$C	L	\	,	<	L	\	,	<	L	\	,	<	L	\	l	|
$D	M	]	-	=	M	]	-	=	M	]	-	=	M	]	m	}
$E	N	^	.	>	N	^	.	>	N	^	.	>	N	^	n	~
$F	O	_	/	?	O	_	/	?	O	_	/	?	O	_	o	■

Table I: ASCII Screen Characters

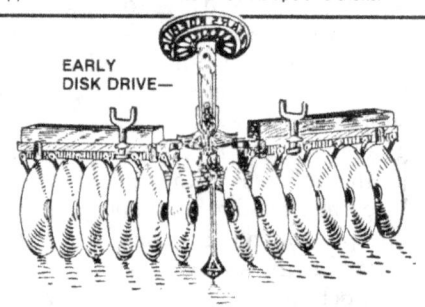
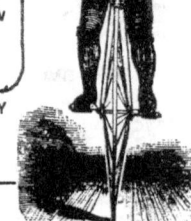

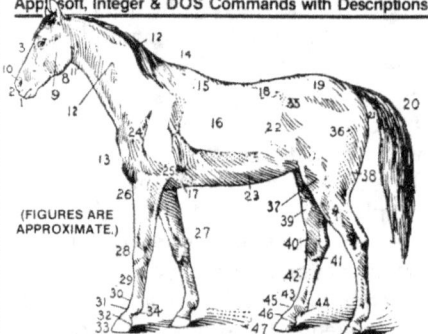

Ask the Wizard

The Wizard of Fairhill Castle

Dear Wizard:

I write a lot of programs, and some of them are pretty big, so I need to renumber them from time to time. Every once in a while, something strange happens that I don't understand: some of my numeric constants get changed. Can you tell me why or provide a fix?

Apple has a habit of sometimes releasing programs that are "almost" bug-free. Renumber is one of them. The bug itself is obscure, and comes into play *only* when a value that corresponds to a line number follows a multiply token (*).

For those interested, the reason is that when Renumber is run, it relocates itself in memory, according to the size of the host computer. In the renumbering process, it must search for tokens such as LIST, GOTO, and GOSUB, etc., so that it may renumber these references. It so happens that a couple of these tokens, when disassembled, look like relocatable code to the relocation routine, thus it attempts to "relocate" what are actually Applesoft command tokens.

The fix is easy. You just load Renumber (do *not* run it), make a couple of POKEs, and save it.

```
UNLOCK RENUMBER
LOAD RENUMBER
POKE 4789,172
POKE 4790,171
SAVE RENUMBER
LOCK RENUMBER
```

These are all direct commands that you type from the keyboard. That's all there is to it.

Dear Wizard:

I'm a real game freak, and I like what what you do in your magazine, but it's not enough for me. Where can I get more information?

There are two magazines that I know of that are devoted entirely to games:
Computer Gaming World
1337 North Merona St.
Anaheim, CA 92803

St. Game
P.O. Box 60
North Hollywood, CA 91603

Dear Wizard:

I've seen programs around that do things like showing deleted files when you catalog a disk, so there has to be a way to do that myself. . . or can I?

Easy as (Apple) pie. There is an instruction in DOS that tells the catalog handler "skip this file — it's deleted." We can defeat that instruction by "NOPing" it out. [A NOP is an assembly language instruction that means literally "do nothing" except go to the next instruction. It is represented by the hex byte $EA.] You can do a couple of POKEs from the keyboard, or you can put it in the form of a short program or an EXEC file. I'll give it to you in the form of a program for a 48k Apple:

```
10  POKE 44505,234 : POKE
    44506,234
20  PRINT CHR$(4);"CATALOG"
30  POKE 44505,48 : POKE
    44506, 74
```

Notice line 30 is important to include, because it restores your DOS to normal after you have displayed deleted files. Incidentally, when you see a deleted file on the screen, there will be an inverse character about 30 characters after the beginning of the title. This represents the track number of the track sector list for the deleted file. It can be handy if you attempt to recover the file. Sometime we'll tell you how to do that, too.

Nobody asked, but I'll Tell:

What with all the Magic Apples that seem to be arriving here at Fairhill, I thought I'd pass along a quick hint that will let you change your disk drive access without doing a CATALOG or VERIFY or anything. Again, one simple POKE does it, and it would be best to include this in your Hello program.

POKE 43624,2

Now your next disk access will be to drive two. To change it back, POKE 43624 with a 1. Either POKE can be done at any time from within a program, whenever you want to change the next drive access. Remember, these POKEs are only for a 48k or greater Apple.

Thanks to those who wrote, and remember no question is too tough or too easy for the Wizard of Fairhill Castle. If you have a problem with your Apple, write to the Wizard of Fairhill Castle, P.O. Box 582-AA, Santee, CA 92071, and I'll try and help you solve your problem.

IF/THEN/ELSE
Spells and Potions

Ralph H. Swerdlow, M.D.

Well, I thought, if my APPLE is so wonderful, why not let it make decisions for me. I always have decisions to make, and a computer is perfect for this task!

Okay, let's ask the computer something. The weather is becoming nice, maybe I should go swimming today. That is a good thought; what does my APPLE say?

So I started up my trusty APPLE and typed in "SHOULD I GO SWIMMING TODAY" and of course a RETURN. Can you guess what happened?

You are right; my APPLE printed "SYNTAX ERROR" because this is not a proper BASIC command! It became obvious that I needed some sort of program to pursue this idea.

Here is my first program:

```
10  TEXT:HOME
20  PRINT "SHOULD I GO SWIM-
    MING TODAY?"
```

Type in this program and then run it. Surprise, for the APPLE prints "SHOULD I GO SWIMMING TODAY?" It doesn't answer a question at all.

Do you see why this program did not answer any question. The program did not ask a question, only instructed the computer to print a statement, which in this case looked like a question. Any characters preceded by the word "PRINT" and surrounded by quotation marks will be printed to the screen or to your printer if it is on. Our computers, while very versatile, have no native intelligence, and do just as they are instructed to do. You and I are smarter, and we are able to recognize the statement in line 20 as a question, but to our APPLES, any string enclosed by quotation marks is a series of ASCII characters to be printed.

Interestingly enough, even if our APPLE was clever enough to recognize this as a question, it could not answer because it doesn't have enough information to make a decision. This is a function of a human, and a realistic answer requires some sort of basis on which to make a judgment!

For example, if I asked you if it was time to eat lunch, you could not answer without knowing the time. Obviously if it was near noon time, the answer would more likely be "YES" than if the time were midnight.

This does not mean that a computer can not make decisions, because they can do so, given some information on which to act. No, they do not do any actual "thinking," but merely compare two values which are placed in the computer's memory by the programmer. Then, depending on these values being equal or not equal, the computer prints an answer which has been supplied by the programmer.

Here is a program to demonstrate this process. It also contains a very little known "CALL" that enables a programmer to erase a complete line from the screen.

```
10  REM IF-THEN BY RALPH H
    SWERDLOW MD
20  TEXT:HOME
30  PRINT "SHOULD I GO
    SWIMMING?"
40  PRINT : PRINT "YOU SHOULD
    IF IT IS WARM ENOUGH"
50  PRINT : PRINT "PLEASE TELL
    ME WHAT IS THE
    TEMPERATURE"
60  PRINT : INPUT "ENTER
    TEMPERATURE —>";DEG
70  VTAB 10
80  IF DEG > 75 THEN PRINT
    "SOUNDS NICE. DO GO
    SWIMMING"
```

Line 10, of course is our standard REM statement, which should always be included in every program. Line 20 sets the screen to full width and then clears it. The main body of the program starts with line 30.

This line first issues a line feed with the "PRINT" command. Note that several commands can be placed on one line if the commands are separated by a colon. The remainder of the line then prints a string of characters which spell out "SHOULD I GO SWIMMING?" The computer does not know this is a question; to our APPLE, this is just a string of ASCII characters. We know it is a question, because we are accustomed to the grammar and form, and by the question mark at the end.

Lines 40 and 50 are the computer's answers. We have, of course programmed the replies, but now it appears as if the APPLE is responding to our question. Line 60 asks us to tell the computer what the temperature is by the INPUT command.

Line 70 cause the answer to be printed on row 10 of our screen, and line 80 then looks at the temperature value the user typed.

Line 80 compares the temperature typed by the user with the value of "75" and if the given temperature is greater than 75, the computer will print out, "SOUNDS NICE. DO GO SWIMMING". This does make it look like the computer is making some logical decisions, but our APPLE is only responding to a program.

Suppose, for a minute, that you prefer to not swim unless the temperature is warmer than 85. Easy enough to reprogram. Just go back to line 80 and change it to "IF DEG > 85...", and it is done.

So far, so good. We now have a program that "makes decisions," using the "IF-THEN" command, but Applesoft lacks an "IF-THEN-ELSE" command that is available in other programming languages such as Pascal.

Let us compare these two commands:

IF-THEN
1. Allows the user to evaluate two strings or values. (Yes, strings can be compared.)
2. If the comparison is TRUE, then the remainder of the command is executed, but if the comparison results in FALSE, the remainder of the command line is ignored!
3. Some examples:
   IF A>40 THEN PRINT "GOOD"
   IF A>=99 THEN PRINT "SORRY"
   IF X<>1000 GOSUB 350
   IF S$="JULY" THEN PRINT "THE MONTH IS ";S$

All of these examples can be tried in the immediate mode by merely typing them, followed by a return. Just give a value to A or to S$ and then type in the "IF-THEN" part. Please note that for strings, quotation marks must be used.

IF-THEN-ELSE
1. The computer first looks at the value or string and compares it with that given.
2. If TRUE, then next part of the command is executed just like the "IF-THEN"
3. If FALSE (OR NOT TRUE), the next part of the command will be performed.
4. Some examples:
   IF A=>100 THEN PRINT "GREATER THAN 100" ELSE PRINT "LESS THAN 100"
   IF N$="SANTA CLAUS" THEN PRINT "IT IS DECEMBER" ELSE PRINT "GO TO THE STORE AND BUY YOUR OWN PRESENTS"

Our computers can be programmed to behave as if they had the "IF-THEN-ELSE" command in a very simple fashion. Here is a modification of the last program to show how:

```
10  REM IF-THEN-ELSE BY RALPH H SWERDLOW MD
20  TEXT:HOME
30  PRINT "SHOULD I GO SWIMMING?"
40  PRINT : PRINT "YOU SHOULD IF IT IS WARM ENOUGH"
50  PRINT : PRINT "PLEASE TELL ME WHAT IS THE TEMPERATURE"
60  PRINT : INPUT "ENTER TEMPERATURE - > ";DEG
70  VTAB 10
80  PRINT "NO, DON'T GO SWIMMING. IT IS TOO COLD"
85  END
90  IF DEG > 75 THEN VTAB 10: CALL - 868: PRINT "SOUNDS NICE. DO GO SWIMMING"
```

Lines 10 to 70 are the same, but line 80 is new. This line prints, "NO, DON'T GO SWIMMING. IT IS TOO COLD" on row 10. Note the END in line 85.

Run this program, and observe that "NO..." will be printed to the screen. This is our "ELSE"!

If line 85 were to be taken out, the program would continue to Line 90 which compares the temperature inputed by the user in line 60 with the value of "75".

Line 90 sets the output of the string "SOUNDS NICE..." to row 10, and will overwrite the statement, "NO, DON'T..." printed by line 80. But what if the statement in line 80 is longer than the statement in line 90. Try this as an experiment and see for yourself what happens. The beginning of line 90's output replaces that of line 80, but the last part of line 80's output is still present on the screen, making a very confusing sentence! What we would like to do is "erase" the entire string produced by line 80!

This could be done several ways, for example by printing a string consisting of 40 blanks. This type of command would look like this:

VTAB 10:FOR N = 1 TO 40:PRINT " ";:NEXT

With a blank between the quotation marks. However, this adds another line to the program. Note the semi-colon. This concatenates (joins together) all of the blank spaces on one row of the screen and effectively erases that row.

Here is another way to do the same thing. Add this line to your program:

```
75  S$ = "NO, DON'T GO SWIMMING. IT IS TOO COLD"
```

Change line 80 to read:

```
80  PRINT S$
```

Change line 90 to:

```
90  IF DEG>75 THEN VTAB 10: FOR N = 1 TO LEN (S$): PRINT " ";:NEXT N:PRINT "SOUNDS NICE. DO GO SWIMMING"
```

This does the same job, but only prints as many blanks as there are characters in S$.

There is an even easier way to do the same thing, and that is by using "CALL -868" as I did in the original line 90. This is a machine language call, that goes to a sub-routine in the monitor of our computer that clears everything from the cursor's position to the end of that row. Using this call, the entire row is "erased" in one graceful swoop, and much faster that printing blanks! We are not limited to choosing between only two alternatives, but can ask our computers to "consider" several possibilities. Here is a program that demonstrates how:

```
10  TEXT:HOME
20  PRINT "SHOULD I GO SWIMMING TODAY?"
30  INPUT "ENTER TEMPERATURE : ";DEG
40  INPUT "IS IT SUNNY OR RAINY OUTDOORS S OR R ?? ";W$
50  VTAB 10
60  PRINT "DON'T GO SWIMMING TODAY"
70  IF DEG >75 AND W$ = "S" THEN VTAB 10:CALL -868: PRINT "SOUNDS LIKE A NICE DAY TO SWIM"
```

In this program, line 70 requires that BOTH DEG>75 AND S$="S" be true or only "DON'T..." will be printed.

These few tricks enable an Applesoft programmer to have the "IF-THEN-ELSE" easily available in their programs. With just a little bit of practice using this technique, you will have no trouble writing more concise programs that require decision making. No longer will you be forced to employ GOTO or GOSUB to control program flow. "IF-THEN-ELSE" is a very useful addition to our Apple's capabilities.

Uncle Bill's Column

Uncle Bill

Off We Go!

Hi kids, I'm Uncle Bill. This column is dedicated to having fun with your Apple computers, making lots of money, becoming famous and seeing what you can get away with while your parents aren't looking. Also, I'll be happy to pass on several tips, hints, gossip, scandal and whatnot. Some of the issues you will all be interested in include software piracy, illegal entry into bank accounts, electronic grade changing and burning down your school with a modem. Naturally, I'll include some tips on how to meet girls and tap telephones.

Getting Weird With the CHR$ Function

Inside your Apple is something called ASCII–Code. (Say As–Key.) They say it stands for American Standard Code for Information Interchange, but I think it is a good way to be sneaky with your computer. For example, let's say you want to pass a note to your friend in class, like "Let's ditch school and go work on our Apples." Now if you get caught writing a note like that, you'll get hollered at, and they may even keep you after school. However, using the CHR$ function, you can get the message across in the guise of passing a computer program. Let's see how it works.

Each character on your keyboard has a corresponding ASCII code. For example, CHR$(65) is the letter "A". By figuring out what CHR$ value is associated with what letter, you can put everything into code that only you and kids with computer smarts can understand. Since the ASCII values are in sequential order of the alphabet, it isn't too difficult to figure out what code goes with what letter. Thus, since CHR$(65) is "A", CHR$(66) would be the letter "B", CHR$(67) the letter "C"

and so forth. That means all the upper-case letters are in a range from 65 to 90. Lower–case letters range from 97 to 122.

So far so good, but how do you use CHR$ in programming? That too is as simple as pie. You use the PRINT statement just as you would with text, but you do not need the quote marks. Try the following:

```
PRINT CHR$(65)
[RETURN]
```

You will get the letter "A" printed on your screen. Now, let's put it in a program and see what we get.

```
10   TEXT:HOME
20   PRINT CHR$(83); CHR$(69);
     CHR$(88)
```

Run that little sucker, and you'll see what I mean about the usefulness of CHR$ codes. You will notice how we used semi–colons to separate the different CHR$ values (letters) in the program. If we had used commas instead, the message would have been spread across the screen.

But there's more you can do with CHR$. For example, let's say you want to print the message "NERD" using the quotation marks. Any jerk can PRINT "NERD", but they get NERD instead of "NERD." However, using CHR$(34), you can print quotation marks to your screen. Try the following program:

```
10   TEXT : HOME
20   PRINT "NERD"
30   PRINT CHR$(34) + "NERD" +
     CHR$(34)
```

Notice how we used the plus sign (+) to tie everything together and mix text with the CHR$. That's called concatenation, just in case you didn't know. (When you forget to do your homework, tell your teacher it wouldn't concatenate on your computer.)

Another secret use of the CHR$ function is to access control characters. When you press the CTRL key along with certain letters, invisible control letters are sent to your screen. Since they're invisible, it is difficult to use them in programming. For example, [Ctrl-G] is a bell, and you can use a descriptive string variable to place it in your program. Try the following little program:

```
10   TEXT : HOME
20   BELL$ = CHR$(7) : REM 7 IS
     THE ASCII VALUE FOR
     CTRL-G
30   PRINT BELL$
```

Use that whenever you want to ring a bell in your programs.

If ringing bells isn't your idea of a good time, you might be interested in accessing your disk drive from a program. (Look kids, if you want to be a real hacker, you gotta learn how to access your disk. Right? So pay attention.) From a program, to make your disk work, you need to use [Ctrl-D] or CHR$(4).

Since your disk access can be anywhere in a program, it is also a good idea to include a carriage return. But how do you get your program to hit the

RETURN key? With CHR$ it is a snap. The ASCII code for a carriage return is 13. Since you want to have the carriage return before your disk command, CHR$(4), define a string variable as D$ = CHR$(13) + CHR$(4). Then when you PRINT D$, you get both your carriage return and your disk command. Try this next little program.

```
10  TEXT : HOME
20  D$ = CHR$(13) + CHR$(4)
30  PRINT D$ "CATALOG"
```

Use that program as your HELLO program on your disk, and whenever you boot your system, it will automatically CATALOG it for you.

Code Writer

Now if you're going to write secret messages, you don't want to spend all your time looking up the ASCII values. To find the ASCII value of a key, use the ASC function. For instance, if you PRINT ASC("A") you will get 65. The ASC function is just the opposite of the CHR$ function. You give ASC a character, and it gives you an ASCII value, and you give CHR$ a number, and it gives you a character. (That's really

neat, huh?) What we need is a program that will encode our messages. Whenever you press a key, it will produce the letter and the ASCII value for it. Once we have all the values, we can enter those into DATA statements and pass all those notes mentioned at the beginning of the column.

Code Writer

```
10  TEXT : HOME
20  X = 1 : Y = 1
30  GET A$
40  IF A$ = CHR$(35) THEN END :
    REM CHR$(35) IS THE # SIGN
50  VTAB Y : HTAB X : PRINT A$;
60  VTAB Y + 1 : HTAB X : PRINT
    ASC(A$);
70  X = X + 3
80  IF X > 39 THEN X = 1 : Y = Y
    + 2
90  GOTO 30
```

When you RUN Code Writer and key in your message, you will be given the ASCII value below the individual letters. Copy those values down after you have written your message and use Decoder to read the message. The last data value should always be a zero so the program will know when to end.

Decoder

```
10   TEXT : HOME
20   READ X
30   IF X = 0 THEN END
40   PRINT CHR$(X);
50   GOTO 20
100  REM ******************
110  REM PUT YOUR DATA HERE
120  REM ******************
130  DATA 83,69,78,68,32,85,78,67
140  DATA 76,69,32,66,73,76,76,32,77
150  DATA 76,76,32,89,79,85,82,32,77
160  DATA 79,78,69,89,0
```

The decoder program simply READs all of the ASCII values from the DATA statements and PRINTs out the CHR$ held in variable X. As it sequentially goes through the DATA, the value of X keeps changing to reflect the next ASCII value for the CHR$ to be printed to the screen. Run the above program and see the secret message it contains. (Do it while your parents are out of the room, though.)

Well, that's all for this time. Next month, we'll get started on software piracy. Naturally the first thing we'll want to learn is how to keep some geek from stealing our programs. We'll see how to mess up disks, prevent listings and even how to prevent your little sister from running your program.

Meet the Turtle

Logo Lingo

Jeff Sandys

Hi-res screens, like the one on your Apple, were very expensive and rare ten years ago. The computer terminal was a noisy teletype and drawings were made on plotters. Logo used a robot with a pen to make drawings. These dome shaped robots were called turtles. You can still buy floor turtles to use with Logo.

We don't use the floor to make a drawing anymore. Thanks to the Apple computer, we can draw on the screen. To see your screen turtle, enter CLEARSCREEN. The turtle lives at the center of the screen. To move or turn the turtle use FORWARD, BACK, RIGHT or LEFT, and input the number of steps. The turtle moves and turns at our command:

```
FORWARD 50
RIGHT 90
BACK 100
```

Some other commands that the turtle knows are HOME, PENUP, PEN-DOWN, SHOWTURTLE and HIDE-TURTLE. These commands do not use inputs. Give them a try! Many of the commands also have short names. Can you match up the short commands with their long names? These short names will save a lot of typing:

FD BK RT LT PU PD ST HT

The Turtle's Home

The turtle turns in steps of degrees. There are 360 degrees in a circle or full turn. When the turtle is at home, pointing straight up, its heading is 0 degrees. When it points to the right, the heading is 90 degrees. This is just like a compass with north pointing straight up. The turtle can tell us its heading. The operation HEADING has no input, and outputs the heading. Try this example:

```
HOME RT 123
PRINT HEADING
LT 33
PRINT HEADING
```

From home, the turtle can move forward about 110 steps before it goes off the top of the screen. This is called the Y direction. The SETY command also moves the turtle up and down. To move the turtle left or right, in the X direction, use the SETX command. X and Y are zero at the turtle's home position. We can find out the X and Y position with XCOR and YCOR. Notice how the turtle wraps around the screen in this example:

```
RT 10 FD 2000
HOME CS
FD 100
PRINT YCOR
PRINT XCOR
SETX 50
PRINT YCOR
PRINT XCOR
```

The turtle can be used to explore geometry. The procedure POLY, listed below, draws a polygon with the angle you give it. Can you draw the polygons shown here? Try different angles, less than 180, until you get a polygon. Count the points on the polygon and multiply by the angle used. Is the result 360?

Color by Numbers

Black and white can be boring on a color TV. We can set the background color and pen color to blue, green, orange or violet with the right number. We can either remember which number is which color or use the procedures below to call the colors by name.

Apple Logo has a different syntax than Terrapin and Krell Logo. To enter the program, type in the Main Listing and the listing for your Logo. Try out the different colors:

```
SETBG VIOLET SETPC GREEN
POLY 80
CS SETPC ORANGE POLY 80
CS SETBG
BLUE POLY 80
CS SETBG BLACK POLY 80
SETPC BLACK POLY 80
LIGHTSHOW
SETBG WHITE POLY 80
LIGHTSHOW
```

Did you notice that some colors do not work together? Were there any weird effects? The Apple hi-res screen will not allow certain colors to mix. Blue and orange will not mix with green and violet. The procedure MESSAGE will write a message on the hi-res screen. But the screen ends up black and the message is invisible. Can you figure out a way to make the message visible? Write and tell me how you did it.

Using the turtle to make pictures is a lot of fun. Sometimes it is hard to figure out how to make a drawing. It can help to pretend that you are the turtle. Ask yourself, "What would I do to draw this?' If your drawing program gets too confusing, break it into small procedures. Learn the angles of a triangle, square and star, then write a procedure for each of these polygons. By keeping your procedures small, your program will be easy to debug.

Logo Lingo
P.O. Box 30668
Seattle, WA 98103

MAIN LISTING, for all Logo's

```
TO BLACK
OUTPUT 0
END                    TO POLY :ANGLE
                       PU
TO WHITE               HOME CS BK 50 LT
OUTPUT 1                     (180 -:ANGLE)/2
END                    PD HT REPEAT 50 [FD
                             100 RT :ANGLE]
TO GREEN               PU HOME ST
OUTPUT 2               END
END
                       TO LIGHTSHOW
TO VIOLET              REPEAT 10 [SETBG 2 SETBG
OUTPUT 3               3 SETBG 4 SETBG 5]
END                    SETBG 0
                       END
TO ORANGE
OUTPUT 4               TO MESSAGE
END                    SETBG BLACK SETPC ORANGE
                       HOME CS HT PG2 PU
TO BLUE                WRITE :MESSAGE SETPC BLACK
OUTPUT 5               PU HOME
END                    WRITE :MESSAGE
                       PU HOME ST PG1
                       END
```

```
MAKE "MESSAGE [[-120 100] [-120 50]
       [-92 35] [] [-80 85] [-66 35]
       [-52 50] [-52 85] [-66 100]
       [-80 85] [] [-12 85] [-26 100]
       [-40 85] [-40 50] [-26 35]
       [-12 50] [-12 65] [-22 72] []
       [2 85] [16 100] [30 85]
       [30 50] [16 35] [2 50] [2 85]
       [] [-40 10] [-40 -55] [-12 -70]
       [] [0 -5] [0 -55] [] [15 -70]
       [15 10] [45 -70] [45 10] []
       [88 -5] [74 10] [60 -5]
       [60 -55] [74 -70] [88 -55]
       [88 -30] [74 -22] [] [100 -5]
       [100 -55] [114 -70] [128 -55]
       [128 -5] [144 10] [100-5]]]
```

Wizard and the Princess

```
APPLE LOGO LISTING

TO PG1
.DEPOSIT 49236 0
END

TO PG2
.DEPOSIT 49237 0
END

TO WRITE :LIST
IF
EMPTYP :LIST [STOP]
IF EMPTYP FIRST :LIST [PU MAKE
    "LIST BF :LIST]
SETPOS FIRST :LIST
PD WRITE BF :LIST
END
```

```
TERRAPIN
and KRELL LISTING

TO PG1
SPLITSCREEN
END

TO PG2
TEXTSCREEN
END

TO SETBG :N
BACKGROUND :N
END

TO SETPC :N
PENCOLOR
:N
END

TO WRITE :LIST
```

The Wizard and the Princess:
Shortcut to Adventure

Cassidy/Katz/Lynn/Waisman

Shortcut to Adventure is a series of excerpts from the first and subsequent volumes of "A Shortcut Through Adventureland," by **Jack Cassidy, Pete Katz, Richard Owen Lynn** *and* **Sergio Waisman**. *It was reviewed in the April Apple's Apprentice, and is copyright © 1984 by Datamost™, Inc., and is used by permission. We extend our thanks to Dave Gordon, president of Datamost, for his generosity.*

The authors designed *Shortcuts* to help you when you are *really* stuck. You could use it as a complete cheaters guide if you wanted, but then that would take most of the excitement out, wouldn't it . . .

Map Notes   Map on Page 24

North is at the top of the map.

Each box □ represents one room or location. An empty box means there is nothing special to do here.

A line with an arrow [→] indicates a one-way passage.

A line with a backward-pointing arrow [←] illustrates that you will wind up in the same place.

A dotted line . . . marks a passage that requires problem solving.

The letter U or D signifies that the passage goes up or down.

The Wizard and the Princess™

In Sierra On-Line's *Wizard and the Princess*, it is the adventurer's goal to rescue the Princess from the evil Wizard and bring her back to safety. This adventure is fairly complicated, mainly because some of the solutions are abstract. In other words, a guessing game might just lead to success, while a logical approach might lead nowhere.

General Hints

During the first part of the adventure, in the desert, you will randomly encounter rattlesnakes. You may either escape or use the stick from #4 to drive them away.

At any point during the game you may be told that you are thirsty. When this happens, drink water.

Towards the end of the adventure you will arrive at a castle. Once you're there the Wizard will teleport you around when you try to do certain things. Do not get frustrated — just work on killing him (see #38).

Procedures

1. This is the start. There is nothing to do in the town of Serenia. You have to find the Princess and bring her here.

2. Although it is not shown on the map, there is more than one spot here. You should go south and east, looking at rocks, until you find one without a scorpion behind it. (This is randomly determined.) Get the rock (that had no scorpion behind it) and go north and west until you get to #1 or #3. Use the rock at #3

3. You must throw the rock from #2 to kill the snake and continue.

4. A stick can be found here. It is used against most snakes by typing "use stick".

5. Looking at the hole will reveal a cracker. This is used in #14.

6. If you get a rock, the snake will thank you by telling you a magical word. Write it down. This word turns you into a snake for a couple of turns.

7. After using the stick to kill the snake, you may look in the hole to find a note. Look at the note and copy what you see onto a piece of paper (real paper, not in the game).

8. Inside the locket, which is found here, is a magical word which is said at #29.

9. There is another note here. Look at it and write it above the first note (#7). This should form a magical word used at #10.

10. Say "hocus" (see# 7 & #9 for origin). This will allow you to cross the chasm.

11. The apple that is found here will be used at #35.

12. The goblin will steal some of your equipment. You cannot stop this. You must retrieve your things from #14.

---

13. You can go through the hole on the tree, and down the stairs (not shown on map). However, the door cannot be opened from this side.

14. Since the crevice is too small for you to go through, you should say the magic word from #6 (hiss) and turn into a snake. You can then go through the crevice and go south (not shown on map) until you find your equipment. You may go back the same way, or unlock the door and exit through #13.

15. When you give the cracker to the parrot, he will give you a vial which is used at #12.

16. From this brook, you can refill your water supply.

17. You may climb this tree to see the boat which you will be sailing (#19).

18. By giving the bread to the lion, you get rid of him.

19. The rope found here is to be used at #22. Entering the boat, you will notice that it has a hole in it. Use the blanket to cover the hole and you will be able to sail off.

20. After getting the shovel from #23 (see below), dig. You will find a chest, but a pirate will steal it and take it to #24.

21. There is an anchor here which is to be used at #22. Also, after finishing this island, drink the liquid from the vial from #15, and go north to #25.

22. Tie the rope from #19 to the anchor from #21. Then throw the anchor which hooks up to the tree, allowing you to proceed to #23.

23. Get this shovel and dig at #20.

24. After digging at #20, come here and get the chest. Inside you will find a harp to be used at #31.

25. The only way to get here is through the action at #21.

26. This ring is to be used at #38.

27. Talk to the woman to get some information. The first time you go west, you'll go to #28. After the first time, the other west path is taken.

28. If you go to the rainbow, you'll find a coin to be used at #32.

29. Say the word found inside the locket from #8 (Lucy) to go west.

30. You can get all of your equipment by going into this cave.

31. You can get past the giant by playing the harp from #24.

32. Buy a trumpet with the gold coin found at #28.

33. Play the trumpet from #32 to lower the bridge. Your next goal is #38.

34. There is a mistake in the game here. It says there is a doorway to the east and one to the south. The doorways are actually to the west and south.

35. Kill the boar. If the Wizard zaps you here, you will see a boar. To kill him, give him the apple from #11.

36. Escape from the cell. If the Wizard zaps you here, you will be locked in a cell. To escape, say the magic word HISS. This lets you exit freely.

37. To open the door to the east, you must use the knife to pick the lock.

38. Kill the Wizard. If this room is empty when you enter, go out and come back in again. You will see a bird, actually the Wizard in disguise. To kill him, put on the ring from #26 and rub it.

39. This frog is actually the Princess. Kiss the frog to change her back. If the Wizard is still alive, he will zap you to a new location out of this room.

40. Look in the closet for a pair of shoes. Take the shoes and look at them. You will see a magic word to transport you and the Princess back to Serenia. Put on the shoes and say the magic word. When you are back in the town, type another command and the game will end.

The Duncan Letters (from page 13)

about my having the Macintosh. The princess here just returned from a camp in the Silicon Valley where they teach young squires and squiresses how to use these Magic Apples, as well as others. Needless to say, the castle is all astir with excitement and anticipation! Oh, I wish that minstrel would return soon with more apples, so that things would get done around here!

Continue your apprenticeship, Duncan, and learn well. Keep me posted on your progress, will you? With knowledge, you can do anything, remember? Ah, but don't let it get to the point of exclusion . . . remember that book I gave you for your last birthday:

". . . Once I had a brain and a heart also; having tried them both, I should much rather have a heart."

Whatever you do, care enough to do your best . . .

Your friend and cousin,

Joseph

Spanish Verb Conjugator

Tim Graham

Here is a program, submitted by 14-year old Tim Graham of Manhattan Beach, CA, that might help you with your homework. It will break down *AR, ER* and *IR* verbs. What it can't handle is irregular verbs. It would seem that perhaps some of Tim's ideas could be applied to other languages. Worth a try, huh?

Incidentally, Tim gets a free 12-issue subscription for his efforts... How about you?

```
JLIST

10  REM

SPANISH VERB CONJUGATER
    BY TIM GRAHAM

100  ONERR  GOTO 600
110  HOME :BS$ =  CHR$ (92)
120  INPUT "VERB TO CONJUGATE? ";
     A$
130  B$ =  RIGHT$ (A$,2)
140  ON B$ = "AR" GOTO 200: ON B$
     = "ER" GOTO 210: ON B$ = "I
     R" GOTO 220: GOTO 120
200  YO$ = "O":TU$ = "AS":EL$ = "A
     ":NO$ = "AMOS":ES$ = "AN": GOTO
     300
210  YO$ = "O":TU$ = "ES":EL$ = "E
     ":NO$ = "EMOS":ES$ = "EN": GOTO
     300
220  YO$ = "O":TU$ = "ES":EL$ = "E
     ":NO$ = "IMOS":ES$ = "EN"
300  HOME : PRINT : PRINT
310  C$ =  LEFT$ (A$, LEN (A$) - 2
     )
320  PRINT "       YO "C$;YO$
330  PRINT
340  PRINT "          ";BS$
350  PRINT "       TU "C$;TU$
360  PRINT
370  PRINT "    ";BS$
380  PRINT "    EL   ";BS$
390  PRINT "    ELLA >"C$;ES$
400  PRINT "    UDS./"
410  PRINT
420  PRINT "NOSTROS "C$;NO$
430  PRINT
440  PRINT "    ELLOS";BS$
450  PRINT "    ELLAS >"C$;ES$
460  PRINT "    UDS. /"
470  PRINT : PRINT
500  PRINT "HIT ";: INVERSE : PRINT
     "RETURN";: NORMAL : PRINT "
     TO CONTINUE"
510  POKE 49168,0
520  KY =  PEEK (49152)
530  IF KY = 141 THEN  POKE 49168
     ,0: RUN
540  GOTO 520
600  IF  PEEK (222) = 255 THEN  VTAB
     23: PRINT "...BYE": END
610  VTAB 23: PRINT "ERROR "
620  FOR PA = 1 TO 1000: NEXT PA
630  RUN
```

Ah, my young friends, I was hoping you would pass this way again soon; I have many new games to offer you. Master Michael, I can not help but notice your brother Matthew is not with you this day. However, I know this is the morn of the Tuldurry Knights Tournament, and I suspect he is eager to attend. I myself plan to be there for the grand championship later today, so we must not allow pleasantries to intercede with our offerings. If you have no other plans, perhaps you may wish to ride with me to the tournament.

Bezare is Bizarre

One of the most unusual games to come my way ever, *Bezare* purports to be from a planet in the Bezardian system. The publishers (Roger Wagner Publishing) inform me they were so impressed by the game that they spent countless hours converting it to Apple format from a Bezardian computer diskette. After all, bits are bits and bytes are bytes, no matter the language. Converting game instructions proved a more difficult task, so the original Bezardian directions have been reproduced in their native tongue, a text that appears to the eye as a combination of Egyptian hieroglyphics and oriental characters. It therefore falls upon the player to do his/her own translation.

Standing on its own, as an arcade game, Bezare deserves at least a B+, but adding the challenge of discovering on your own *how* to play the game must add at least another full point. I've discovered quite a bit on my own in a limited period. There are three distinct and repeating arcade games, or levels of play.

At this point I have not become fluent in Bezardian, so the current and high scores — which I rely on heavily — are of little help, since they are displayed in Bezardian pictograms. Like any other game, though, practice and familiarity produce the technique required to win.

I've at least figured out that some of the standard arcade commands like "P" for pause and [Ctrl-S] for sound, do work. In addition, should you be playing at the office, a [Ctrl-W] instantly converts your display to a dummy spreadsheet! The graphics are simple but effective. The intrigue of what the game does is as exciting and as effective as the game itself. I don't think this is for the casual game–player, but for anyone above that first elementary level, the challenge is first cabin.

As we go to press, I've just made a deal with the publisher to offer Bezare at a reduced price to Apprentice subscribers only, along with a full–color 17" x 24" poster! I'll put a notice elsewhere in this issue.

Bezare
Roger Wagner Publishing
10761-E Woodside Ave.
Santee, CA 92071
$19.95

Hanky–Panky with Hinky Pinky

Now here's a game with a . . . never mind those cobwebs, they're not hurting anything — pay attention now . . . a game sold on the honor system. You pick up a copy of the game from the supplier or a friend; if you like it, you send them 25 dollars, and they send you back a registered copy, as well as future updates. You are encouraged to make copies and give them to your friends, along with the request, of course, that they too send in their money or pass the copy on.

Now, let's see, I haven't told you about the game itself, yet, have I? The Hinky Pinky Game is a rhyming game with a large dictionary containing mated syllable groups. You take a hint and try to guess the hinky pinky rhyme pair. For example, a hint reading "Wizard's abode" might lead to "power tower" or the hint "noisy insect inhabiting a bushy area" could mean "cricket thicket" and so on. This is lots of fun, but the really good part is when you flip the disk over to create your own rhyming pairs. Now you have a complete rhyming dictionary at your command. You can type in a word, then select from the menu a list of words that rhyme with yours. It's great for the budding poet.

The Hinky Pinky Game
The 22nd Avenue Workshop
P.O. Box 3425
Eugene, OR 97403
$25.00 (see story)

Once Over Lightly

More for our puzzled (puzzling?) readers: a trio of word games from *Hi–Tech of Santa Cruz*, $25 each or all three for $60. Word Search, Word Match and Word Scramble. In the first, you locate words in a block of characters. The second matches words to definitions, while the third, does as its name implies. Looks neat.

Chez 21, by *Microlon, Inc.* P.O. Box 1529, San Marcos, TX. A moderately good blackjack game with an excellent tip book (when to split, when to stay, etc.)

Though the day is still young, it is time to shutter the windows; I must be off to the tournament. You, young Michael, may ride with me on my steed if you desire, and all of you are welcome to return at another time. The sorceror tells me he has heard from one of his Hexels that a stranger rides toward our land, his satchels filled with new games and Magic Apples, so do hurry back.

Cross Words

Don't be angry, let's not have words . . .
Unless, of course, they are cross words . . .

Hints

You should read the *Apple's Apprentice* carefully. Many of the answers appear in the stories. Watch out for puns and word plays. For example, the clue "job" might mean "tasc" (the compiler). When you think you have an answer but are not sure, look it up in a dictionary or a BASIC manual.

Answers appear on page 6. Good luck!

Across

1. Came before Applesoft
5. Code word is "sesame"
8. Recollect
9. Condition when bit = 1
10. Held at Tuldurry
13. Command to get a binary file
15. A reader
16. Programmer's program
17. Spoil
20. Take apart
22. Mom's mate
23. What we confess
26. Not now
27. Slang for bad
29. Little used BASIC command
30. Opposite of 13 across
32. Instructs the microprocessor
34. A beam
36. What a lion does
37. A student magician
41. What you do with a telephone
42. Made from a tree
44. Name for the character "@"
45. In graphics, to erase
46. Apples often have 64k

Down

1. What you get in school
2. Goof-off or thug; Alice was one
3. In radio or tv, delete
4. Alphabetize
7. Cartoon character
11. Grows underground
12. Condition of a spoiled apple
14. Not too bright
18. There's a bug in it
19. They are often hatched
21. System with only two values
22. Made from apples
23. This command rhymes with 23 across
24. Distress signal
25. Brand name of bacon
28. Popular soft drink
29. A structured language
31. A measure of energy
32. What most opcodes need
33. In some systems, a loop
35. Known to plunder
38. A test
39. Alternative to THEN
40. Opposite of few
43. A sticky mess

The Crystal Ball

Earn-it/Play-it Unique Concept

Earn-it/Play-it from Dynacomp, is an automated "contingency management" program for the classroom. Access to computer games is contingent upon the student's behavior.

Each use of Earn-it/Play-it with a student is called a session, generally one school day. The teacher may identify up to nine objectives for each student during each session (e.g., completes homework, passes quiz, zero misbehavior rate). At the end of a session, the teacher records whether or not the student has achieved each objective. If a specified proportion (say 65%) of the objectives is achieved, the student is rewarded with game credits.

Game credits give the student an opportunity to play one of the games contained on the Earn-it/Play-it disk. The student may choose to save the game credit or use it immediately (if the teacher permits). The program keeps track of each student's game credit balance. To maintain the student's motivational level, new games become available at certain milestones. There are a total of six different games on the disk. At game time, the student can select any available game for which he/she qualifies. Naturally, the more interesting games cost more game credits. Price $29.95 from Dynacomp.

Dynacomp also offers Coach's Corner at $29.95, a realistic computer football game which allows you to coach rather than play. Coach's Corner teaches football strategy by "first hand" experience, and helps you better understand what is happening on the real field.

Dyslectic Learning Package

Dynacomp's Primer 83 is a very unique and effective learning package designed for people with impaired reading skills. It was originally written to aid in the rehabilitation of a 30-year old man suffering from "word blindness" or dyslexia. He had a brain tumor which, after removal, resulted in selective memory loss. He worked with many traditional exercises with only

limited success. With the incentive of sponsorship from John Hopkins University, Primer 83 was developed to handle the needs of this individual and other people having this handicap. Primer 83 worked. It also appears to be effective with individuals having reading problems in general. Primer 83 is the culmination of the combined effort of several people, including the original "student," an expert programmer, a grammaticist, a musician and several others. It is well thought out and tested.

Requirements

- The user *does not* need to have prior experience with a computer or have typing skills.
- A cassette recorder is needed: The instructions given in the manual are also recorded on tape.
- A black and white monitor.
- A paddle connected to port #0 to control display speed
- A printer (optional) to print out test statistics and analyses.
- An ECHO II speech synthesizer (optional) for letter and word prompting. Nice, but not vital

Note that a black and white *monitor* is required. Color televisions do not have the resolution of a B&W monitor. There is no point in *further* handicapping the student with a poor display.

Module Descriptions

Primer 83 contains several program modules. The main ones are:
- **Talkwriter** — a program designed to familiarize the user with the keyboard. If an Echo II is present, the letter will be spoken.
- **Letter Flash, Word Flash, Sentence Flash** — Letters, words and sentences are flashed on the screen. Words come from a 600 word vocabulary of common words. 6000 grammatically correct

sentences may be displayed or spoken. Each of these modules have many additional features to aid use.
- **Music, Music Editor** — You may create your own tunes and words: load, save or play a song; add, change, insert or delete a note. Notes range over two octaves and can be full to 1/32. Four tunes come with the Music module.
- **Sci-Fi Story** — A nearly infinite variety of short science-fiction stories can be created and displayed.
- **Trouble Shoot** — All of the question and answer modules have the option to save statistical results. These include number of presentations, %errors, average response times and specific errors. Trouble Shoot will also analyze specific errors to determine possible perceptual or motor difficulties of rotation, inversion, correct key/ wrong hand, etc.

Other Features

- Upper or lower case letters
- Alternate character sets. ASCII, Roman, Collasal and Flow are currently available; you may also design your own font.
- Re-defineable keyboard. Keys may be put in ABC order instead of QWERTY.

Additional information from Dynacomp, Inc. 1427 Monroe Avenue, Rochester, NY 14618, (716) 442-8960, (716) 442-8731.

Contests Galore!
Daze of The Knights

David Sparks

Right now, in county Tuldurry, the Knights Tournament is taking place. Many prizes will be awarded to the bravest and most ingenious of the knights. Here are two more special contests, designed to bring you hours of fun and challenge, while at the same time showing you some of the powerful things your Apple can do as you learn about its internal workings.

We want to hear from you: we want to know how you like the contests; we also welcome your contest submissions. Most of all, we want you to enjoy the *Apple's Apprentice* and have fun learning about computing. Preliminary rules follow; the complete rules and prizes will be published next issue.

General Rules

*   Be sure to include your name, address and *age* with each entry.
*   Duplicate prizes will be awarded to each of two age groups: under 15 and 15 and older.
*   In the event of a tie, the earliest post-marked entry will receive the prize.
*   Winner's names will be published in the *Apple's Apprentice* and added to our "honor roll"
*   No more than one entry to one contest may be enclosed in the same envelope.
*   Envelopes must be marked on the outside with the number and/or name of the contest, and addressed to:

> Apple's Apprentice
> P.O. Box 582-AA
> Santee, CA 92071

Contests 3 and 4

Many thanks to David Sparks, the author of this month's contests.

Type each in, exactly as listed with no space after "REM," save and run, then list. Tell us why they did what they did. Note each program should be saved to disk before running.

Extra Special . . .

If you can write a good explanation that can be understood by others and help them learn about the Apple, we will consider it for publication! And now, it's time to get to work. Good luck!

```
]LIST

10  REM DAZE OF THE KNIGHTS: #3
20  X = 2: POKE 2049,59: POKE 2082
    ,178: RUN
30  PRINT : PRINT "X=";X
```

```
]LIST

10  REM DAZE      OF THE KNIGHTS #4

20  X = 2
30  FOR Y = 2053 TO 2060: READ Z:
    POKE Y,Z: NEXT
40  GOSUB 10
50  FOR Y = 2053 TO 2060: READ Z:
    POKE Y,Z: NEXT
60  PRINT : PRINT "X=";X
70  DATA 88,208,88,202,50,58,177,
    0,178,83,79,32,87,72,65,84
```

Crystal Ball (from Page 31)

Home Cataloger

The Home Cataloger is an efficient and easy to use filing and cataloging program, allowing up to 1,500 individual entries (depending on hardware). The user can create customized filing systems, or select one of the program's ten pre-designed cataloging lists. These include telephone list, inventory, travel planner, insurance policies, studies and book lists.

The Home Cataloger has the capability of totaling numbers in any or all numeric categories. Additionally, the program can generate whole lists of selected categories in any order, as well as custom printouts.

Suggested retail is $49.95. For information, contact Continental Software, 11223 South Hindry Avenue, Los Angeles, CA 90045, (213) 417-8031.

Dija Know

Deja vu describes a scene you have seen before — perhaps in your dreams; *Dija know* is our way of describing a simple hint you may have heard before, but forgotten.

Dija know— typed from the keyboard, **FP** will completely re-initialize Applesoft (and wipe out your program).

Dija know— typed from the keyboard, **MAXFILES 3** will reset HIMEM and *will not* wipe out your program.

Dija know— **DEL 1,0**, when typed from the keyboard, will reset LOMEM.

Look for *Dija know*'s in each issue of *The Apple's Apprentice*.

Penguin Scores Again!

	Releases	Hits	Errors
Fantasy	2	2	0
Arcade	1	1	0

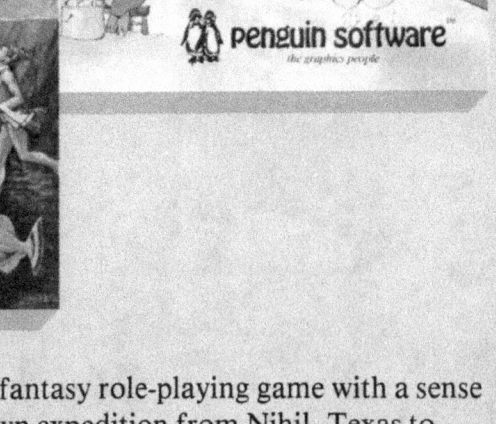

Expedition Amazon—A fantasy role-playing game with a sense of humor. Guide your own expedition from Nihil, Texas to Pedro's Trading Post and through the jungles of Peru in search of priceless treasures and the fabled lost city of Ka!

Arcade Boot Camp—Tired of getting 30 seconds of arcade play for your quarter? Face forward, Civilian, and march over to your dealer for this one. Train in five areas vital to arcade skills: Driving, Chopper Flying, Shooting, Jumping & Ducking, and Obstacle Course.

Xyphus—Explore the Lost Continent of Arroya as you develop a band of warriors and spellcasters in preparation for the final confrontation with Xyphus, Lord of Demons! This fantasy role-playing game features four-player independent movement and six separate scenarios, each set in a different region with different types of creatures, weapons, and spells. A true breakthrough in its genre, **Xyphus** is destined to become a classic.

penguin software ™

the graphics people

830 Fourth Ave.
P.O. Box 311
Geneva, IL 60134
(312) 232-1984

Expedition Amazon, Arcade Boot Camp, Xyphus, and Penguin Software are trademarks of Penguin Software, Inc.

Apple owners shouldn't be jealous of integrated software like Lotus 1-2-3.
Now you can have something better. Magic Office System.™

Now you can have four of the most powerful programs for the Apple IIe and Apple IIc computers—all in one fully integrated package.

You'll be able to quickly and easily produce letters and reports—complete with spreadsheets and graphics interspersed—with every word spelled correctly.

Using one disk. No shuffle.

WORD PROCESSING: you'll have a greatly enhanced version of an already popular program for creating and editing any kind of document. Printing and formatting are automatic.

SPELLING CHECKER: you'll have the first ever, on-line automatic checker with plenty of room to add words special to your business.

SPREADSHEET: this one is more powerful than VisiCalc and includes variable width columns and output formatting.

BUSINESS GRAPHICS: you'll be able to create pie charts or multiple bar charts to enhance your reports and presentations.

What's especially convenient is how Magic Office System uses icons to simplify your work.

It's all organized into drawers containing file folders, stationery and documents. You can even place folders in other folders, or "cut" parts of documents and "paste" them to others. Or move or copy documents anywhere in the system.

Lotus should be so easy!

Want a Magic Office System immediately? Check with your local dealer. If he doesn't have it, send in the coupon below.

You'll need 64k, an 80-column display, two disk drives and a whole new level of expectation about great software for Apple!

artsci™

I can't find Magic Office System at my local dealer.
- ☐ Please send me more information right now.
- ☐ I can't waste time. I want _____ copies of Magic Office System now. Enclosed is $295 per package, plus $19.18 sales tax per package for California residents.
- ☐ Enclosed is a check for _____ .
- ☐ Charge to my ☐ VISA ☐ MasterCard.

Acct. No. _____

Exp. Date _____

Name _____

Business _____

Address _____

City/State/Zip _____

Telephone _____

Mail to: ARTSCI 5547 Satsuma Avenue
North Hollywood, CA 91601
Or call: 818/985-2922   AA8

Sorry, IBMers, Magic Office System is only for the Apple IIe and the IIc.

Magic Office System is a trademark of ARTSCI, INC.